SHELTON STATE COMMUNITY.
COLLEGE
JUNIOR COLLEGE DIVISION
LIBRARY.

DISCARDED

D0846109

JK
2391
.S6
B87

Burbank, Garin
When farmers vot-
ed red

DATE DUE

SHELTON STATE COMMUNITY.
COLLEGE
JUNIOR COLLEGE DIVISION
LIBRARY.

WHEN FARMERS
VOTED RED

DISCARDED

When farmers voted red THE GOSPEL OF SOCIALISM IN THE OKLAHOMA COUNTRYSIDE, 1910-1924

Garin Burbank

Contributions in American History, Number 53

GREENWOOD PRESS
WESTPORT, CONNECTICUT ● LONDON, ENGLAND

Library of Congress Cataloging in Publication Data
Burbank, Garin.
When farmers voted red.

(Contributions in American history; no. 53)
Includes bibliographical references and index.
1. Socialist Party (U.S.). Oklahoma—History.
2. Socialism in Oklahoma—History. 3. Oklahoma—
Politics and government—1907-   I. Title.
JK2391.S6B87   329'.81'021109766   76-5259
ISBN 0-8371-8903-9

Copyright © 1976 by Garin Burbank.

All rights reserved. No portion of this book may be reproduced, by any process or
technique, without the express written consent of the publisher.

Library of Congress Catalog Card Number: 76-5259
ISBN: 0-8371-8903-9

First published in 1976.

Greenwood Press, Inc.
51 Riverside Avenue, Westport, Connecticut 06880

Printed in the United States of America

To the memory
of
John M. Burbank (1912-1973),
who practiced the virtues of self-help all his life

Contents

Acknowledgments

Many people have helped me write this book over a period of almost eight years. Brief mention of their names here will hardly repay them for their many kindnesses. At the Oklahoma Historical Society Louise Cook and Mary Moran of the Newspaper Department eased my way to most of the newspapers I used in this study. In the library of the society Manon B. Atkins and Willa Doty helpfully pointed out many useful items in their special file on Oklahoma. Milton Ream, a graduate student at the University of Oklahoma, helped me with the research on numerous occasions. Donald R. Graham and Douglas McCashin, graduate students at the University of Sackatchewan Regina Campus, did some laborious statistical calculations for me. Jeff Harding of the University of Winnipeg's Graphics Department designed and photographed the maps.

Richard M. Abrams of the University of California at Berkeley encouraged me to continue my work on this subject long after I had written it off as a futility. He insistently reminded me that when liberals and socialists argue the merits of their philosophies, they must address the opposing contentions honestly and without resort to cheap shots at conveniently created straw men. Arthur Donovan of West Virginia University, and Walter Stein and Ross McCormack, both of the University of Winnipeg, made me aware of ambiguities in my understanding of social processes and social history. Peter Griffiths of Northern Ireland Polytechnic College taught me much of what I know about the evolution of British and European social democracy. When James R. Green of Brandeis University and I discovered that we were working on virtually the same subject at the same time, we tended to react as if we were rivals. Fortunately, our good sense prevailed at an early date; we have cooperated, as scholars should, ever since.

My friends and advisers will undoubtedly be relieved to know that they are not to be charged with responsibility for any errors or eccentricities in this book.

The University of Winnipeg provided me with small but useful sums, which facilitated completion of the work. I am grateful to the administrators of the University of Saskatchewan Regina Campus (now the University of Regina) for having been gracious enough to release me from some residual obligations on their campus, thereby permitting my departure to the University of Winnipeg, where I subsequently met a number of historians who lent important inspiration to my work. Finally, the editors at Greenwood Press showed me how to pull weeds out of a manuscript.

Permission to use previously published material has been granted by the following: the Organization of American Historians, for "Agrarian Radicals and Their Opponents: Political Conflict in Southern Oklahoma, 1910-1924," *Journal of American History* 58 (June 1971): 5-23; Cambridge University Press, for "The Disruption and Decline of the Oklahoma Socialist Party," *Journal of American Studies* 7 (August 1973): 133-152; and the Oklahoma Historical Society, for "The Political and Social Attitudes of Some Early Oklahoma Democrats," *Chronicles of Oklahoma* 52 (Winter 1974-1975): 439-455.

Preface

In these days when the circumspect scholar is quick to identify the taint of
"political advocacy" in scholarly work, it may seem eccentric for a
historian to admit by way of preface that his studies were inspired by his
angry dissatisfaction with the directions of American politics in the
1960s. But those were the years in which I began to think about the
American social order; and, as virtually everyone knows, those were the
years in which many thousands of Americans met their untimely deaths
or suffered disabling injuries because their elected leaders misled them
into an imperial war in Vietnam. Anyone privileged enough, as this
writer was, to have spent those years in graduate school instead of in
Vietnam or a federal prison can testify that the sense of social crisis
engendered by American intervention in Vietnam moved many students
to look at the nation's past with a more critical—and occasionally
jaundiced—eye. Students so minded produced a variety of works chal-
lenging a regnant view of our history that seemed unwarrantedly benign,
optimistic, and complacent. The leading scholars in the guild have now
acknowledged the challenge. No one has framed the issue with greater
pith than Edmund S. Morgan, who suggested in his presidential address
to the Organization of American Historians in 1972 that scholars
"interested in tracing the rise of liberty, democracy, and the common
man have been challenged in the last two decades by other historians,
interested in tracing the history of oppression, exploitation, and
racism."

At the outset of my own studies I believed that my interpretation of the
Oklahoma socialists and their opponents during the 1910s would be very
much part of the attack that Morgan was to pronounce both provocative

and salutary. Though the subject of my first publication, which appeared in the June 1971 issue of *Journal of American History,* was sharply restricted as to time, place, and social circumstance (as indeed the subject of this book will be), I had intended to address the same historical question as had Morgan: what substantive advantages and penalties has American liberal capitalism allotted to different social groups? For many of the country people of Oklahoma during the Progressive era, the results frequently had been impoverishment and degradation. My conclusion at that time obviously verged on exhortation when I insisted that it was "by their political actions and goals that southern Oklahoma's agrarian radicals should be known and judged." No one was supposed to overlook my political sympathy and admiration for the agrarian radicals and their program. That hortatory expression reflected the enthusiast's hope of discovering in the American agricultural hinterland a popular insurgent movement whose participants could be seen and well remembered as worthy exemplars of resistance to exploitation in the capitalist marketplace.

Authors who burden their histories with their hopes, however, may find later that they have obscured complicated issues. This has been so with my original considerations of the "socialism" in the Socialist party of Oklahoma. From the British social historians of Marxist persuasion I have since learned an important lesson: one may indeed sympathize with the men, women, and children who have laboriously used up their living energies in mine, mill, and field while also recognizing that those laboring people have often seen their world from cultural perspectives that limited their ability to envisage a fully revolutionary transformation of industrial capitalism. Inherited ideas are notoriously difficult to dislodge when they seem "natural" to people. But they can and do change in enduring periods of social tension and disruption. And we have been made aware, thanks primarily to E. P. Thompson, that when the cultural inheritance of ordinary people is invaded and their customary sense of justice offended by new practices, the shock of disruption can sometimes fuel a fierce resistance. In the introduction to his monumental book, *The Making of the English Working Class*, Thompson avows his intention "to rescue the poor stockinger, the Luddite cropper, the 'obsolete' handloom weaver, the 'utopian' artisan . . . from the enormous condescension of posterity. Their hostility to the new industrialism may have been backward-looking. Their communitarian ideals may have been foolhardy. But they lived through these times of acute disturbance, and we did not.'' That is a historical and political purpose worthy of emulation. No one is constrained to argue that militant, collective protest from exploited groups has always propelled the social order toward some ineluctable future of equality. However, if we study particular instances of popular mentality and activity, no less than the attitudes and abilities of those who consider themselves worthy rulers (and who may be popularly accepted as such), we may find the clues necessary to explain the origins, character, and consequences of specific episodes of social disturbance or quiescence.

Authors should foreshadow their themes and forewarn their readers of difficulties ahead. The organizing themes have been influenced by major historical controversies of recent years: whether populism in its ideology and program was socially nostalgic or forward looking; whether the Socialist party of America was achieving political vitality or declining into feckless sectarianism after 1912; whether local agrarian discontents such as land hunger and low crop prices can be transformed into long-term support for radical social change; whether evangelical Protestantism, especially in its revivalist forms, has helped or hindered the growth of radical democratic movements; and whether the Protestant emphasis upon individual moral responsibility and personal diligence sets limits upon the absorption of collectivist ethics stressing the social character of labor and responsibility. Well-informed students will not need an elaborate description of the significant works that have canvassed these related issues.

It would be foolish to claim that Oklahoma, with its late settlement, its unusual social development, and its heavily rural population, provides a typical instance of the meeting of those clusters of values associated with Protestantism, liberalism, and socialism. It would be difficult to maintain that Oklahoma was a decisive episode in the failure of the Socialist party of America. But even if gains and losses in Oklahoma were not typical or decisive for American Socialists, the experience of the Oklahomans who were trying to become socialists in the midst of the mobilized biases of liberal capitalism may yield important historical and political insight into the problem of building a socialist movement in America. Although it was a colonial hinterland in the North American economy, Oklahoma did not exist apart from liberal capitalist society.

The Socialist party of Oklahoma did make some remarkable gains, winning 17 percent of the statewide vote in 1912, 21 percent in 1914, and 16 percent in 1916. A heavily disproportionate percentage of this vote came from the rural precincts, a surprising result in the light of traditional European and eastern American socialist expectations, which led Socialists to scorn country folk as unpromising candidates for conversion to proletarian politics. But some American Socialists looked at a different kind of countryside and had to confront the hollering presence of discontented southwestern farmers ready to support the party. In 1912 the Socialist party of America, after years of ideological dispute, followed the advice and example of the Oklahoma comrades and invited the "working farmer" to join the struggle against capitalism. Significantly, the platform advocated the collective ownership of land "wherever practicable" and the heavy taxation of land held for speculation and exploitation. This stratagem seemed to leave a vague middle ground for small private ownership where collectivism was "impracticable" and the farmer's intentions and behavior were deemed neither speculative nor exploitative. No doubt this was a studied vagueness on a controversial issue.

What follows is an attempt to ask questions previously only reconnoitered (critics may say "skirted" or "ignored") in my journal articles. How much "socialism" was there in the spectacular and regrettably brief gains of the Oklahoma Socialists between 1910 and 1918? To what extent were the ideas of the party's supporters influenced by the dominant tradition of liberal individualism and by an emergent collectivism? Was there an oscillation between these competing conceptions of human development? Which of the imported socialist ideas, if any, were adapted and assimilated into the inherited folk wisdom of the southern country people? How much weight sould be given to conscious cognition and to subliminal perception, to the imported ideas taught in a rationalistic and catechetical manner and to familiar notions received from the mother culture? Did the socialist persuasions of leaders correspond to the understandings of followers in the movement?

Undoubtedly the alert reader must now be impatient to ask what is meant by socialism with a small "s" when it is distinguished from the Socialist party and its program for Oklahoma. It is one of those difficult matters. If the historian's model of socialism is derived from the unambiguous collectivism of European Marxism, with its origins in the communal life and shared struggles of industrial proletarians, then the varieties of socialist expression to be found in the Oklahoma party will appear to be unschooled and provincial, if not so heterodox as to be cashiered from the ranks. A socialist would hope to find a basic understanding of the first principle: the market in labor and goods—with its competition, its unequal results, and its justifying ideology of individualism—is a social construction and not an invariable "natural" phenomenon. From this principle we may deduce that market distributions of reward for the exertion of human powers are simply one way of dividing the fruits of collective labor. The market can force the poor to do without, but it cannot oblige the propertyless to concede the moral justice of a process dominated by the proprietors of land and capital. Historically the minimum postulate of socialism has been that capital is socially produced by all who work and therefore may be socially owned by all in equal shares.

Most Socialist leaders in Oklahoma were not literal minded in their application of socialist principle to the local and regional circumstances. While affirming that wealth belonged equally to those who created it, the leaders did not advocate the public ownership of every garden plot, corn crib, and plough team. In giving conception to the ideal of an agrarian socialism, the leaders recommended the eventual cooperative use of the land and the tools of production. Their suggestions of the possibilities of cooperative labor for social ends introduced much tension into the Oklahoma movement. What came to be known as the "land question" was frequently and controversially discussed, as much by their opponents (significantly) as by the Socialists themselves. Where we find the local Socialists visualizing the hard-working farmer as the fee simple lord of his home and acres, as the worthy yeoman privately possessing his moral earnings, we may ask whether the older tradition of acquisitive individualism had ever been displaced by socialist conceptions, however vaguely and incompletely articulated. Did the local Socialists of Oklahoma acquire the "proletarian perspective" attributed to them by one recent student of the movement? Were they learning to be socialists before the events of 1917-1918 had their shattering and lethal effect upon the Socialist party's prospects?

Difficult questions may produce answers that sometimes sound like confessions of doubt and uncertainty—but hopefully not so doubtful as to be easily dismissed and ignored. One thing is certain: the evidence of mentality among the Oklahoma Socialists is thin, obscure, necessarily ambiguous, and probably inconclusive in any strict sense. Apart from a few letters to a governor, in which tenant farmers awkwardly disputed the terms of work and rent or condemned the indifference of governing Democratic politicians to their plight, there is little surviving literary evidence from a countryside that was as inarticulate (for historical purposes) as it was impoverished. With the addition of a few letters to Socialist weeklies and a few more to agricultural "business' journals, social historians have soon accumulated the complete—and utterly disappointing—body of direct verbal expression.

So we must rely on firsthand description shot through with a partisan intensity seldom matched anywhere. In a day when printers carried their presses in their wagons from one town to another, they often reflected, with their engaging combination of eloquence and scurrility, the variety and eccentricities of the public mind in the villages. Socialist editors and their more "respectable" opponents, when seeking the approbation and support of the country people, often spoke to them and about them. If we avoid laboring the evidence in search of an illusory certitude, we can gain something from listening to the local accents, inflections, emphases— listening, weighing, and then comparing the indigenous attitudes with those imported from outside the region and its culture. This requires study of those who feared the politically unpredictable, economically "backward", and morally "disgusting" country people. It demands no less study of the Socialists who hoped that a small farmer educated with the "right dope" would join with men and women from the Colorado mines, the Milwaukee breweries, and the New York City garment districts in a grand effort to build the cooperative commonwealth. This book will have succeeded in its purpose if it clarifies the particular visage of the Americanized socialism that grew up, struggled mightily for a time, and died out in the hinterlands of Oklahoma.

                                                                            GARIN BURBANK

The social setting ————————————————1

Before Oklahoma became a state in 1907, Americans knew it best as a somnolent refuge for displaced Indian tribes, a likely haven for desperadoes fleeing from the authorities in the surrounding states, and a new frontier lately opened to furious land rushes. The new settlers initially made life problematical and ultimately intolerable for the outlaw and the Indian alike. Oklahoma repeated much midwestern and southern history. On the west side of the present state, the tribal reservations that had existed since the end of the Civil War were extinguished by 1889, with the tribesmen being allotted individual parcels of land under the Dawes Act (1887); the vast remainder of the land was thrown open to settlement by whites. The land hunger of the "Boomers" and "Sooners" was satisfied in large measure in the now legendary scramble for homesteads in the 1890s. It was a fearfully competitive process in which the race had gone to the swift and the fortunate. By 1900 well over 300,000 people had occupied the best parts of 25,000,000 acres on the west side. The Indian inhabitants, themselves unwilling migrants in the preceding generations and now fewer than 17,000 in number, were inundated by the acquisitive new society.

In Kansas, Nebraska, and the Dakotas, it had already happened: the swift influx of population, the rapid acquisition of land and minerals, the hasty erection of jerry-built towns, and, above all, the pervasive willingness to plunge for a cash crop or a speculative tract. Only the self-absorbed local chauvinist would claim that Oklahoma had a unique history. The land rushes into the west side (Oklahoma Territory after political organization) permit us to characterize this as one more episode in the long, rolling real estate boom that was, in many significant ways, the quintessential American experience.

Yet there was another side to Oklahoma, which gave its early history a somewhat peculiar flavor. Until the extinction of their tribal governments in the early 1900s, the Five Nations—Cherokees, Creeks, Choctaws, Chickasaws, and Seminoles—had led an autonomous existence as United States protectorates in what is roughly the eastern half of the present state. In the years after the Civil War, the governments of the nations leased land to white developers, who could not permanently settle and own title. White capitalists laid railroad and sunk coal mines in southeastern Oklahoma between 1870 and 1900. Poor whites, fleeing from the poverty of postwar southern agriculture, leased small holdings on comparatively advantageous terms from the nations and practiced a diversified agriculture. Compared with their earlier experience, the operation of leased land must have been at least sustaining if not handsomely profitable, because whites did arrive in large numbers, their population rising from an estimated 8,000 in 1879 to 302,000 in 1900, while the Indian population declined from 59,000 to 52,000. This imbalance portended the grimmest of fates for the tribal autonomy and the non-capitalist way of life the Five Nations enjoyed. The whites set up a clamor for the dissolution of tribal governments, the allottment of tribal lands to individual Indian owners, and the opening of the Indian Territory to white settlement and "enterprise." The land was too promising to allow it to lie "idle," as the "lazy" Indians were wont to do. The results of the clamor were predictable. Between 1900 and 1910, the Indian Nations saw their governments disbanded, their lands "allotted," their venerable and richly textured social fabric torn beyond repair. The tragic consequences for the Indians of eastern Oklahoma have been captured in Angie Debo's *And Still the Waters Run,* which refers, of course, to the treaties that were to last as long as the rivers flowed.

The consequences of the dissolution and the subsequent creation of Indian Territory were almost as damaging for many of the small farmers who had formerly held leases from the Indians. Enterprisers who were quick on their feet and burdened only lightly with moral scruples finessed appointments as "guardians" of legally incompetent Indians. Now in control of the land "owned" by many hapless Indians, the guardians seized the opportunity to raise rents and demand quick returns while providing dubious accounts of the proceeds to the federal authorities charged with the Indians' protection. Angie Debo has described the devices and deceits real estate men used to acquire not only the "surplus" but much of the "restricted" land (not to be sold for twenty-five years) allotted individually to the Indians. So common were these maneuvers that whites in eastern Oklahoma frankly used "grafter" less as a term of abuse than as a term of description.[1]

It is only to be expected that those who had done well in mercantile and professional pursuits during the days of Indian Territory would have the wherewithal to acquire large amounts of land as it was made available. There were no cultural sanctions that would have prevented the despoliation of the Indians and the subsequent exploitation of white tenants. By 1910 the county seats of eastern and southern Oklahoma had their local elites of bankers, lawyers, merchants, and landlords who largely set the terms of work and credit for tenant farmers. The customary southern emphasis upon cotton as a cash crop supplanted the diversified crop and pasture farming practiced by white leaseholders when they lived under the less demanding, noncapitalist regime of Indian landlords. Cotton acreage doubled in the Indian Territory between 1900 and 1910. A continuing influx of new migrants, stimulated in part by the general rise in agricultural prices after 1900, served to inflate land values beyond the reach of most croppers who aspired to farm ownership. Thus what one sociologist has aptly termed a "labor repressive" system of farm tenancy emerged in the former Indian Territory, with the tenant farmers suffering an important loss of their sense of competence and hope as their energies were made tributary to the unrestrained capitalistic impulses of the new local elites.[2]

Oklahomans may claim that their state was special in that it saw the development of both midwestern homesteading and southern cropping "on the shares." But there was nothing unique in the response of its wheat and cotton farmers as they struggled with declines in commodity prices, recurrent droughts, the boll weevil, and population pressures that tended to push farm rents above customary levels. The embattled farmers turned to politics. Among those who had sought a new beginning in the new state were large and growing numbers sufficiently discontented and disillusioned to bear willingly the stigma of supporting a novel and radical movement.

Students of political behavior have done their work so well that further research and extensive tabulation of the Socialist vote between 1910 and 1918 would be superflous. The social basis of the Socialist vote is readily identifiable: correlations can be made with low farm values, high rates of farm tenancy, greater percentages of rural population, slower rates of population growth, greater percentages of mortgaged property, and dependency upon cotton and wheat as staple crops. In general, the so-called Red River counties in southern Oklahoma and the wheat counties of western Oklahoma were most likely to support agrarian radicalism.[3] In addition the coal counties in eastern Oklahoma also produced Socialist votes. Except for coal-mining towns like Krebs and Wilburton, the Socialists received very little consistent support in urban areas.

Their failure to make significant gains in Oklahoma City was a troublesome and frustrating experience for the Socialists of Oklahoma. Trade union leaders who called for "more" in the spirit of Gompers were able to persuade the city's workers to support a Democratic Party that had delivered some basic labor reform legislation. Only in 1911, when militant businessmen united to crush an embryonic streetcar motormen's union, did the Socialist party find a receptive audience among city workers. Even in the midst of a defeated strike's bitterness, the Socialist candidate for mayor could gain only 23 percent of the citywide vote, although he did win small majorities in working-class districts. Contrary to their theory, Oklahoma's Socialists found much more enthusiasm for their program among small farmers than among city-dwelling workers.[4]

Partisans and opponents of the Socialists knew that southern Oklahoma was the setting in which agrarian rebellion occurred. High rates of farm tenancy and heavy dependence upon cotton as a cash crop typified the economy of most of the Red River counties. "Renters," as they were called, supplied labor and work animals and paid rents of one-third of all corn and one-fourth of all cotton harvested. In their efforts to come out ahead, the renters mined the soil for cotton. Although these tenants were generally younger than owners of the land, indicating some ability to climb the ladder of farm success, fully 35 percent of the tenants in the state were at least forty-five years old in 1930 and nearly 60 percent were more than thirty-five years old. In south-central and southeastern Oklahoma, tenants moved so often (one study found that approximately 60 percent of the tenants in the sample moved to a new farm annually) that they could not have had the advantages of a settled social life.[5]

It may be useful to look more closely at Marshall County, where the Socialists obtained their largest percentages of the vote between 1910 and 1916. Here the rate of tenancy was 81 percent in 1910, 67 percent in 1920, and 72 percent in 1930.[6] The high rate of tenancy, the lack of sustained increase in both number and percentage of owners, and the age of many tenants indicate that most tenants advanced slowly—if they advanced at all—to farm ownership. And tenants were no better situated in the surrounding southern counties. Farm tenancy was a condition of important political consequence, creating an identifiable and frustrated lower class in southern Oklahoma.

In four south-central Oklahoma counties—Bryan, Johnston, Marshall, and Murray—the ownership of tenant farms was concentrated to a considerable extent, although not to the extent found in the Deep South states. Landlords owning three or more farms comprised only 12.5 percent of the total number of landlords, but they owned 36.3 percent of the farms, 34.2 percent of the acreage, and 35.8 percent of the total value of rented farm property.[7] Those landlords holding five or more rented farms held 19.4 percent of the total number of farms. Holders of ten or more farms owned 6.4 percent of the total number, indicating that the plantation style of agriculture typical of Alabama and Mississippi was not typical in Oklahoma.[8] While 75 percent of the landlords held fewer than 200 acres, landlords owning more than 200 acres held fully 57 percent of the total acreage.[9] Seventy-two percent of the landlords held farm values totaling less than $10,000, but landlords owning more than $10,000 worth of rented farm property held no less than 67 percent of the total value of rented property.[10] Ninety-two percent of the landlords lived in the county where they owned or in adjacent counties. Seven percent lived out of the state.[11] The presence of landlords probably intensified political conflict.

Marshall County had only four incorporated towns, whose population comprised roughly 30 percent of a county total of 14,500. More than 90 percent of the people were native-born whites with native-born parents. Statistics on religious affiliation show a preponderance of southern Baptists and southern Methodists, sugesting, as do other sources, the predominantly southern origins of the population. Marshall County, typical of most of southern Oklahoma, was white, Anglo-Saxon, and Protestant.[12]

Although the Oklahoma Socialists never attained a plurality in any election for a state office, they increased their vote in the southern cotton counties in every election from 1907 to 1914, finally throwing the Democrats into panic. While Eugene V. Debs gathered 6 percent of the national vote in 1912, he secured 16 percent in Oklahoma. At the height of Socialist insurgency in 1914, when cotton prices had been reduced to $.06 a pound by the eruption of European war, the party's candidate for governor received 21 percent (52,000 votes) of the state total; he received more than 25 percent of the vote in thirty-five counties and slightly more than 33 percent in thirteen counties. The Socialists elected five state representatives, one state senator, a few county officers, and numerous rural township officers.[13]

The electoral pattern in Marshall County during the period of agrarian insurgency can be seen in the tabulation of the Socialist vote between 1910 and 1916 shown in Table 1. The strongest Socialist precincts—Lark

TABLE 1

Percentage of Socialist Vote in Marshall County Precincts, 1910-1916

PRECINCT	1910	1912	1914	1916	Average
Madill, First	*	20.2	35.7	19.3	25.1
Madill, Second	*	23.2	9.8	5.4	12.8
Madill, Third	*	11.2	7.0	3.3	7.2
Madill, Fourth	*	1.9	7.6	4.0	4.5
Oakland	40.9	42.7	45.8	33.7	40.8
Kingston	13.1	19.5	16.1	8.2	14.2
Woodville	0	14.5	14.8	8.9	9.6
Grantham	18.5	28.0	32.9	13.7	23.3
Durwood	*	28.8	34.0	21.0	27.9
Powell	34.2	40.0	63.0	29.3	41.6
Aylesworth	19.1	13.9	18.8	10.5	15.6
Linn	48.4	68.3	65.7	46.9	57.3
Lebanon	40.3	41.9	56.0	38.1	44.1
Willis	52.2	49.6	58.4	31.8	48.0
Tyler	51.0	41.3	55.1	32.8	45.1
Simpson	50.0	41.0	56.8	38.0	46.5
Lark	48.0	78.8	75.2	69.2	67.8
Isom Springs	47.5	62.6	79.1	56.3	61.4
Shay	53.1	72.5	65.7	64.3	63.9
Cumberland	29.7	44.8	68.4	39.1	45.5
McMillan	48.8	52.9	62.5	41.7	51.5
Lone Elm	46.6	31.5	47.3	27.7	38.3
Kinlock	15.6	26.3	42.5	2.0	21.6

*Not available.

(67.8), Shay (63.9), Isom Springs (61.4), Linn (57.3), McMillan (51.5), and Willis (48.0)—were all crossroads centers that served as the polling places in the rural areas. Lark, Shay, Isom Springs, and Willis nestled in the sandhills adjacent to the Red River in the far south end of the county, an area of poor soil connected to Madill and Kingston only by rough and poorly tended clay roads, which were impassable in wet weather.[14] Simpson (46.5), Cumberland (45.5), Tyler (45.1), Lebanon (44.1), and Powell (41.6) were other farming communities that gave strong support to the Socialists.[15] The lowest Socialist percentages came from the town precincts of Madill, Kingston, Woodville, and Aylesworth, with only Oakland (40.8) departing from the norm of town antiradicalism.[16]

Before one studies local Socialist propaganda it would be wise to examine the formal program that the Socialist Party in Oklahoma ratified and offered to the voters in 1914. The platform affirmed its allegiance to the principles of international socialism and then set forth its demands for the "working class" of Oklahoma. Socialists demanded that industries "collectively used" by the people should be collectively owned. The purpose of state ownership was not to make profit but to ensure "the full social value of their labor" to workers. There were demands for "here and now" legislation to regulate the hours, conditions, and wages of workers in numerous nonfarm industries.

Declaring that the working class of Oklahoma consisted primarily of "agricultural workers," the platform proposed a "Renter's and Farmer's Program", which was strongly agrarian radical in its insistence upon various measures to put land into "the hands of the actual tillers of the soil." Although it did not propose to nationalize privately owned land, it did offer numerous plans to enlarge the state's public domain, from which land would be rented at prevailing share rents to tenants until they had paid rent equal to the land's value. The tenant and his children would have the right of occupancy and use, but the "title" would remain in the "commonwealth", an arrangement that might be aptly termed "Socialist fee simple."[17] They proposed to exempt from taxation all farm dwellings, animals, and improvements up to the value of $1,000. The state board of agriculture would encourage "cooperative societies" of farmers to make plans for purchasing land, seed, and tools and for preparing and selling produce. In order to give farmers essential services at cost, the Socialists called for the creation of state banks and mortgage agencies, crop insurance, elevators, and warehouses.

Demands for immediate political reform were made. The Socialists favored women's suffrage; proposed to make initiative, referendum, and recall procedures easier; demanded that schoolhouses be opened to public meetings for discussion and recreation; and condemned a proposed poll tax as a device to disfranchise tenants and "propertyless workers." On the question of the "colored worker," the platform declared that the Socialists "emphatically" reaffirmed their stand of 1912, which had recommended equal political rights for the "colored members" of the "working class". But the 1914 platform did not restate the position, and the Socialists may have tried to de-emphasize their earlier strong avowal that blacks and whites were equally members of the working class.[18]

Leaders of political parties are occupationally inclined to see their own efforts in organization and propaganda as being more consequential in political results than they really are. Without doubt the leaders of the Socialist party had created an effective organization in the two years after the 1912 election. Notwithstanding a serious schism in the leadership of the party in 1912, the party's secretary could happily report to the convention in December 1913 that there were 3,025 members fully paid up, 342 locals in good standing, and an anticipated large number of new charters soon to be issued.[19] The same secretary offered an explanation of the increased Socialist vote in 1914:

The heavy Socialist increase was due to a campaign of intellectual propaganda which has been carried on by the Socialists. When a man once sees it is a class fight it is very easy for him to take sides with the class to which he belongs.

The increase in our vote is also due to the personal sacrifices that are being made in the organization. Our workers give what little means they have, and their time, to carry the message to the unconverted . . . . who would benefit by the adoption of just and right and they are willing to meet with jeers and ostracism in order to promote the movement. They willingly face the ridicule and opposition which has met great reforms from the days of Jesus down to the present time.[20]

The historian could simply adopt this explanation and attribute Socialist growth to the intentional activities of the agitators who were reportedly making people conscious of their tangible interests in a class fight. Such an explanation would tend to assume a correspondence between the socialism offered in official platforms and the mindful choice made by the voter in a backcountry precinct. We should examine the reality of the relationships between leaders and followers instead of simply assuming a natural correspondence of perceptions and hopes. This is not to suggest that the followers in the movement were incapable of grasping complicated political ideas. That suggestion may be left to those who make a vocation of disparaging particular popular intelligence. Here we will try to discover the combination of attitudes and ideas that motivated dangerous political dissidence.

Socialist voters were indeed jeered, threatened, and ostracized in their own communities. Their local leaders and followers were hardpressed to contribute material support to the party, amid the chronic afflictions besetting agriculture in Oklahoma. But they supported the Socialist party, warded off disruption, and resisted intimidation until finally overcome by the demands of officially sponsored patriotism and the allurements of delightfully high commodity prices between 1916 and 1920. Why did country people associate themselves with a movement condemned by all the commanding and influential people in their localities?

NOTES

1. Angie Debo, *And Still the Waters Run: The Betrayal of the Five Civilized Tribes* (Princeton, 1940, 1972), 61-125, 230-257. The reference here is to the paperback reissue of the original work.

2. These introductory remarks are based upon two dissertations: Ellen Rosen, "Peasant Socialism in America: The Socialist Party in Oklahoma Before the First World War" (City University of New York; 1976), and James R. Green, "Socialism and the Southwestern Class Struggle: A Study of Radical Movements in Oklahoma, Texas, Louisiana, and Arkansas" (Ph.D. diss. Yale University; 1972). Both works place the early history of Oklahoma within theoretical frameworks designed to explain the emergence and character of a rural Socialist movement in Oklahoma. For a standard history, see Edward Everett Dale and Morris L. Wardell, *History of Oklahoma* (New York; 1948).

3. Oliver Benson et al., *Oklahoma Votes, 1907-1962* (Norman, 1964), 25-27 and Green, "Socialism and the Southwestern Class Struggle," 225-228. Benson's work is available from the Bureau of Government Research, University of Oklahoma.

4. See Garin Burbank, "Socialism in an Oklahoma Boom-town: 'Milwaukeeizing' Oklahoma City," in Bruce M. Stave, ed., *Socialism and the Cities* (Port Washington, N. Y., 1975), for a discussion of the Socialist party's 1911 foray in Oklahoma City.

5. J. T. Sanders, "The Economic and Social Aspects of the Mobility of Oklahoma Farmers," *Oklahoma Agricultural Experiment Station Bulletin No. 195* (August 1929), and John H. Southern, "Farm Tenancy in Oklahoma," *Oklahoma Agricultural Experiment Station Bulletin No. 239* (December 1939): 6-7.

6. U.S. Department of Commerce, Bureau of the Census, *Fourteenth Census of the United States Taken in the Year 1920* Vol. 6, *Agriculture* (Washington, D.C.,1922), pt. 2: 633; *Fifteenth Census of the United States Taken in the Year 1930*, vol. 2, *The Southern States* (Washington, D.C., 1931-1932), pt. 2: 1287.

7. U.S. Department of Agriculture, *The Ownership of Tenant Farms in the United States*, Department Bulletin No. 1432 (Washington, D.C., 1926), 9. The use of these statistics may be vulnerable to the criticism that they reflect early or mid-1920s conditions. True enough, but basic patterns of tenancy did not change much between 1910 and 1930.

8. Ibid., 13.

9. Ibid., 14-15.

10. Ibid., 16-17.

11. Ibid., 23.

12. Bureau of the Census, *Fourteenth Census of the United States*, Vol. 3, *Population* (Washington, D.C., 1920), 821; and *Religious Bodies: 1916* (Washington, D.C., 1919), pt. 1: 299-301.

13. The election statistics were obtained from the State Election Board, *Directory and Manual of the State of Oklahoma, 1967* (Oklahoma City, 1967). The computations of percentage are mine.

14. L. C. Snider, *The Geography of Oklahoma* (Norman, 1917), 293, provides a description of Marshall County's topography.

15. Socialist locals were active at Lark, Shay, Powell, Lone Elm, Lebanon, McMillan, Tyler, Simpson, Linn, Cumberland, Oakland, and Madill precincts. *Oklahoma Pioneer* (Oklahoma City), May 4, 1912. After the 1914 election, the *Marshall County News-Democrat* conceded, "You've got to hand it to them, boys—the Socialists of Marshall County have some organization." *Marshall County News-Democrat* (Madill), November 6, 1914.

16. The voting percentages discussed here are for Governor and President. The precinct results in all counties, for state and national offices, can be found in the State Election Board Archives, Oklahoma City. The high rate of tenant mobility described by Sanders, "The Economic and Social Aspects of Mobility of Oklahoma Farmers," leaves the student of voting behavior in a thicket of difficulties. We cannot assert that the same people stayed in the same precincts between 1908 and 1918. But we can say that tenants did not necessarily move far when they moved. They moved, but did not migrate, as an old song put it. We can also be fairly sure that tenants were replaced by other tenants, not by clerks from town and city stores. The social and economic situation of the voter, be he tenant Jones or tenant Smith, is the important point to be established.

17. Socialists used this non-Marxian but politically well-adapted program in Texas as well. See Green, "Socialism and the Southwestern Class Struggle," 79-86, and James Weinstein, *The Decline of Socialism in America, 1912-1925* (New York, 1967), 17-19.

18. For sharp disagreement among Socialists on a party member's proposal to support jim crow legislation, see the *Oklahoma Pioneer*, February 10, March 2, 16, 1912. Democrats belabored Socialists with the cry of "nigger lover," and some Socialists responded with charges that the Democrats were much the greater practitioners of "Nigger Equality" and miscegenation. See chapter 4 below.

19. *Social Democrat* (Oklahoma City), December 31, 1913.

20. *Oklahoma City Times*, November 12, 1914.

The gospel according to ———2
local socialists

In January 1911 R. E. Dooley, secretary of the State Executive Commit-tees of the Socialist party of Oklahoma, felt constrained to address the issue of "Socialism and Religion" in the notes that he published weekly in the *Oklahoma Pioneer*. There was a hint of exasperation when Dooley reported that "day after day we receive letters from comrades from over the state asking that we arrange debates between some Socialist speaker and an opponent . . . the question for debate being, 'Resolved, that Socialism is opposed to Christianity.' " [1] Dooley's reply made it obvi-ous that the compatibility of socialism and Christianity was not one of his major concerns. He suggested that if Socialists "would take some time to consider before writing these letters they would realize that it is abso-lutely impossible for the state office to comply with any such requests. The reason is apparent." [2] He then lectured the local letter writers on the duties of the Socialist party in the class struggle. He warned them that the "attempt to drag in theological argument while supposedly discussing socialism, draws away the interest from the essential principles, clouds the main issues, diverts the attention of the general public and even the Socialists themselves from the very objects for which the Socialist Party was organized." [3] Six months later, the State Executive Committee which was strongly influenced by German-born Socialists who practiced a European style of centralized direction, formally admonished the local Socialists to observe the party constitution's ban on religious discussion and to avoid "odious personalities and offensive sarcasms in pursuit of their agitation work." [4] In December 1911 Dooley was obliged to inform local agitators that their use of quotations from the Bible was acceptable practice but that they could not, as they were sometimes claiming, "prove" the need for socialism from biblical texts.[5] State leaders in later years delivered similar reproofs. [6]

The necessity of these repeated admonitions was apparent. Much of the local Socialist expression in Oklahoma was literally saturated with the arresting imagery of the area's many Protestantisms. This intense religiosity would be unsurprising even to the most casual observer of the American South, for Protestantism was an enveloping ideology that gave meaning to the world of the country folk. It was a system of inherited ideas that was their habitual resort when they tried to explain the rights and the wrongs, the good fortune and the bad, the beauties and the terrors that they encountered in this life. Like other dominant cultural forms, the available configurations of Protestant belief could persuade people to withhold their approval from novel ideas and activities. Many local Socialist spokesmen found it personally difficult to separate their older faith from their new-found political convictions. To many it would have seemed unnecessary, if not actually blasphemous, to make the distinction between politics and religion recommended by the State Executive Committee. One could anticipate that their newspapers would be frequently and heavily laden with affirmations of the Christian character of socialism. If nothing else, the adherents of socialism had to maintain self-esteem in a consciously Christian community. To the charges of atheism and immorality ceaselessly leveled against them, they developed a conventional response: socialism would create better conditions for the promotion and practice of Christian faith.

It is necessary, therefore, to distinguish the two socialisms circulating under the auspices of the Oklahoma party. These may be usefully designated as the imported orthodoxy and the indigenous variation. The outsiders who brought the Marxian idea of class conflict and historical progress to the country realized that capitalism could be attacked on moral grounds, but they concerned themselves far more with the social setting of moral action. They did not see significant possibilities for progress in isolated cases of personal reformation. But if enough working people would agree to abolish private capital, then the necessity for them to engage in selfish and invasive actions to protect personal interests would be reduced and eventually eliminated. This imported version of socialism was completely secular and addressed exclusively the major "industrial and political" issues.

Outsiders like Oscar Ameringer, an Austrian-born immigrant who became a close associate of Victor Berger and the Milwaukee Socialists, saw people linked together in class relations that determined their collective fates. Ameringer pronounced the crowds in the Oklahoma encampments to be among the most intelligent students of socialism that he had taught in a long career of agitation.[7] His listeners were often captivated by his plain speech and his humorous deflations of the Democrats, but it may well be that their understanding of his socialist advocacy was altogether different from what he imagined. The *Oklahoma Pioneer* (which Ameringer greatly influenced) permitted no discussion of Christianity and socialism, an editorial practice that contrasted sharply with the local Socialist weeklies' preoccupation with the subject.

Local Socialists adapted the lessons of the outsiders to their own idiom, creating what was effectively an unschooled variant of the social gospel. This socialist gospel of the countryside was tougher than the more well-known urban middle-class version because the country people could not permit themselves the luxury of a faith in gradual persuasion. In a word, they were more doctrinaire. They envisaged the coming of universal harmony and well-being under the reign of Christ only after standing at Armageddon to battle with an oppressive and wicked capitalist class. Their experience with well-furnished and snobbish townsmen, when combined with their evangelical urgency, sufficed to persuade them that the property-owning lions would not lie down with the shorn lambs.

No one who has studied the evidence of Socialist activity would hastily conclude that the movement in Oklahoma was merely a surrogate for a missung religious experience. There could have been less arduous substitutes. And their conscious attempts to wrestle with the ideas of class conflict, cooperative production, and public ownership suggest that the local Socialists were looking for something other than simple moral transformations unconnected with, and unaffected by, particular social realities. But it would be equally erroneous to argue that, in spite of the remarkable religiosity of these people, they were looking for essentially political solutions unconnected with any inward longings to restore and revitalize a familiar moral order. In light of the wide variations in ideological comprehension and absorption present in the local movements, the historian might be better advised to look for evidence of a genuine syncretism, composed of incongruous elements that generated internal tensions and probably contradictions. This formulation does not foreclose the question of the actual historical relationship between political radicalism and evangelical Protestantism in this particular instance. It does not force us to conclude that one or the other—the imported socialism or the indigenous religious feeling—must have been the determining "base" or the predominant "source" of perception and action.

Socialism promised immediate aid and eventual triumph to farmers who had known little but desolating defeat. Among those farmers the Socialists saw potential sympathizers who were

> mostly renters and laboring men and while they vote all right they are transient and don't care to join a local; and now that we are turned out many are leaving; many are leaving and it is hard to get them to think of anything but their woes.[8]

A correspondent of the *New Century*, published at Sulphur (Murray County) in southern Oklahoma, reminded the tenant farmers of their dreams when they arrived in Oklahoma: "of acquiring and fitting a snug little farm home . . . for yourself and family. How did your plans pan out? The fact that you are still renting is deemed sufficient answer."[9] The editor of the *New Century* pointed to the dismal consequences of rural transiency and poverty:

> School has begun in the towns but the children of the tenant farmers of Oklahoma are in the cotton field. For two months more they will be there. In the meantime the children of the bakers and landlords are getting the benefit of the best educational advantages obtainable. The workers pay for these facilities, but through rents, interest, and profits their children are kept from their enjoyment.[10]

The advantages the townspeople enjoyed excited feelings of intense hostility among the country people because they believed that their own hard work should have earned them similar advantages. The *Madill Socialist-Herald,* published for the benefit of the "red" tenants of Marshall County, dramatized the felt disparities of condition:

> the $25.00 a bale rent you pay the landlord would buy lots of biscuits and calico for the wife, but then it enables the landlord's wife to wear silk and ride in an automobile, and no matter if your wife does walk.[11]

To the *Otter Valley Socialist,* published at Snyder in southwestern Oklahoma, the solution to these injustices was obvious:

> . . . will we be content to permit the gang of interlocked parasites that infest the electric light towns of this county to continue to fatten their sleek hides at our expense, while we who do the work of the world feed on the crumbs from their table.[12]

The *Boswell Submarine,* citing a flyer written by the party's U. S. Senate candidate in 1914, identified and prepared to sink the political enemies of the small farmer: "Our Bulletin entitled 'The Interlocked Parasites,' showed beyond question, that the democrat party in Oklahoma is a political tool of the banker-ginner-merchant-landlord class."[13] These astringent comments typify the efforts of the articulate local Socialists to draw what they saw as class lines between the farmers "who farmed the land" and the farmers "who farmed the farmers." They knew their local world well. Their descriptions of the privations endured and the sense of dispossession created were seldom echoed by their local opponents.

Major business spokesmen in the state, concerned about the long-term implications of perennial rural poverty, sometimes provided analyses of the objective conditions of Oklahoma tenant agriculture that explained the local discontents dramatized by Socialists. The editor of the *Oklahoma Farmer-Stockman,* an affiliate of the state's leading daily newspaper, reported that a careful survey of cotton tenant farming in southwestern Oklahoma revealed the cost of production to be twice the price of cotton (per pound) sold on the market in late 1913.[14] The same editor gave heavy coverage to a 1915 report by the comptroller of the currency that among 7,615 national banks throughout the country, there were 1,022 banks receiving an average of 10 percent or more interest on their loans: of these, 317 were in Texas and 300 were in Oklahoma. Among the many banks claiming heavy losses on small chattel notes, the comptroller singled out one that had lost less than $6,000 in a five-year period while returning dividends amounting in aggregate to 700 percent on its original capital in fifteen years of operation.[15] Even the editor of a conservative business weekly had to be impressed: "I wouldn't think so much about it if the record showed that interest rates are high everywhere. But why should Oklahoma and Texas alone be the earthly paradise of the grasping banker?"[16] Were Oklahomans, he asked, poorer and less reliable than the people of Arkansas, Louisiana, Mississippi, and Alabama, where only forty national banks in all four states charged an average of 10 percent or more of interest? He did not think so. [17]

The economic analysis of the local Socialists, which found some confirmation in (at first glance) strange places, was often equaled, if not exceeded, in volume by enthusiastic reports of vibrant activities among the sorely pressed countryfolk attending the local meetings. In these reports a different idiom frequently appeared. The poor became the Lord's own poor. Socialism became an agency of salvation and seemed destined to perfect the world in anticipation of the coming of the Lord. In what other terms can we understand the feelings of the people gathered at the Caney encampment in 1914? The editor of the *Boswell Submarine* was exultant upon learning of the progress of these pilgrims:

> Comrade Mrs. Cartwright, the Anti Catholic, gave us a history of her life as a Catholic, and I wish I could deliver that lecture all over the state. . . . In short, will say that the encampment was one of the best in the state. They opened with prayer. We had the finest singing you ever heard. I saw old men and women weep like children. They shouted for joy for the coming victories through cooperation. About 1500 were in attendance. [18]

The wayfaring evangels who were trying to bring the wandering tenant farmer home were themselves very much at home within the structure of Protestant thought. Their tradition told them to look for the appearance of certain signs, such as a "baby orator" who would have a

> good grasp of the fundamental principles of Socialism, and is himself an ardent revolutionist with his heart, mind, and spirit in the great cause. . . . He fulfils the scriptural pronouncement: "A little child shall lead them." [19]

The socialist revolution would lead to the kingdom of Christ. Such was the expectation of a Socialist prayer proposed by a writer in the *Sword of Truth*, published at Sentinel in southwestern Oklahoma:

> Permeate our souls with divine discontent and righteous rebellion. Strengthen within us the spirit of revolt; and may we continue to

favor that which is fair and to rise in anger against the wrong, until the Great Revolution shall come to free men and women from their fetters and enable them to be good and kind and noble and human!

O Lord, hasten the day![20]

Marx, too, hoped that the socialist revolutions of his time would introduce a diversity of human excellence and happiness, but his language of expectation was very different.

Postmillennial expectations in Oklahoma were founded upon the popular belief that the Socialist party would improve the earth and perfect its fullness so that the advent of Christ became a real possibility. A western Oklahoma Socialist appealed to his brothers to raise their eyes:

> Socialism will remove poverty and all its hideous train of limitations. Socialism will remove the unhealthy surroundings. Socialism will remove the struggle for mere animal existence. Socialism will remove the lack of hope. Brother, let us have Socialism IN OUR DAY.[21]

When a Christian minister in western Oklahoma denounced the Socialist party for holding meetings on Sundays, Hattie Poling of Lone Wolf, whose husband was an activist in the Kiowa County organization, retorted that the farmers had to keep up the "struggle for existence" during the week. She asked the minister how he could be so certain that God had not sent the Socialist movement to lead mankind into "the Christian Millennium."[22] Another evangelist took his listeners to the mountaintop:

> Complete victory for the reds. The plutes [plutocrats] didn't reach first base. Comrade Curry knocks a home run wherever he goes. The Dubs [Democrats] are stricken dumb when Currie takes the Bible and unmercifully flays the system they support. Then he eloquently pleads with them until they raise their heads. When, by his masterful logic, he carries them with him to the highest pinnacle on the mountain of hope, as he points out to them the beauties of a co-operative commonwealth and the blessings that will be theirs in that day when all humanity will be made free by the workers' vote.[23]

In the *Ellis County Socialist,* Andrew Spratt was an effective proponent of postmillennial socialism. His prayer was that

> . . . the Kingdom come, on earth. While men are underpaid, while women are overworked. While children grow up in squalor, while exploiting and social injustice remain, the Kingdom of Heaven can never come on earth and never will.[24]

In order to begin the improvements here on earth, two Socialists advertised "the primitive gospel of applied christianity." They encouraged people to begin the practice of cooperation. "The holy benefits of co-operation and brotherhood may be realized now to a large extent in any community where enough believers reside to organize for the actual practice of the principle. . . . Theorizing only gets old and brings discouragement," they wisely warned.[25]

One historian has suggested recently that sectarian revivalism was weak in the Southwest during this period and that the poor people who attended Socialist meetings were "interested in radicalism not religion."[26] Religious revivalism, however, was certainly not weak among the Socialists themselves. People were urged to give themselves to the uplifting experience of the revival. The *Ellis County Socialist* was eager to publicize the visit of the Rev. H. Cloud, an "Indian Evangelist, who is holding a revival meeting at the M.E. Church."[27] The same paper gave its evaluation of a census conducted by the Christian churches of Shattuck, Oklahoma. As a result of the census

> the Christian people are intending to do some active work now in trying to increase the interest in christianity and church work. The church organization stands for a great principle, for life itself. The work, therefore, should be pushed with such fervency that no stone will be unturned that will help to save a soul, or encourage the growth and development of those in Christ.[28]

The *New Century* had similar concerns: "The Baptist people of Sulphur have begun a protracted meeting down at the Culbert Well in West Sulphur, with Rev. Moosehead and Rev. Ogle in charge. These gentlemen should receive the encouragement of all right-thinking people in their efforts.''[29] The *Constructive Socialist* of Alva, Oklahoma, recommended that its readers pay attention to the former pastor of the First Christian Church in Alva. He was reported to be a ''red card'' Socialist as well as a consistent Christian. ''This week he opens an evangelistic meeting in the county west of us and we certainly wish him great success,'' the editor concluded.[30]

The forms and functions of politics and religion sometimes seemed barely distinguishable. The *Ellis County Socialist* announced that their comrades at nearby Fargo would hold ''a three days political revival at that place.''[31] And when the Rev. O. E. Enfield reported to the *Ellis County Socialist,* the line between the revival of Christian faith and the promotion of worldly socialist reform blurred into insignificance. His ''Sermonette'' contained three items:

> We have just closed a good meeting at Merrit Okla. Five were added to the church and three were restored. This was my third annual meeting at this place and the church made me promise to return next year.

> We are in a three days encampment here at Wheeler Tex. Now this is the home of Bro. G. A. Lambreth a noble Christian preacher and an ardent Socialist. . . .

> Next Saturday evening we begin a week's meeting at Pixley school house . . . after which we go to Kiowa County for four weeks, making three socialist lectures daily thru the week and preaching on Sundays.[32]

Out of the unpromising landscape and disconsolate lives they encountered, the local Socialists drew out yet another version of the Protestant doctrine of equality in the sight of God. They laid reform within a sacred and millennial context. Trying to reform this world, they tended to revert to categories long familiar to them, thus infusing a transcendental impulse into their doctrines. They had begun to instill a new sense of self-esteem and perhaps even a new sense of identity in their followers. If they did not feel equal to the ''big men'' in their communities, they could begin to feel the confidence of equality in the communal excitement of the revival. The Socialist revivals of Oklahoma had the same leveling effect as their precursors. Once the essential segregation of the "interlocked parasites" had taken place, social distinctions would no longer matter as "the Social Souls of earth are about to roll away the stone that has hid the Christ of Humanity from the working class of the world."[33]

Preachers and their preaching were an important point of reference and a source of legitimacy for country people protesting their conditions. The preacher's authoritative pronouncement shielded religiously sensitive people from the wounding accusations of atheism, quieted the doubts of would-be adherents, and gave the Socialist movement the urgent impulse of revivalism. With the preacher patiently prodding and occasionally lashing his flock, paradise seemed possible where all was now gray and fearful. The vision of a boundless future served to sustain local Socialists in the face of widespread community disapproval whipped up by the respectable and notable among the town middle class.

Although there were almost certainly more preachers who opposed socialism, the minority of preachers who supported it were recruits whose significance far surpassed their numbers. The *Social Democrat* of Oklahoma City reported that "T. J. Minnis is an orthodox minister and his explanation of Socialism from a Bible standpoint is effective. He is just the man to reach the Christian element."[34] No less enthusiastic was a letter writer from Marlow in southern Oklahoma who reported to the *Oklahoma Pioneer* readers that the Rev. Thomas W. Woodrow had given local Marlow "six lectures on Socialism from the Bible standpoint, while his presentation of Marxian Socialism was so clear that a child could understand." Marlow Socialists could therefore recommend him "as being a worthy, clean, and deserving brother and a staunch teacher in economics, Marxian and Christian . . . the Socialism of both Marx and Jesus Christ, and for the Kingdom of God on earth."[35] Local Walter endorsed Comrade S. C. Stair with this humorous accolade: "He has been in the ministry fourteen years—and for five years has had as bad a case of socialism as one needs to have. . . . He is a Christian Socialist."[36] Although the writers distinguish "Marxian" from "Christian" socialism, the elements are so mixed as to be functionally inseparable in their minds. Perhaps the most revealing endorsement of this kind came from eastern Oklahoma. A letter to the *Oklahoma Pioneer* announced that

Sam Baldwin, the poet preacher and Socialist agitator, is once more in this county, preaching, singing, and expounding Socialism in a way that is attracting great crowds.

Few men in our country are equal to Comrade Baldwin in expounding true, scientific Socialism. . . . Now, comrades, get on the firing line. Keep your eyes on the enemy, trust in the Lord, and keep your powder dry.

The principles of Socialism stand for justice, equity, and the Golden Rule.[37]

This writer knew that socialism is supposed to be "scientific," but he did not have a secular conception of historical progress from lower to higher stages of development. The advent of socialism becomes vivid when the poet-preacher invokes the Christian ideal of justice in the Lord's name and faith in the Lord's proffered protection when enemies surround and threaten God's people. The figure of the preacher bringing the gospel to the oppressed is effectively represented by the *New Century*'s story of a Socialist preacher who was driven from his pulpit in the town of Bokoshe. Recalling the experience of the "Son of Man" for an audience that probably did not need the reminder, the editor reported that

in our own state of Oklahoma the sordid tragedy of 2000 years ago is reenacted. The elements entering into the case are the same. A man dares speak for the oppressed. The result is the same, Failing in their efforts to curb the man, the ruling class have crushed him.[38]

An egalitarian ministry emerged in the course of what might be termed the Socialist revival; it was proud to identify its aspirations with the ordinary people whose speech, clothes, and social manners made them unwelcome in many town churches.[39] The local Socialists frequently distinguished a true and democratic Christianity from what they happily termed "churchianity." The Woods County Socialists claimed that the old-time churches "were not endowed by mine and factory owners. The meeting house was built by the brethren. The pastor was a workingman."[40] The Rev. G. G. Hamilton reported to the *Oklahoma Pioneer* that the Hughes County movement was healthy, with its twenty-five locals and 250 cooperative cotton patches whose yields were intended to finance party work. Hamilton was pleased to note that another "element of great power in the Hughes County movement is the large number of preachers. . . . They are the kind of preachers who till the soil, pound iron, and build houses." He guessed that the majority of preachers in the county were Socialists.[41] One such minister was W. L. Thurman, who was, in the estimation of a southern Oklahoma Socialist

> the best man we have to clean up on capitalist-minded preachers. He whips them with their own book—the Bible. He shows beyond the shadow of a doubt that Christ did not bring the Gospel to grafters, interest, profit, and rent takers, but to the working class; that Christ's church was a working class church and that grafters were not eligible for membership in it.[42]

When accused of infidelity, one of the spokesmen of Marshall County socialism offered this rebuttal:

> DO WE OPPOSE CHRISTIANITY?
>
> Does Christianity interfere in any manner with honest labor in the production of necessaries of life?
>
> Does Christianity decree that "he that hath not the cash to pay rent on a seat in church," is debarred from the Kingdom of Heaven?
>
> Does Christianity decree that the men who pay the preacher should select texts and direct his preaching to suit their worldly interests? . . .
>
> But you say that this is all the fruit of hypocrisy? Well, then, it is hypocrisy that we are opposed to![43]

These replies, Marxian in neither inspiration nor substance, were radical enough in the context of local society. The suggestion that the Christian message could favor the bedraggled "wool hats" of the countryside more than the bankers and landlords in the "electric light towns" flew directly against the conventions of respectable opinion, which held that the tenant farmer had failed to meet the test of self-help and was, on that account, unlikely to have the favor of a God who rewarded the diligent with a comfortable prosperity.

The careers of two ministers who became evangels of socialism illustrate the experience of conversion. Both G. G. Hamilton and O. E. Enfield emerged from the obscurity of the small-town ministry to become powers on the platform in the Socialist encampments. Hamilton was a Methodist minister who had won local acclaim in the Red River Valley for his frequent attacks upon "infidel" socialism. Afher one debate he accepted the challenge of a socialist minister to read Walter Rauschenbusch's *Christianity and the Social Crisis.* Overwhelmed by the book's argument that a people could be held collectively responsible for the derelictions and oppressions in their midst, Hamilton walked through the valley of death and emerged a Socialist, a transformation that stupefied his church elders and astonished his erstwhile opponents. The Halletsville, Texas, *Rebel* sent out a special flyer to announce Hamilton's conversion and to publicize his explanation for rejecting religious complicity in a sin-ridden society.[44]

Abruptly dismissed from his Crowell, Texas, church, Hamilton quickly won a following among the Socialists, with the *Oklahoma Pioneer* reporting numerous requests for his services. A reader from Local Short Grass informed *Pioneer* readers that Hamilton

> appeals to the brotherhood of man. His argument is not against men, but against methods. He does not believe that men are so bad as you would believe, but that the system under which men and women are forced to live is what drives them to crime and to the houses of ill fame.[45]

Exhorting readers to secure Hamilton for a meeting, the correspondent from Short Grass concluded, "And watch that old hypocritical fur fly. Hamilton does not fight religion, but he unmasks hypocrisy, and shows you what a true Christian he is."[46] To be a Christian and a Socialist was, in the minds of Hamilton's admirers, to reject the airs of moral and social superiority adopted by well-to-do town Christians. A Socialist in Cordell reported that Hamilton had given the local a speech and had stayed overnight in one of Cordell's "humblest" homes, in contrast to the luxury afforded by the town judge and local businessmen on a previous visit when he was opposing socialism. The correspondent was not disturbed by the news that the Methodist church was preparing to expel Hamilton for his discordant preaching. It was more important that Hamilton had aligned himself with the "working class."[47]

O. E. Enfield was probably the most chiliastic Socialist in Oklahoma. In mid-1915 he had apparently been a conventional Presbyterian elder in the town of Shattuck in northwest Oklahoma.[48] He seemed to be looking for new opportunities, for he had studied and sucessfully passed the state bar exam.[49] In February 1916 he availed himself of the columns of the *Ellis County Socialist* to explain his conversion to socialism:

> When I became, in fact, a socialist, I beheld for the first time the monstrous evil—the source of unspeakable misery—of a very few men owning and controlling the means of production and distribution. . . .
>
> Today one man does nothing and has millions. Today millions do everything and have nothing.[50]

When his coreligionists remarked upon the changed tone of his sermons, Enfield replied somewhat solemnly: "I admit that also and that new, and to some ominous, ring is the note of sympathy for the workers of the world."[51] With a new world to evangelize, he would find the need to testify on the trials of his new faith. In affirming that he wished to be called "comrade", he wrote that very often "someone sneers 'kumrid' at a socialist. The person who does so, however, is ignorant as well as unkind. There is only one title at the sound of which my heart throbs with greater joy, and that is the word Christian."[52] In reply to the recurrent criticism of Socialist meetings on Sundays, Enfield said that the meetings were no worse than his opponents' drunken parties. Besides, he argued, Sunday was the only day of rest Socialists enjoyed. And, with a stormy and egalitarian fervor, he leveled the accusation that was heard so often and revealed so much about the relations of town and countryside: "You have robbed them of four-fifths of their wealth till they cannot dress themselves and their families so but some of your snobocracy who attend church would give them the cold shoulder."[53] False preachers had offended and driven away the hard-working faithful: "Your Capitalistic preachers with purchased lips have condoned and covered the sins of the rich by preaching 'submission' to the poor till the workers become disgusted with these holy humbugs."[54] The organized churches might offend, but Socialists nonetheless should not neglect their Christian duties for local meetings. Enfield suggested that the Socialists of Ellis County did, in fact, "arrange their local meetings so as not to conflict with church services."[55]

As an agitator, Enfield's strength was his impeccable Christianity; his weakness perhaps was his tendency to leap toward the apocalypse. Local Socialists lionized him for his debating successes against the Democrats' favorite "socialist-eater," W. C. Witcher. As the *Otter Valley Socialist* saw one of the encounters, "Enfield is a preacher, he and Witcher belonging to the same church, so Rev. Witcher was robbed of his favortie 'infidel' howl and, having nothing else to talk upon, fell down completely. So long, Witcher."[56] Enfield's vision, outwardly socialist but inwardly and powerfully millennarian, could be too high flown for local Socialists concerned with mundane matters like their tax bills. When the Socialist commissioners of Roger Mills County were being attacked for levying high taxes, Enfield quickly admonished the disgruntled constituents to remember that socialism was an international movement and "perfect Socialism" was consequently impossible in a county or even a nation until it "comes to all the world."[57] Enfield was waiting for the Lord to end all local grievances, but the voters were not willing to wait so long, for they used their votes to oust the Socialist commissioners in the November 1916 election. Enfield, himself defeated in a congressional race, maintained a preternatural optimism. He was with Jesus in the dungeon at Jerusalem, steeling himself for the final battle against iniquity. Jailed for sedition in 1917, he preached from his cell:

> The coming of the jubilee
> When workers of the world are free.[58]

With their command of orotund expression and the confidence of their convictions, the Socialist country preachers delivered a message that resonated in the minds of poor country folk famished for expressions of genuine respect for their efforts and endlessly waiting for the good news of salvation from their ill-rewarded drudgery. If the imported, secular idea of socialism reached any accommodation with the inherited evangelical traditions of the countryside, it was accommodated through the energetic, sometimes fanatic, activities of the preachers. This adaptation of a major European idea to the local cultural landscape was only another of many such accommodations in the history of America. The particular contingencies of life in the Oklahoma countryside and the particular configurations of belief substantially transformed a formally stated secular socialism into a millennarian and transcendant faith in the possibility of universal harmony and perfection. The urgent expectations generated by the communal experience of the meetings and encampments produced incipient strivings for a new identity among the country people. It was not so much that new socialist ideas were emergent as that an old Protestant optimism had been rekindled, with all its lightning and fire now crackling through the language of social protest.

Following the preacher to the highest peaks was an arduous, sometimes exhilarating, experience, not meant for daily repetition. As local Socialists moved about in their localities, doing their daily work and their errands, they had to make judgments on how their neighbors lived, approving or condemning as their moral lights required them. Their acquired Socialist politics had given them an effective, if very simplified, explanation of the class cohesion among the leading townspeople. But their various Protestant beliefs imbued them with standards of personal morality and with a sense of duty to assert those standards. The concern to distinguish individuals as moral (or immoral) beings often made the local Socialists revert easily to a preoccupation with perceived evils of long standing—the Catholic Church, the theory of evolution, the perils of irreligion, the horrors of drink, the wages of sin. The evidence is scattered but suggestive, and anyone who would wish to portray the local Socialists in Oklahoma as the possessors of an unambiguously modern, class-conscious mentality must examine it.

There was, for example, much hostility expressed toward the Catholic church—hostility engendered less by the well-known papal antiradicalism than by an older Protestant fear of "popery" and its Roman seat. The *New Century* advertised subscriptions offers from its editorial comrades in this way: "The *Appeal* is a national weekly and no socialist feels just right without the *Appeal*; The *Menace* is an Anti-Catholic paper published at Aurora, Missouri, and it is a dandy."[59] The *Strong City Herald* reprinted an article from "The Gospel Trumpet" on its front page, apparently approving the article's attack upon the Wilson administration's appointment of Catholics to important national offices.[60] From Marshall County came the same complaint. The *Madill Socialist-*

Herald, upon seeing that Cardinal Gibbons had given a benediction at the Democratic national convention, wished to know if the Democrats were intentionally catering to Catholics. If one or both of the old parties were "guilty," then the *Socialist-Herald* would be obliged to conclude that freedom of speech and press were in grave danger.[61] The *Social Democrat* of Oklahoma City expressed a fear that was definitely not to be seen in Oscar Ameringer's *Oklahoma Pioneer.* "A Protestant businessman does not last long in Shawnee," the editor alleged. "The church controls the town, the ship, the factory, and the public schools." Suggesting that nuns and priests were assembled for precinct duty on election days, the *Social Democrat* became furiously patriotic in putting forward an obvious but revealing fabrication. Hoodlums tore up the American flag, the writer solemnly stated, and threw it in the street, "where the automobiles of the parasites passed over and crushed Old Glory in the dirt, while they speeded on their way to Romanize our public schools."[62] The Socialist candidates, so it was claimed, were the only ones opposing the employment of Catholics. A Protestant and an old republican fear of despotic religious establishments, combined with a ready opportunism, characterized the response of some local Socialists to the few Catholics present in Oklahoma. It was an altogether predictable response from an overwhelmingly evangelical Protestant area.

At least one local editor directly confronted the anti-Catholic attitudes surfacing in the Socialist movement. Noting the growing popularity of the *Menace* in his area, Vernon Rhodyback, the editor of the *Otter Valley Socialist,* advanced this caution to the *Menace* readers:

> We find many socialists working devoutly for the "Menace", an anti-catholic publication. We are not denying the truth of some of its statements, but it is only antagonizing one religious sect against others and in no way presents any solution to the bread and butter question that the Socialist philosophy is interested in.

> We don't care whether a man is a Catholic, Baptist, Hindoo, Heathen, or Jew, what we wish all these fellows to know is that their interests are all the same if they are wage workers.[63]

Only a week later Rhodyback acknowledged the saliency of the religious issue and implicitly flirted with the anti-Catholics when he asked why the

Governor of the state, Robert L. Williams, had attended the dedication of a Catholic school in Shawnee:

> The great mass of voters who elected these democrats hate catholics worst [sic] than a fly does tanglefoot. And these same folks used to hold up with green vehemency, President Taft, because he had appointed several catholics and had a catholic cardinal to shower blessings on our national congress. We are just asking for consistency.[64]

The issue of tolerance for Catholics, with its potential for backlash from angry readers, was not susceptible to facile evasion. It distressed a man who clearly wanted to discuss the economic and political issues. Socialists, he admonished, were bound to oppose the "master class" everywhere. He warned his readers: "Do not become confused. The issue is not religion, it is exploitation."[65]

Since there were so few Catholics in Oklahoma, their possible recruitment by the Socialist party would not become the basis of an active controversy. It would have been understandable for Socialists to feel some antagonism toward an institutional church known for its opposition to socialism in general. But modern versions of that old cry, "No Popery," were far more potent among country Socialists. Such sentiment provides another rough measure of cultural persistence among people who were being introduced to a new scheme for understanding their world.

For the same reasons Darwinism was a divisive issue for the Socialists. The fear of the "monkey" theory could arouse angry protest whenever parents gave thought to their childrens' education. The *Strong City Herald* complained that the Democrats were corrupting the minds of schoolschildren with modern textbooks. To this frightening development the *Herald* responded with the following proposal for debate:

> The democratic party was founded by an infidel and does now compel our children to study textbooks that teach things directly contrary to the teachings of the Bible, therefore the democratic party is teaching infidelity to the children of Oklahoma.
>
> The Socialist Party offers more to the working man than the democratic party.[66]

"More" in this context embraced a local reality that the "bread and butter" advocacy of the major Socialist leaders could not easily or comfortably address. Here a rural conservatism found its voice. The *Ellis County Socialist* published a letter from a man in Gage, Oklahoma, who accused the Democrats of being the real infidels and home-wreckers because they were allegedly removing the teachings of the Bible from the school lessons.[67] The *Otter Valley Socialist* also yields some evidence of local response to teachings that would erode confidence in a literal understanding of the Bible. Reporting that a Socialist speaker had claimed, in debate with a Democrat, that the theory of evolution had proven the Bible wrong, the editor offered this evaluation: "In the debate Mr. Warlick [Democrat] had the advantage of general accepted ideas, while Mr. Clark [Socialist] had the evidence of science and historians."[68] The same editor gives us another useful clue to popular attitudes:

> One of the chief arguments used against socialism by the "campaign opponents" is that most socialists are evolutionists. If it be so, the socialists surely class high, for . . . the theory of evolution stands mighty high with the scholars of America.[69]

It is a reasonable guess that the "scholars of America," armed with their formidable learning, would not have been able to intimidate the Democrats or reassure wavering Socialist voters. The agitator did not tamper lightly with his audience's deeply rooted belief in the authority of the Bible. The *Otter Valley Socialist* editor, with his disturbingly novel learning, stood at considerable distance from his literal-minded Protestant readers. As late as 1925, long after the demise of the organized Socialist party in Oklahoma, former party members argued that the aggressive advocacy of evolutionary theory and atheism by some Socialists had damaged the cause in its most promising constituencies.[70]

In a state where the voters would not approve the legal sale of spirituous liquors, or even limited sales under a physician's prescription, the suppression of bootlegging became a desideratum for those seeking to improve the moral quality of life. Local Socialists often sought answers to the "booze" no less than to the land, usury, and labor questions, which were formally recognized in the party platforms. For many of them it would have been incomprehensible that a Socialist should feel embarrassed about his support for prohibition. The *Woods County Socialist* argued that good citizens would vote for men who stood "for prohibition and the enforcement of law." Among other reasons for voting the Socialist ticket, the editor claimed that "there is not a 'boozer' in the whole bunch."[71] On the other side of the state, the *New Century* had the same perception of the linked moral questions. "Socialism," it proclaimed, "offers the only solution to the white slave traffic. It has a favorable plan for doing away with land tenantry. It proposes to make it possible for a man to worship God according to the dictates of his own conscience. It offers a solution to the whiskey question, and would do away with gambling in farm products."[72] On another occasion the *New Century* told the voters that a vote for the Democrats was a vote for whiskey because they "peddle booze."[73] A correspondent to the *Johnston County Socialist* posed the starkest possible alternatives: it was for the people to choose between "socialism or hell." In addition to ending wage slavery and poverty, socialism would eliminate "the profits from the sale of whiskey," thereby diminishing drunkenness.[74] In the *Constructive Socialist,* "Little Locals by Herb" proposed the same Christian nostrums:

> What have the two old parties done to appeal to a Christian? Have they not built up the liquor traffic by congressional enactment? Have they not protected the white slave traffic? . . . What are they doing to stop the divorce evil?[75]

Ladies who appeared to be straying down an errant path also came under the moral scrutiny of the *Tishomingo News*:

> We got the idea from an old Sunday School book that Eve didn't think so much of her immodest appearance until she had eaten the apple, and while wending our way through the City's streets and seeing the throngs of Women in the cafes, movies, and dansants, it occurred to us that it's about time to pass the apples again.[76]

It is far from easy to decide how much interpretive weight to lay upon these occasional calls for personal and community reformation. They do not bulk large when all of the local writing on socialism has been canvassed. But even if occasional, they are not necessarily uncharacteristic. One may be permitted the suspicion that there was, at the heart of local socialism, a conservative and wholly understandable resistance to incursions that threatened to disrupt and rearrange the neighborhood ways. Someone like the Rev. W. L. Thurman, praised as the man to whip the "capitalist-minded" preacher with the Bible, could move from a discussion of class conflict to a discussion of the vice-ridden classes with no apparent sense of incongruity. He wished to keep the city at a distance. The Democrats were a

cesspool of graft . . . one thing can fitly represent the national democratic party. That is a moving picture show of the slums of the great cities; for the slums dominate the democratic party and take the lead in nominating their presidential candidate.

Tammany Hall, New York is its governing force. But for their slum element Woodrow Wilson would not have been nominated nor elected.[77]

This was altogether a curious attitude for a Socialist agitator, for the slums were presumably the home of impoverished working people who, by his own profession, had a claim on his sympathies. Although there were numerous instances in which local Socialists expressed concern for the plight of workers in distant locales, there is much evidence to suggest that they had not achieved the proletarian perspective exemplified in the nationwide agitations of Eugene Debs.[78] Not that their task was the same, of course. The country people of Oklahoma, so clearly white, so faithfully Protestant, must have seemed so much more worthy than the Catholic denizens of Tammany's precincts. If the country people followed their lights, they would never sink to the level of the "slums," which were less a social than a moral condition.

Endlessly buffeted by accusations of immorality in their own communities, the local Socialists would have needed an endless resilience to endure and survive the abusive treatment they met. Having had neither the broader experience nor the secular mentality of party leaders, they could not accept the leadership's argument that socialism had nothing to do with their religion. Their religion had to do with everything encountered in this life. They were wounded to the quick by the persistent allegations of "infidelity."

Some Socialists, feeling obliged to respect the sentiments of their

constituents, undertook to explain themselves. T. H. McLemore, Socialist state representative from Beckham County for 1915-1916, said that he
did believe in a "Supreme Power", which some would call God. This
would be a God of "love and mercy" who had given the world Jesus and
his ethical ideas. But he could not believe in hell and found much to
dislike in the "narrow-gauged" and "selfish" religions whose devotees
were too eager to condemn the suspected "infidel."[79] The *New Century*
sought to explain away the avowed hostility of some Socialists to Christian belief:

> It goes without contradiction that some Socialists, as individuals, do
> condemn the church. There are also others who are or were not
> Socialists, who have not affiliated with the church, among them you
> will find Jefferson, Darwin, Lowell, Hugo, Ridpath, Edison, and
> scores of others. . . .
>
> In the platform adopted in 1912 religion is not mentioned, neither is
> there anything contained in this platform, that should be odious to
> adherents of the church.[80]

Some Socialists simply expressed exasperation at their opponents'
tactics:

> A member of one of the old parties was heard to remark on the street
> recently that "if we can get the socialists to fighting religion and the
> church it will be an easy matter to beat them." This is dirty politics.
> Why do you not come out squarely and meet us on the real is-
> sues?[81]

The *Ellis County Socialist,* when confronted with the "free love" theme,
asked the Democrats to come to the "front door." The editor warned, "If
you insist on a back door handout, we will try and satisfy your craving to
the best of our ability."[82] In Alva, Oklahoma, the Socialists, after
delivering another long explanation of why socialism was not antagonistic to Christianity, threw up their hands and concluded that people were
"prejudiced" on the question.[83]

The more Socialists claimed to be affiliated with an international
movement, the more their enemies emphasized that some of the major

thinkers and leaders in that movement had been indifferent or hostile to religious belief and institutions. So the Socialists in Oklahoma were kept busy at the "back door," supplying indignant refutations to incessant criticisms. They wondered why the Democrats were unable to appreciate their faith and piety. At North Burns schoolhouse in Washita County on March 14, 15, and 16, 1912, there occurred a three-day debate on the proposition that socialism led to "the overthrow of faith in Christ and is dangerous to morals, the monogamian [sic] family, the salvation of mankind from sin, and loyal citizenship." After hearing the debate, one local Socialist writer had had "enough":

> Look at the men and women around you who are socialists and then can you look them in the face and say that they stand for everything that is degrading and low. I believe that my father and mother are Christian people and the man that says they are all those mean things is a willfull and malicious damned liar.[84]

Since no one was consciously "lying" in these debates, initial bewilderment had to give way to a steadily intensified anger and vehemence. The Socialists were forced to define their attitude toward the evangelical patriotism of the citizens of God's country. The foreign and secular reputation of socialism was no advantage in these latitudes.

The native village atheist who found his way into the Socialist ranks could do his eccentric best to polarize the issue. A Beckham County editor, not at all frightened of offending the Christians, contended that the Socialists were not concerned about "a man's origin or his destiny, where he came from or where he is going." They only wanted "the Shylocks to get off the workingman's back while he is on the road."[85] Always ready to speak more in anger than in sorrow, this tempestuous editor rebutted criticisms of those who made exclusive claims to moral superiority with counterassaults upon traditional patriotic symbols:

> We socialists have been accused of being the worst moral perverts that ever ambled down the pike; and to get back at you we are going to tell a few things about the highfalutin heroes of society.[86]

His readers were probably astonished to learn that George Washington had died of syphilis, that Grover Cleveland had frequented honky-tonks, and that David had ravished Uriah's wife! In light of these "facts," he suggested that the "irresponsible nincoompoops that are running at large and braying about socialists being free lovers should turn the hose upon some of their own cattle and wash off the stink."[87]

When no reply was easy, the least difficult tended to be, "You're another." Whatever such replies had to do with socialism, they at least kept the party's followers on the local battlefield. The condition of the individual as moral (or immoral) being was a widespread concern. The editor of the *Sledge Hammer* in Okemah was very brief with an annoying Democratic rival: "Gaston knows no more about Christianity than a tumble bug knows about the nebular hypothesis."[88] After alleging that some local Democrats had participated in some "free love stunts" themselves, the *Tishomingo News* hastened to assure its readers that if they took "all the religion that that crowd and their cohorts have and put it in a balloon . . . you wouldn't have enough to waft a chigger's soul to heaven."[89]

Like the mingling of waters at the confluence of a smaller with a larger stream, the ideas of socialism flowed into, and were absorbed by, the roiling currents of evangelical emotion. Socialist weeklies like the *Sword of Truth* and the *Sledge Hammer* spent the better part of 1913—a year of organizational prowess and leaping optimism for the party—in trying to dissuade their readers from believing the accusations of socialist immorality and then to persuade them that socialism in Oklahoma would indeed make them far better Christians.[90] The *Sledge Hammer's* statement of purpose asserted that although socialism as such had nothing to do with religious belief, "under socialism you might find it much easier to put your religious belief into practice."[91] This line between politics and religion, drawn with a delicate stroke, must have seemed casuistical to the opposition; and it perhaps bemused the faithful who would have seen any legitimate means of encouraging Christian practice as an integral part of God's intelligent plan for converting sinners. The Rev. E. F. McClanahan, the *Sledge Hammer's* specialist on the historical and moral connection between socialism and Christianity, stated the preferred local solution to the great conundrum:

> On every hand there is a sweeping demand for a righteous government, the toiling thousands of earth's homeless burden-bearers are demanding it, and the socialist movement is the concrete expression of this demand. For the first time since Christ, there is an intelligent

movement toward the conscious organization of a just society. Then children can enjoy childhood, women can be womanly, and men can be manly. The men can organize and cooperate industrially. Then all true Christians will follow the Great Galilean from conquest to victory.[92]

An extensively domesticated and non-Marxian socialism, McClanahan's synthesis did good service. Without disturbing their view of the origins and purpose of the world, it provided an understandable explanation of the source of oppression and a justification of resistance. It subordinated the agency of deliverance to the one and only Source of Deliverance. And it promised to preserve the home, the family, and the fruits of their labor.

Those who were in step with the Great Galilean tended to fall out of step with their worldly leaders. Even after the expulsion in early 1913 of Oscar Ameringer and the group of "centralizers" who gave the *Oklahoma Pioneer* its dominant tone, the local people found themselves at odds with the new, indigenous leadership whose views can be found most readily in the *Social Democrat*, the successor to the *Pioneer* and one that was more congenial to the local temperament. At first the party's new tacticians were inclined to criticize only those who "drag religious questions into our political movement." And how were these disruptive elements identified? They were the speakers who "indiscriminately denounce the Church, the Bible, and the Christian religion."[93] This tactical advice was more consonant with local religiosity than were the directives to avoid religious discussion entirely that had come from an earlier central committee. Now explicitly antireligious Socialists were declared to be in error while the Socialist advocates of the coming kingdom on earth received no mention and apparently no reproof. By April 1914 the continued eruptions of abusive debate over the religious implications of socialism threatened to crowd out discussion of the "bread and butter" issues close to the hearts of more secular-minded Socialists. The Socialist state women's committee, anticipating the 1914 campaign, proposed "to show up the capitalist schemes of poising the minds of the people on religious and the Socialist movement." They would "let the people know that the Socialist party is an economic movement and is not concerned in matters of religious belief and that it is a well laid scheme of the politicians to inject this matter on the unthinking mind."[94] After touring the 1914 summer encampments in Oklahoma,

Socialist lecturer Caroline Lowe complained to her Kansas comrades that in "every encampment more than half the groups gathered in discussion were arguing about the Bible and Socialism."[95] Instead of discussing biblical events, the Oklahomans should have been clarifying "the one and only working class issue. Socialism, pure and undefiled."[96]

Unfortunately for the Socialists, it was the bent of many local minds that transmuted socialist goals into controversies among Christians over the nature of their religion. At the end of 1914 the Committee on Resolutions of the state convention, having seen further consequences of rampant religiosity, was ready to grasp the nettle, as R. E. Dooley had back in 1911. The committee believed itself justified in using stern and imperious language:

> We wholly disapprove of the tendency manifested by a few socialist speakers to attempt to instill into their associates and audiences their own particular religious beliefs or lack of belief, while they are supposed to be presenting socialism; we also disapprove of the practice of engaging in ecclesiastical debates which are not germain [sic] to the question of socialism. Once more we call attention to the fact that socialism deals primarily with the bread and butter question.[97]

The evangelists, no less than the atheists, were now put on notice. But the evidence of the local newspapers would suggest that the directives, as always, were repeatedly honored in the breach.

If socialists wished to form an association of working people who had become politically conscious of the exploitation they suffered at the hands of property owners, they had to tamper with the roots of identity felt by the people who worked in the country. Socialist outsiders had to argue that socialism could not be proven by reference to biblical "laws"; that socialism should encourage the merger of individual small holdings with larger, cooperative holdings of land; and that socialism would succeed only if working people of all races and religions united to oppose and defeat property owners. It was inevitable that a proletarian socialism would generate internal tension within the movement. The only community the country people knew was based upon their religious, their racial, and their "landed" identity.

It may seem strange and inappropriate to use a conception like community to explain the attitudes and behavior of a people so frequently in motion, so precariously unsettled, so naggingly insecure. Certainly nothing like the traditional European rural community existed in the Sooner's state. There were no ancient villages, no families who had lived in one place for generations, no venerable communal rights and obligations, no ruling gentry with time-honored privileges. There were only new towns full of hustling businessmen and a countryside full of small farmers shifting about in a struggle to survive. Everywhere social life was intensely competitive and uncertain.

Yet if the feeling of community is, in part, created from the common images people carry in their heads, there were many Oklahoma country folk who could visualize the moral and ethical community they wished to enjoy. The ingredients of rural communal feeling in an American setting were to be found in the patriotic Fourth of July, the evangelical inspiration, the southern suspicion of outsiders, the ideal of the producer's independence, and the purity of the white race. The Bible, the land, and the energy of the people, combined in a providentially directed union, would make life good, long, happy, and prosperous. When the markets beyond the villages and the country neighborhoods all too often yielded disappointing returns, the country people searched for an explanation. Socialism, uncomfortably novel in its cultural implications but politically appropriate for their oppressed circumstances, could help them identify and understand the propertied power of the local elites. Socialism, represented by the bewhiskered visage of Marx, could not, by itself, dry their tears. There was only One who could.

NOTES

1. *Oklahoma Pioneer* (Oklahoma City), January 28, 1911.
2. Ibid.
3. Ibid.
4. Ibid., July 1, 1911.
5. Ibid., December 23, 1911.
6. *Social Democrat* (Oklahoma City), December 31, 1913; Tishomingo *News*, January 5, 1917.
7. Oscar Ameringer, *If You Don't Weaken: The Autobiography of Oscar Ameringer* (1940; reprint ed., Westport, Conn., 1969), 262-263.

8. *Oklahoma Pioneer*, June 10, 1911 (letter to the editor from W. J. Crawford).

9. *New Century* (Sulphur), September 6, 1912.

10. Ibid., October 4, 1912.

11. *Madill Socialist-Herald*, quoted in the *Kingston Messenger*, September 22, 1916.

12. *Otter Valley Socialist* (Snyder), March 22, 1916.

13. *Boswell Submarine*, October 9, 1914.

14. *Oklahoma Farmer-Stockman* (Oklahoma City), February 26, 1914.

15. Ibid., October 25, 1915.

16. Ibid.

17. Ibid.

18. *Boswell Submarine*, August 28, 1914.

19. *Fairview Republican*, July 17, 1914.

20. *Sword of Truth* (Sentinel), March 5, 1913.

21. *Carter Express*, October 16, 1914.

22. *Otter Valley Socialist*, May 24, 1916.

23. Ibid., January 19, 1916.

24. *Ellis County Socialist* (Shattuck), May 4, 1916.

25. Ibid., September 28, 1916.

26. James R. Green, "Socialism and the Southwestern Class Struggle" (Ph.D. diss., Yale University, 1972), 153.

27. Ellis County *Socialist*, March 30, 1916.

28. Ibid., November 23, 1916.

29. *New Century*, July 7, 1911.

30. *Constructive Socialist* (Alva), August 21, 1912.

31. Ellis County *Socialist*, September 28, 1916.

32. Ibid., September 21, 1916.

33. *New Century*, January 6, 1911.

34. *Social Democrat* (Oklahoma City), July 16, 1913.

35. *Oklahoma Pioneer*, April 6, 1912 (T. N. Pritchard to the editor).

36. Ibid., April 13, 1912.

37. Ibid., February 4, 1911.

38. *New Century*, November 22, 1911.

39. Green, "Socialism and the Southwestern Class Struggle," 254-255.

40. *Constructive Socialist*, August 2, 1911.

41. *Oklahoma Pioneer*, May 18, 1912.

42. *Social Democrat* (Oklahoma City), October 8, 1913 (Monroe Jones to the editor).

43. *Madill Socialist-Herald*, July 26, 1912.

44. Green, "Socialism and the Southwestern Class Struggle," 149-152, for the episode of Hamilton's conversion.

45. *Oklahoma Pioneer*, April 27, 1912.

46. Ibid.

47. *Cordell Herald-Sentinel*, February 8, 1912 ("Social Democrat" page).

48. *Ellis County Socialist*, July 15, 1915.

49. Ibid., July 22, 1915.

50. Ibid., February 3, 1916.

51. Ibid.

52. Ibid., March 3, 1916.

53. Ibid., May 11, 1916.

54. Ibid.

55. Ibid.

56. *Otter Valley Socialist*, May 3, 1916.

57. *Strong City Herald*, August 7, 1916.

58. *Otter Valley Socialist*, August 23, 1917.

59. *New Century*, January 19, 1912.

60. *Strong City Herald*, September 21, 1916.

61. *Madill Socialist-Herald,* July 26, 1912.

62. *Social Democrat* (Oklahoma City), April 16, 1913.

63. *Otter Valley Socialist*, November 24, 1915.

64. Ibid., December 1, 1915.

65. Ibid., June 7, 1916.

66. *Strong City Herald*, September 7, 1916.

67. *Ellis County Socialist*, March 9, 1916.

68. *Otter Valley Socialist*, May 31, 1916.

69. Ibid., November 22, 1917.

70. *Oklahoma Leader* (Oklahoma City), May 29, August 7, 1925.

71. *Woods County Socialist*, October 29, November 5, 1910. This is the predecessor of the *Constructive Socialist* mentioned above.

72. *New Century*, November 3, 1911.

73. Ibid., August 23, 1912.

74. *Johnston County Socialist*, February 2, 1912.

75. *Constructive Socialist*, July 17, 1912.

76. *Tishomingo News*, January 5, 1917.

77. *Social Democrat* (Oklahoma City), July 2, 1913.

78. To be sure Thurman could deliver a ferocious assault upon capitalism as such. See *Oklahoma Pioneer*, May 18, 1912, and *Social Democrat* (Oklahoma City), May 14, 1913. But see also his 1920 letter comparing Debs with Christ and A. Mitchell Palmer with Judas. *Oklahoma Leader*, August 16, 1920.

79. *Elk City News-Democrat*, August 19, 1915.

80. *New Century*, June 7, 1912.

81. *Cordell Herald-Sentinel*, April 11, 1912 (''Social Democrat'' page).

82. *Ellis County Socialist*, March 9, 1916.

83. *Constructive Socialist*, July 24, 1912.

84. *Cordell Herald-Sentinel*, March 21, 1912 (''Social Democrat'' page).

85. *Social Democrat* (Sayre) February 28, 1912.

86. Ibid.

87. Ibid

88. *Sledge Hammer* (Okemah), June 15, 1913.

89. *Tishomingo News*, November 8, 1916.

90. *Sword of Truth* (Sentinel), January 1, May 28, June 18, October 8, 15, 1913; *Sledge Hammer*, June 15, 19, 26, July 24, 1913.

91. *Sledge Hammer*, June 19, 1913. For similar hopes, see the *Social Democrat* (Oklahoma City), September 3, 1913, and *New Century*, March 8, 1912.

92. *Sledge Hammer*, June 26, 1913.

93. *Social Democrat* (Oklahoma City), December 31, 1913.

94. *Boswell Submarine*, April 10, 1914.

95. *Workers Chronicle* (Pittsburg, Kansas), August 21, 1914. Neil Basen called my attention to Lowe's report on Oklahoma.

96. Ibid.

97. *Proceedings of the Socialist State Convention, Dec. 29-31, 1914*, 13-14. Available in the Library, Oklahoma Historical Society.

The land question ——————3

In the fall of 1911 an Oklahoma City Socialist reported to the readers of the *Oklahoma Pioneer* that she had seen a new cotton-picking machine at the state fair that would sharply reduce the need for labor and the cost of production in the countryside. The advent of the machine would mean "good-bye little cotton farmer," for even now he earned only enough "to hold soul and body together by working his whole family, and if the cost of production is (still further) reduced, he will be absolutely unable to compete with the machine work."[1] The writer then delivered a socialist lesson. No one would wish to return to the age of hand manufactures and, anyway, resistance to the introduction of labor-saving machinery was futile: "The breaking up of the models of the sewing machine only paved the way for the garment factory of today."[2] Socialists should remember that the nearer they came to perfection in production, the sooner they would solve the problem of "DISTRIBUTION." It only remained for them "to go in and possess the land."[3]

A coming state of perfection, shimmering in the imagination of the socialist ideologue, was without doubt less easily imagined by those under the sentence of obsolescence. The editor of the *Oklahoma Pioneer*, George Owen, recognized that the soon-to-be "mere farm hands" would need to be encouraged with a plan of immediate action. "Let the renters in the state get together in all haste and let every renter become a member of the renter's union if he hopes to save himself from immediate disaster," Owen advised.[4]

For as long as the Socialist party survived in Oklahoma, it proclaimed in its official platforms that its most important purpose was to serve the interests of the "agricultural workers" who comprised the vast majority of the "working class" of Oklahoma. In Socialist minds, the tenant farmers and the small owners working on their individual parcels of land were absorbed, by means of a tricky mental traverse, into the body of industrial workers more commonly accepted as the potential, if not the actual, constituency of Oklahoma, and especially the tenants of the southern and eastern counties had few worldly possessions. A plough team, a few implements, and some meager furnishings were all that most could claim as their own. They had little to sell but the labor capacity of their families. Propertyless people, however, are not necessarily or naturally proletarians. These rural poor neither lived in closely packed neighborhoods nor worked beside each other in great factories, learning from their common and collective experience to resist the capitalist's organization with varied collectivisms of their own. The inherited notions and habitual experience of country people emphasized self-rule and self-help; the new ideas of the Socialists emphasized collective progress through an enlarged, more efficient process of production and especially through fairer distribution of the increased product.

Not all farmers held views that were proof against all Socialist prescriptions for a new style of agriculture, but judging from the complaints of Socialists who took agricultural collectivism seriously, many farmers did seem loath to accept socialism as anything other than a scheme of relief devised to deliver land into willing hands and to make its yields worthwhile. Indeed some local Socialist editors, better schooled in their party's philosophy than were their readers, themselves reflected the ambivalence of a countryside being asked to alter its cherished ways. The Socialist platform envisaged productive land as a public utility, with the title ultimately residing in the commonwealth. Farmers could transfer possession of their parcels, but only to other working farmers or to sons intending to follow father's footsteps down the furrows. But for southern farmers who thought of their acres as their home, the idea of land as a collective public utility was disturbingly uncertain.

The sense of unease and perturbation may be traced in the local newspapers. There was enough heterodox departure, even from the "farmer's program" of the formal platform, to make the historian's obligation to provide concise description a demanding one. In southern and eastern Oklahoma, where the *New Century* and the *Sledge Hammer* held forth, and in western Oklahoma, where the *Ellis County Socialist,* the *Strong City Herald,* and the *Otter Valley Socialist* mounted their propaganda, editors and their readers discussed the conditions that would permit farmers to exert their energies in fruitful and satisfying activity.

All agreed that the landlord who speculated in the rich earth and "farmed the farmers" was not a useful citizen. His was an unproductive and disharmonious presence. But in the rebuttals directed at Democratic critics and in the lessons and reproofs directed at erring tenants who did not vote Socialist, we can discern the tensions induced by the collectivist implications of socialism.

Some of the most eloquent discussion of the land issue came from the successive editors of the *New Century* during its publication in rack-rented Murray County between 1911 and 1913. In October and November 1911, when the experimental cotton-picking machine was the object of much curiosity, the *New Century* commented, "A sane system would welcome a machine of this kind but our present insane method of doing things cannot see much good in its introduction."[5] After reprinting the *Pioneer* article on the machine, the *New Century* dared to hope that it would become a boon to the farmer:

> Much depends upon its use. If the people would but control this machine, but make it work for them instead of against them, what a blessing it would be, if they would but awaken to the fact that that machine was for the reduction of labor without taking from labor the right to live, it would be a blessing. If that machine was owned collectively instead of individually all humanity would be benefited.[6]

This observation, more plaintive than hopeful in tone, was notable for its lack of ambiguity. But even where the Socialists were careful to be clear, they could still reveal their ambivalence about the extension of public ownership into the commonly accepted private spheres of life. In February 1912, the *New Century* noted an error in its earlier publication of a local platform. Mines, mills, and factories were to be "collectively owned and democratically managed, while the home, which is private property, would remain the same today."[7] What would be the disposition of fields attached to farm homes and of machinery used to work the fields? The answer in this instance was silence. A correspondent of the *New Century* conceded that the tenants' habitual practice of mining the soil for a cash crop was "wofully antiquated" but insisted that the blame lay with the system which enables non-producers to own the land, and through the control of wealth, dictate as to the crops to be planted by the farmer. There can be no radical change in the methods of farm production except through the producer owning his own land, and that can only come through Socialism.[8]

Here socialism is summoned to restore the producer's independence and private control, to diversify crops, and to increase returns; but it is apparently not summoned to extend public ownership and collective operation to the capital resource of land. There is little in the comments of these local discussants to suggest that the Socialists would have compelled a private producer and potential supporter actually to abandon his hopes for a rising market in cotton. At most they might have encouraged the self-directing producer to try new crops and new methods.

In the latter half of 1912 an eloquent young writer named Grady Milner took over the editorship of the *New Century* and immediately began to heighten the sense of urgency in the paper's message to the tenants of southern Oklahoma. He and his correspondents ceaselessly attacked the system of intensive labor extraction fashioned by the banking and real-estate interests in the years after Indian lands had been made alienable to whites. One letter writer warned of the dark night now descending upon the tenants' hopes:

Ten years ago you were eager to unfold your plans of acquiring and fitting a snug little farm home for the maintenance of yourself and family. How did your plans pan out? The fact that you are still renting is deemed sufficient answer.[9]

And how were the tenants going to acquire their snug little farm homes? Milner's version of socialism supplied a curious answer:

The Socialist Party says that when all the means of producing all things necessary to life are socially owned Mandy can primp up, and rest assured that this useful little machine [a milker] is doing the dairy work she used to. When the Socialist have abolished rents, interest, and profit, and each man receives the full social value of his toil the eight-tenths he now doesn't get will enable him to install improved machinery on his farm and thereby cut his working day into half.[10]

Here the shift from a formally learned collectivism back to an inherited individualism occurred within one brief editorial paragraph. Having begun with an affirmation of the idea of social ownership and cooperative activity, the young editor argued for it as a device to support and enhance the profitability of private operation. It was the private action, independently adopted on his own farm, that would enable the farmer to cut his working day. The social sharing of costs, tasks, hours, and profits did not enter the discussion.

The idea of possession as complete and privatistic moves furtively through Milner's thought even when he explicitly endorses the justice of use values:

> Use and occupancy should be the only true title to land. With each man secure in the knowledge that the land he is using remains in his possession while he uses it, he will then take the necessary steps to erect a decent home, get telephone communication with the outer world, and prepare to enjoy life.[11]

It is not easy to fathom the emotional resonance of the notion of possession in this writer's mind. Possession need not have been antisocialist, need not have led to a capitalist privatization of property. But for a man to invest his long-term efforts in creating a farm and building a "decent home," he would want (if he were at all influenced by the dominant tradition) his property to be something private and basically familial. It was on this issue that the Socialists, with their talk of "possession for use," perhaps found it most difficult to allay the conscious fears of the small farmer. A hint of these difficulties is found in Milner's melancholy assessment of the 1912 election results in Oklahoma, in which he wrote, "We have to put up with the evils of tenant farming for another two years. The fellows who had no land were still afraid that Socialism was going to take away the land."[12] Such reluctance and such results were to frustrate the great expectations of the Socialists year after disappointing year.

In late 1912 and early 1913 the Socialists were anticipating a thoroughgoing mechanization of Oklahoma agriculture that, in fact, did not take place until the 1930s. The *New Century* writers tried to awaken their readers to the imminent threat and opportunity of farm consolidation, citing the creation of a few large-scale "bonanza" farms in Texas. They noted that discussions had taken place among Oklahoma's bankers and commercial men, with a view to the replacement of the "shiftless" tenant farmer by a supposedly more provident husbandman.[13] The possibility of successful resistance seemed to recede daily:

> Our land is gone from us, an industrial giant has robbed us of our subsistence. What matters it to us if modern science has relegated the crude horse-power machinery to the rear, and has supplanted it with machinery 100 times superior in point of efficiency? We are penniless; we cannot buy it.[14]

The fate of the penniless men would be harsh when there was no longer any demand for their labor. "Having rendered their full measure of tribute to the masters," Milner fumed, "these tenants are to be dispossessed of everything and set adrift, homeless and destitute wanderers upon the face of the earth."[15]

The *New Century* men asked themselves how this gloomy end could be forestalled. Their answers, refined and summarized in the writings of editor Milner, were revealing. Milner continued to be divided against himself when facing the issue of consolidation. One week he would argue that capitalism would soon "confiscate" the small farm while socialism would save it by assuring the worthy small holder "the full value of all he produces."[16] Individualized and private ownership seemed to be the implicit goal of this socialism. In succeeding weeks, however, Milner was able to articulate the idea of a social response to capitalist progress and inequality. On at least two occasions he suggested that the big farm, whose advance was seemingly irresistible, could be turned into a boon if its title was conferred upon those who used and occupied it and if the users, in turn, were prepared to have the farm "operated socially."[17] Six months later, after the *New Century* had gasped its last breath, Milner reappeared as a writer in the *Social Democrat*, and his writings revealed an unmistakable reversion to the belief that socialism was the salvation of the small farmer.[18]

It is important to see the inward struggle of the local Socialist clearly. His particular form of socialism effectively located the source of agrarian discontent in the experience of work made oppressive by scant returns and numbing poverty. But in his search for a response that small farmers could feasibly make to the massed holdings of the speculator and the corporate farm, he naturally found it difficult to look the idea of social ownership fully in the face. He could not accept the collective implications of a socialist response to a new technology, an enlarged scale of production, and a transformed style of rural life.

One hesitates to say that this was diffidence in the face of changes that were clearly perceived and considered; it may well be that there was a cultural inability that kept the local Socialist from fully understanding the possibilities of change in the accustomed style of rural life. It would surely be otiose to look for proposals that the modes of farming be grandly changed when few local people had grand changes in mind. The Okemah *Sledge Hammer,* whose motto was ''to hammer the system, not the individual,'' called for the elimination of rent and interest but not for the end of individualized farming operations. While attacking a Democratic editor who had proposed that the renters around Okemah be replaced with more efficient farmers, the *Sledge Hammer*'s editor offered this defense of their capability: ''Our farmers are alright. All they need is an opportunity and God's sunshine and showers, which it is fortunately beyond the power of any political system to give or withhold.''[19] To the ever-recurring accusation that socialism would interfere with individual operation of the farm, the *Sledge Hammer* hastened to reply, in effect, that socialism would remove the alien and artificial forces that prevented the farmer from exerting his natural energy upon nature's bounty:

> Socialism will not interfere with the farmer who owns and farms his land. On the contrary it will render his possession of it far more secure than it can possibly be under capitalism, for he cannot lose it by debt, crop failure, or sickness. Co-operative farming will gradually develop under socialism, but the feature of the program that should appeal to the tenant farmers with the greatest force is the fact that the occupancy of the land will be in the hands of the men who work it, and they will have permanent homes without having to pay rent.[20]

The apposition is significant: cooperative farming as an unelaborated ideal of the future placed beside an immediate demand for land for the individual working farmer. From the backcountry along the county roads the working farmer could assert his competence forcefully. An "associate" of the *Sledge Hammer*, writing from the village of Quasada, spoke in the accents of legendary southern men who were quick to resent insult. No one could tell him that he was "shiftless" and dispensable:

We all feel the sting of such treatment as this, and . . . we resent such a move as this with all the energy of our American manhood. The wayfaring man, though feeble minded, can see the motive behind a move like this.[21]

Unable to gain access to their chosen means of living unless they paid the customary rent of "a third and a fourth," the renters in many country districts were predictably enthusiastic about the Socialist attack on land-lordism. Where the Socialists seemed to support public insurance and subsidies for their private farming efforts, the renters in many instances were ready to follow the reds. But where the Socialist editors spoke, usually in brief, undeveloped, and noncontroversial terms, of the cooperative or "social" operation of farms, they were greeted with silence or skepticism from their readers and livid denunciation from the Democrats.

Local Socialist support for the small farmer's aspiration to own and control his land did not seem to vary by locality. In northwestern Oklahoma the *Constructive Socialist,* by reputation less "revolutionary" than the *New Century* and by its name and practice closely identified with Victor Berger's gradualism, assured its readers that socialism would spread property among the many:

Instead of socialism being opposed to the ownership of private property by the individual, Socialism would make such ownership much more secure, but, most desirable of all, it would diffuse much ownership among ALL the people, where under our present system, millions do not and cannot own any private property because of the concentration of so much property in the hands of a few.[22]

This assurance was repeated a number of times during the 1912 election year.[23] A discussion of cooperative farming communities made only a rare appearance in the *Constructive Socialist.*[24]

In Washita County the *Sword of Truth* was obviously encountering the same questions concerning the Socialist position on land ownership. It duly noted the national platform proposal that land would be collectively owned "wherever practicable" and then denied (correctly) that there was anything in that platform that would threaten the small farmer with confiscation. On the contrary, land held for speculation would be seized, and thousands of homeless men and their families would be placed upon it.[25] "Practicable" collective ownership was narrowly defined here, as elsewhere in Oklahoma, to give the widest possible latitude to the private—and traditional—aspirations of the country people.

On at least two occasions controversy over the proposed dispossession of landlords reverberated through the columns of major Socialist newspapers. In November 1911 Willis Bonner, a well-known Socialist agitator from Stephens County, proposed in a letter to the *Oklahoma Pioneer* that payment of rents should cease the day the Socialists carried the state, with confiscated land going to "bonafide farmers" and previously unused land to be made available in homestead portions as quickly as possible.[26] A Socialist named Isaac W. Phillips wrote to protest that an elderly man like himself would be deprived of his rental income if Bonner's "foolish crank proposition" were adopted as policy. He predicted that 90 percent of the farmers would leave the party in that event, largely because the party would acquire a fatal reputation for "dividing up." He believed that Socialists would do best to increase the money supply while leaving the farmer "in possession of the fruits of his hard life's toil until the new conditions are at least formulated."[27] Bonner then rejoined with the prediction that tenants would hardly be appalled by a proposal that would let them retain the fruits of their toil and build their own homes. He concluded, "No master, no slave, no landlord, no tenant. If that means dividing up, I believe in it."[28]

Within three weeks nine men had written letters on the topic, which the *Pioneer* had published in a regular section designated "For the Good of the Party." The length of the letters prompted the editor to request that the comrades shorten their contributions so that he would not be obliged to do so and perhaps truncate their thoughts in the process. It was a hot issue. Most of the letter writers were critical of the old farmer's argument; some accompanied their criticism with the sensible suggestion that a Socialist government would provide support for older workers. One suggested that socialism would "give him something better before it deprives him of his livelihood." And socialism would surely not be introduced without "a constructive plan that will care for just such victims of the present system . . . while it also cares for the renter."[29] To these critics Phillips replied that he did believe that the public should take over all land not cultivated in a "useful and bonafide manner." If the Socialists would "make it good to him," (compensate him), he would be prepared to give up ownership of his 160-acre farm. Socialists should honor contracts made under the present system while endeavoring "to change the system for future use."[30]

There were consistent defenders of outright confiscation in the Socialist party of Oklahoma. J. M. Pilcher, many years a leader in the Kiowa County movement, entered the "Phillips discussion" to see that the party should "stand true to its principles than to see it win in 1912 on a reform platform."[31] In his view not only rents but interest-bearing notes should become null and void at the moment of victory. Nor should revolutionaries draw back at the certainty of federal interference with a Socialist attempt in one state to dispossess robbers of their spoils. Pilcher concluded with the prediction that there

> never will be a time when we can institute the co-operative commonwealth without interfering with the vested rights of some petty landholder who has spent a life of toil for his small holdings. Such men should be taken care of by pension or in some other honorable way, but they should not be permitted to collect rent from their fellow man.[32]

And if the proposal to abolish both rent and interest did drive 90 percent of the farmers out of the party, then Pilcher was prepared to argue that the event "simply proves that 90 percent of the farmers are not ready for Solcalism [sic]."[33]

The evidence is slender as to how the small holder received Pilcher's abrupt dismissal of the "vested rights of some petty landholder," but the occasional eruption into print of the evident disagreements over the sensitive land issue does suggest that the collective and "industrial" implications of the cooperative commonwealth perturbed many of the party's potential and actual supporters. No doubt there were Socialists in Oklahoma who were ready to endorse the vision of a countryside in smoking upheaval. There was certainly enough resentment and a sufficiently deep sense of oppression to be kindled into angry resistance and ultimately open rebellion. The existence of rebellious feeling we can take for granted, but we will still be required to ask whether the local rebels were doing more than resisting an invasion of their agrarian dreams.

The land issue always threatened the surface of party unity. Almost four years after the *Pioneer* debates on land tenure, the same J. M. Pilcher found himself locked in another ideological combat, this time with H. H. Stallard, one of the most popular agitators in southwestern Oklahoma. Their debate in the *Otter Valley Socialist* proceeded upon the assumption that local attitudes toward landed property could not but help determine the electoral strategy and the ultimate political goals of the Oklahoma party. Pilcher had accused Stallard of advocating compromise on the question of absolute land ownership in order to attract "middle-class" votes. For backsliding of this sort Pilcher had only scorn:

> Wouldn't it be a job for the working class to get up a party that would catch the interlocked parasites and still be controlled by the workers?

> The landlords of Oklahoma are largely the bankers, the real estate grafters, and the professional men about the towns. We do not want them in the socialist party unless they will humbly come on our terms. . . .

> We must keep our heads and not go crazy on "carrying." Should we carry every state we could not establish the cooperative common-wealth if the people are not ready for it, so let us educate the people in scientific socialism and say less about our immediate demands.[34]

It was still his conclusion that "confiscation" in one form or another was the only effectual method to abolish capitalist property.

By way of refutation, Stallard anchored his position in the national party's 1912 platform, citing the plank that would limit the collective ownership of land to those instances where it was "practicable." The Socialist program, Stallard claimed, did not "condemn private titles only when such titles are used to exploit. . . . I have shown Comrade Pilcher you are out of line with the socialist platform. . . . I only wanted to exempt the homestead from the application of the law and you wanted to do away with all private titles."[35] He doubted that the small holder struggling to pay his mortgage interest, his county taxes, and his general upkeep was "in any better condition than a renter."[36] He would join Pilcher in advocating "the collective ownership and democratic management of the monopolized industries," but he thought that the landlord system was "the least cog in the capitalist wheel. . . . So long as the capitalist class owns the mills, mines, factories, etc., and can price what I grow and what I buy, they can give me land and take it away, together with all I create."[37]

As a lesson in political economy, Stallard's formulations were exemplary. He perceived that lack of access to the means of production left a person demoralized and diminished in market society. He also saw that local small holders, both farmers and merchants, contributed their bucketfuls to the river of wealth that flowed out of the colonial hinterland to the leading commercial, industrial, and financial centers. Rightly suspected of wishing to blur the lines and mute the antagonisms between possessor and nonpossessor in local rural society, Stallard was, in reality, only taking a "revolutionary" like Pilcher at his word: if the local farmers were accustomed to the notion and practice of private acquisition, then there was no use in baying at the moon, no use in refusing to compromise on the issue of property rights if the "working" farmers were inclined to cherish those rights. If 90 percent of the farmers wanted reform that would assure them of the opportunity to acquire property, then an intelligent political movement should offer them reform rather than offense.

The Stallard-Pilcher debates took place within a rural society whose cultural traditions held that the creation of a home was the result of honest labor, with the land one controlled to serve as the setting of the work and the site of the home. Work rewards were at the heart of the controversy, as the opponents of the local Socialists tirelessly reiterated. According to one of these critics, the Socialists were proposing to reward the improvident and the unworthy:

> You socialists say that a man should receive the full product of his labor. Suppose a man over here plants 10 acres of bad land to corn, and over here a farmer plants 10 acres of good land. One raises 200 bushels of nubbins, the other 500 of good corn, and both have used the same amount of labor.[38]

Not so, replied the *Otter Valley Socialist*, invoking the ideal of social labor for common ends:

> Mr. Elkins cannot get it into his noodle that under Socialism, farming would be cooperatively done. The individual would not lose because of bad lands or bad crops, but the whole society just as society would gain by good crops. The illustration is absolutely capitalistic, and not socialistic.[39]

Elkins had presumably raised the question because he believed that his listeners would find it difficult to accept cooperation as a mode of operating farms and distributing the results. Impoverished and aggrieved the farmers may have been, but they would cling to their belief that a man with land, once freed from the unnatural and unfair exactions of monopolists and speculators, was responsible for helping himself.

The discussions of the forms and functions of landholding should have helped the Socialists to achieve a well-informed and reflective understanding of the term "working class" as it was used to describe the hard-working people of the country districts. Such an understanding was, however regrettably, not achieved. So accustomed were the local Socialists to the perennially depressed condition of the small producer that they did not, for the most part, think through a political response to a possibility that became reality in 1916-1917: not socialism but a rising market might appear to be the quicker route to the possession and ownership of a farm home. Promised a good price for 500 bushels of good corn, the farmer might not wish to keep step with other members of the rural "working class" who, for one reason or another, did not have equally good prospects in the market.

Socialist leaders, whether outsiders like Oscar Ameringer or local boys like Grady Milner, could agree on one major point: the farmers were akin to wage workers in that they would surely do better for themselves if they owned the means of production. Ameringer said simply, "A farm tilled by its owner is a means of life, the possession of which insures to him the product of his labors."[40] The *New Century* editor asked whether the farmers were not in the same position as the city wage workers. He was convinced that they were: "The city wage worker is exploited because he does not own the tools with which he must work, and the farmer is exploited because he does not own the land he must till."[41] Socialists who were less conversant with the ideological conception of the "proletariat" were less persuaded of the similarity. A correspondent from Edmond, Oklahoma, who signed himself "Plough Boy" said that the propaganda "which appeals to the wage worker of the city does not reach the average tiller of the soil. We want literature that tells the farmer just how he is exploited, renter and home owner alike, the selling of the raw farm products on a closed monopoly owned market, and buying back our manufactured . . . products at the other fellow's prices."[42] This preoccupation with the malefactors who would manipulate the markets to the farmers' disadvantage was a major element in local Socialist consciousness. The Ellis County *Socialist*, to take but one example among many, carried numerous articles on how the farmers might vote their particular interests, rid the marketplace of "parasites," and thereby advance themselves as individuals and as a socially worthy group. But the same newspaper printed only one article conveying a vision of cooperative farming in which farmers would work as a class toward common ends and social "shares."[43]

Many of the Oklahoma Socialists characterized their ideas as "scientific," but their "science" was far removed from the analytical understanding of ineluctable social process that has been characteristic of Marxism. The local reds appealed more to old-time religion, to a proven morality, to a sense of righteous conviction. From the exemplary moral character of the "producer's" arduous efforts they drew the standards with which they ruthlessly measured the activities of the "interlocked parasites." A major Socialist spokesman like Patrick S. Nagle, the party's candidate for the U.S. Senate in 1914, could present his essay, "The Interlocked Parasites of the Electric Light Towns," as a simplified and dramatic description of the class cohesion among the propertied and professional townspeople. But when the local Socialists took over the analysis, they tended to shift the accent, placing it more heavily upon the moral meaning of parasitism. The *Sword of Truth* yields a text worthy of full examination:

This was an exposition of the class struggle and class lines between the farmer who farms the farm and the parasites of the county seat and electric light towns. The farmer as the producer is forced to bring the product of his labor to the markets. The banker, the money shark, the merchant, the petty grafter . . . the court house ring,

their slaves, such as clerks, deputies, stenographers, etc., are waiting for the harvest of the farmer. They are of the class that produces
not. They get their living out of the sweat and toil of the farmer, the
working class. It is the height of folly to expect them to work in the
interest of the farmer. It is the height of folly for the farmer to vote
the ticket proposed by these parasites. . . . It is worse than idiocy to
expect these parasites to count the vote that will forever end their
opportunity to feed and fatten on the toil of others.[44]

As a description of the hard feelings experienced when buyer and seller
haggle over prices in straitened circumstances, this passage will serve; as
an exposition of the class struggle, it becomes a problematical document.
"Class" is surely something more than discontent with the prices one is
compelled to accept and to pay. It is founded not only upon differences in
short-term market conditions but upon permanent structural relationships
between owners and nonowners of property and upon different perceptions of the consequent social arrangements.

It is questionable whether the numerous local critics of "interlocked
parasitism" differed substantially from their opponents in their basic
perceptions and explanations of human motive and activity. They
believed that men exerted energy to satisfy their private wants and
desires. Any good man would do so. Wicked men, consumed with malice
and greed, sometimes misappropriated the fruits of labor. They could
retain their ill-gotten gains if they could maintain their corrupt monopolies. Was it merely "bad men" who were at fault or was it the
"system" itself? The answers from the countryside, while often talking
of the system, tended to focus on the little groups of bad men who had to
be rooted out before the farmer would get his due. The countryside's
emphasis upon removing the incubus of parasitic "monopoly" from the
marketplace leads one to suspect that it really wished to free the track for
those energetic runners who had been immorally, if not illegitimately,
shunted aside and deprived of their God-given opportunity to win themselves a home. Equality in the eyes of God should have made men equally
free to help themselves in the marketplace.

It would be an ill-informed historian who asserted that socialists, in
many different times and places, had not condemned capitalist practice
on moral grounds. Their moral critique of capitalists hardly made the
Oklahoma Socialists unique. Socialists everywhere have asked men to

exert themselves to the full extent of their abilities and to be prepared to share equally in the rewards of productive labor. Socialists have promised a free ride to no one except the disabled. It was the requirement of social sharing as a basic principle of distribution that presented the leaders with a virtually insoluble dilemma when they tried to move the country people beyond moral condemnation of the banker-landlord to a socialist reconstruction of the countryside. "Dividing up" the bad and the good corn was not easily comprehensible to people who had a deep-seated religious belief in personal responsibility. No matter how many times Oscar Ameringer told the farmers that the "Socialist Party . . . does not propose to separate the actual farmer from his farm," many remained doubtful.[45] After all, the basic principle of socialism seemed to require that a man would be "separated" from his particular contribution, whether it was 200 bushels of bad corn or 500 bushels of good.

If the Socialist party muted the disturbingly innovative implications of socialism, it could only advocate demands for immediate relief from hardship and measures to improve the market position of individual farmers. But then the market itself might improve, and formerly disadvantaged interests could become newly advantaged. Even if the profit-seeking bankers, landlords, and middlemen were put out of business (which they never were), the countryside would still be full of small holders whose livelihoods would always be decisively affected by commodity market fluctuations. At some point, Socialists who held power and believed in socialism would have had to approach the small holders to propose an enlarged scale of production, along with cooperative operation and ownership. That the Oklahoma Socialists never got the opportunity does not prevent us from speculating that the promotion of a socialist modernization of the countryside would have been a difficult political task.

Socialist leaders did encourage tenant farmers to join renters' unions, which were to represent the rural "proletarians" in collective negotiations with landlords for better terms of rent and work. Modelled after the industrial coal miners' and timber workers' unions of the Southwest, the new renters' unions were envisaged as an industrial arm of the movement for political socialism.[46] But even though Socialist leaders ceaselessly repeated their prescriptions to the proletarianized countryside, they found it difficult to persuade country people to act like proletarians. If the numerous complaints of Socialist editors about the indifference of the tenants to the collective purpose of the unions are at all indicative, the idea of a union was problematical for country people. They were being asked to unite and seek improvements in their condition as tenants when they really wished to become the owners of land and homes.

Two Socialist renters from southern Oklahoma, Sam and Luke Spencer, had founded the Oklahoma Renters' Union in 1909.[47] In 1910 the *Oklahoma Socialist* was portraying the union somewhat implausibly as a "nonpolitical" agency to win improvements for tenant farmers.[48] By October 1911 Sam Spencer reappears in the pages of the *Oklahoma Pioneer,* denying that the union had expired, pleading that it needed new stimulation and organization, exhorting the renters to make the required effort.[49] In January 1912 the *New Century* advised its readers that

> every tenant farmer in Murray county should take steps to organize. . . . There are less than one hundred landlords in the county and about seven hundred tenants, organization is the only remedy. Just so long as you act independent of your neighbor he is your competitor, but when organized you become each other's protectors.[50]

The advice had apparently proven unpersuasive. Two months later the *New Century* was obliged to ask why the renters of Oklahoma were not responding to the union.[51] In early 1913 the *New Century* was still drumming the message of the renters' union, still imploring the tenants to join before the huge corporate farms engulfed them.[52] It gave a realistic appraisal of the effect of an important "external" impediment to unionization: "Too many of the renters in this state are afraid of their jobs. They haven't backbone enough. Any galoot can see that if the renters are organized they are bigger than the fellows who own the jobs."[53] Intimidation (willingly employed by the Democrats) was undoubtedly effective, especially when piled upon the cumulative pressures of hard times and drought that weighed upon Oklahoma farmers between 1910 and 1913. Yet an explanation stressing the external disruption of unionism may obscure or even ignore attitudes within the potential union constituency that impeded union just as much. The coal miners and timber workers of the Southwest were able to build organizations and mount strike actions in the face of repression, though it certainly must be admitted that the timber workers' union in Louisiana fell victim within three years of its inception to the combined disruptive measures of the company owners and their allies among public officials.[54]

Another reason for tenant reluctance to join the renters' unions is not far to seek: many tenants wished to progress in a "business" way, as the columns of the agricultural business weeklies amply testify. The *Oklahoma Farmer-Stockman* encouraged its readers to discuss the question of land tenure and agricultural production. The debate lasted through the spring of 1914. While there were some contributions, reminiscent of those in Socialist papers, that attacked the landlords' refusal to offer more than a one-year contract and to provide well-improved farms, there were other contributions from tenants who accused their fellows of lacking the sense of responsibility and the diligent habits necessary for profitable operation of farms. These, of course, were not the kind of letters that appeared in the Socialist press. One man who had become a farm owner wrote:

> We have some good and fair-dealing men on both sides but am sure that many of our renters are lacking in both energy and honesty. They don't seem to try to accumulate wealth. If they make a good crop they spend all the proceeds and don't save anything for the bad years.[55]

Other writers suggested that the profit-seeking tenant should diversify into turkeys, livestock, fruit trees—anything to escape the curse of King Cotton. Instead of demanding cotton, landlords should give tenants contractual security, and encourage them to diversify, thereby achieving success as business farmers.[56] This was a debate without end in Oklahoma: whose burdens were onerous, whose demands were unfair, whose energies were slack, whose word was worthless? And it revealed a substantial body of tenant opinion that endorsed individual much more than unionized effort.

To the tenant farmers who responded favorably to the renters' union and the Socialist party, Leviticus 25:23 carried the great message of righteous inheritance: "The land shall not be sold forever: for the land *is* mine; and ye *are* strangers and sojourners with me." This traditional belief gave a strong tincture to the general ideology of protest that issued from the renters' union and the local Socialists. Innovative proposals occasionally saw the light of day, but they seldom went abroad in the local world without the company of traditional understandings, which could usually be found in uneasy proximity. The official resolutions of the Texas Renters' Union, reprinted and endorsed by the *New Century*, illustrate the incongruous coexistence of an indigenous "moral" economy and an imported political economy. The Texas Renters began with a defense of the customary rents: they would "destroy the bonus and cash system and refuse to rent for more than a third in grain and a fourth in cotton."[57] Next they would change farming practice by promoting "co-operative farming and co-operative enterprises related to farming *as far as possible,* realizing that the machinery needed to farm in the modern style, is beyond the reach of the individual renter."[58] A hint of what was possible—or, more likely, what was not possible—in the way of innovation is found in the eloquent coda reasserting the ideals that their culture and experience had given to the southern small holders. Here indeed were the ideas that ruled their hearts in the deepest and most inward reaches:

> To bind ourselves together in one great army of emancipation from landlordism and all its attendant evils so that the American home may be builded on a rock, that the teachings of the Bible be lived up to in our daily lives, to the end that we shall live under our own vine and fig tree and raise our children so that they may receive a thorough education as befits the sons and daughters of the producers of wealth.

> Finally, we believe with the good book that "the land is mine and shall not be sold forever, for ye are strangers and sojourners with me."[59]

These were not negligible ideals. When pronounced with an honest fervor, they could revive a people's battered pride while intensifying their eventual disappointment. The soulful hopes generated were, in the dismal circumstances of rural poverty, not likely to be realized. But for a time, some rural people would be inspired to vote Socialist because socialism seemed to promise equality in the sight of the Lord. In the end, these selfsame ideals, expressive of a strong sense of individual independence, would have conflicted with the socialist collectivism offered to the rural community by secular-minded Socialists. People are ruled by their ideas no less than by physical force and material constraint. And these traditional ideas, which could arouse diffuse social resistance and a more focused political insurgency in local society, were so saturated with the obsolescent individualism of the small land user that they set limits upon his capacity to understand and absorb socialism.

Nothing measures the distance between the Socialist outsider's conception of positive public policy and the parochial Socialist's concern to be restored to private prosperity and competence quite as effectively as their respective attitudes toward public taxation. The local Socialists frequently bewailed high taxes and called for rigid economy in governmental operations.[60] The *Ellis County Socialist* complained of the extravagance of the Democrats and implored the voters to "give us a Socialist legislature and we will give you laws to relieve."[61] The same newspaper was pleased to report five months later that the Socialist commissioners of Roger Mills County had "decreased the salary expense by $327.65."[62] J. T. Cumbie rhetorically asked his readers if they would like to see a 25 percent reduction in the salaries of all state and local officials.[63] A Woods County Socialist heartily wished that tax monies for education would be dispensed only for the teaching of humble arts relevant to the activities of country people. He wrote:

Only the useful in the course of study will be emphasized. Folderol to sell books and apparatus will be discouraged. Hundreds of older pupils quit every year because of the nonsense attempted. Education must be toward the country and away from the city. The school must become the social center from which will radiate a saner and happier country life.[64]

Given the townspeople's tendency to scorn the country people when they were not ignoring them, these feelings of resentment are understandable. But it should be clear that this was also a resentment of the new ways that were intruding into the old countryside. What it once was is what it still should be.

By contrast, local Socialist proponents of an expanded public service were thinly scattered. One was the redoubtable revolutionary, J. M. Pilcher, who was ready to set himself against cherished local preferences. He considered his Harmon County comrades foolish for having proposed a reduction in educational expenditures and abolition of the county superintendant's office, with its duties to be assumed by the county judge. Pilcher pleaded for more and better supervision of schools. "The county judge is always a 'jackleg' lawyer, and knows about as much about educational matters as a hog knows about religion."[65]

As in so many other controversies, it was left to the *Oklahoma Pioneer* to teach proper socialist doctrine. Ameringer and his happy band of "German centralizers" informed the country locals of the necessity to pay high taxes if the Socialist party was to fulfill its promises of public service to the farmers and workers.[66] One lesson was delivered in October 1912 when Ameringer and the *Pioneer* group were under steadily mounting pressure from the rural decentralizers to resign from the state executive committee, suspend the publication of the *Pioneer*, and take their leave from the Oklahoma movement. On the edge of extinction after two years of excellent service to the movement, the *Pioneer* fired a withering blast of grapeshot at local departures from socialist principles and policies. The *Pioneer* sneered at the local platforms, which

hasten to assure the property owner that the Socialist Party will reduce the taxes he has to pay, and that the workers in the county offices will work long hours for small pay.

The Socialist Party will do nothing of the kind. It believes in short hours and high pay. It believes not in low taxes but in high taxes. . . .

In the meantime low taxes mean low wages and unemployment to the workers, and an increased amount for the property owner.[67]

Pressed by critics to explain this emphatic and unqualified language, the *Pioneer* offered these clarifications in its next issue:

It does not mean that two men should be employed where there is work for only one, or that offices should be maintained at public expense which do not give an adequate return to the public. . . .

It is not a question, therefore, of how high the taxes are, but of who gets the benefit of the taxes. . . .[68]

After reciting the long list of public services proposed in the state platform, the *Pioneer* inquired of its readers:

> Is any Socialist so foolish as to imagine we can do all this and "reduce the taxes?"

> Is any farmer or wage worker so foolish as to prefer a little reduction in taxes to the tremendous good which would come to him from the adoption of this program? . . .[69]

These strictures were symptomatic of the fissures that had opened up within the Socialist party of Oklahoma during 1912. Local definitions of the public good tended to be parochial and too inelastic to include the measures of positive public policy so readily acceptable to Socialist leaders. The "tax question," intimately related to the "land question," served to divide followers from leaders. The basis of division was the same: country people wanted to own land unencumbered by any financial snare of a private or public character.

This interpretation of the local Socialist response to the land question must inevitably remain controversial. The evidence that might reveal the mind of the countryside is slender and inconclusive. To search for the inward side of thought so poorly documented even in its manifest forms would seem to be all the more hazardous; but not to hazard anything would leave us with little more than a summary and explication of formal party platforms and catechetical restatements of acquired learning. This suggestion is not put forward to disparage the laboriously acquired learning of the local Socialists but it is intended to question how much the new learning flowed beneath the surface of conscious thought into the hidden currents of "natural," habituated moral emotion.

In the currents of feeling that flowed through the Socialist gospel of the country communities, there was very predictably more of Leviticus than of Marx, more evangelical enthusiasm for encouraging righteous behavior than intellectual comprehension of a class war upon a contradictory social system. Too many bad men had usurped the land. There was only one great Landlord, and He was preparing to cast out the strangers and sojourners, the impudent intruders who had misappropriated the patrimony of the hard-working and God-fearing poor. Once He declared the land His own, the Lord, acting through His Socialist movement, would vouchsafe it to those who lived up to the teachings of the Bible in their daily lives. Socialist leaders, having come to Oklahoma to promote socialism, found themselves incongruously summoned to perform the matchless feats of Moses.

NOTES

1. *Oklahoma Pioneer*, (Oklahoma City), October 28, 1911.
2. Ibid.
3. Ibid.
4. Ibid.
5. *New Century* (Sulphur), October 6, 1911.
6. Ibid., November 10, 1911.
7. Ibid., February 16, 1912.
8. Ibid., March 29, 1912.
9. Ibid., September 6, 1912.
10. Ibid.
11. Ibid., January 17, 1913.
12. Ibid., November 29, 1912.
13. Ibid., January 3, 10, 17, 24, 31, February 7, 1913.
14. Ibid., September 27, 1912.
15. Ibid., January 3, 1913.
16. Ibid., January 10, 1913.
17. Ibid., January 24, 31, February 14, 1913.
18. *Social Democrat* (Oklahoma City), July 16, 1913. See "The Farmer Under Socialism" by H.G.M.
19. *Sledge Hammer* (Okemah), June 5, 1913.
20. Ibid., July 10, 1913.
21. Ibid., June 15, 1913.
22. *Constructive Socialist* (Alva), August 14, 1912.
23. Ibid., July 10, 1912.
24. Ibid., August 2, 1911.
25. *Sword of Truth* (Sentinel), December 18, 1912.
26. *Oklahoma Pioneer*, November 11, 1911.
27. Ibid., November 25, 1911.
28. Ibid., December 2, 1911.
29. Ibid., December 9, 1911.
30. Ibid., December 23, 1911.

31. Ibid.
32. Ibid.
33. Ibid.
34. *Otter Valley Socialist* (Snyder), October 21, 1915.
35. Ibid., November 10, 1915.
36. Ibid.
37. Ibid.
38. Ibid., December 1, 1915.
39. Ibid.
40. *Oklahoma Pioneer*, September 24, 1910.
41. *New Century*, January 24, 1913.
42. *Oklahoma Pioneer*, January 6, 1912.
43. *Ellis County Socialist*, December 30, 1915, for the article "Cooperative Farming in the Future." See also January 6, March 9, April 13, May 11, 18, 1916, for repeated arraignments of monopolists and "parasites" who thwarted the farmer's natural energy.
44. *Sword of Truth*, August 26, 1914.
45. *Oklahoma Pioneer*, September 24, 1910.
46. James R. Green, "Socialism and the Southwestern Class Struggle" (Ph.D. diss., Yale University, 1972), 98-103, 202-204.
47. Ibid., 98.
48. *Oklahoma Socialist* (Duncan), February 3, March 3, 1910.
49. *Oklahoma Pioneer*, October 7, 1911.
50. *New Century*, January 5, 1912.
51. Ibid., March 8, 1912.
52. Ibid., January 31, February 14, 1913.
53. Ibid., February 28, 1913.
54. Green, "Socialism and the Southwestern Class Struggle," 160-208.
55. *Oklahoma Farmer-Stockman* (Oklahoma City), May 7, 1914.
56. Ibid., February 26, March 5, 12, April 2, May 7, 1914.
57. *The New Century*, February 7, 1913.
58. Ibid., my italics.
59. Ibid.
60. *New Century*, January 19, February 16, 1912; Cordell *Herald-Sentinel*, August 2, 1907, November 9, 1911, January 4, February 8, 22, 1912; *Social Democrat* (Sayre), February 28, 1912; *Oklahoma Labor-Unit*, December 27, 1913; *Strong City Herald*, September 7, 1916.
61. *Ellis County Socialist*, December 30, 1915.
62. Ibid., May 25, 1916.
63. *New Century*, January 19, 1912.
64. *Constructive Socialist*, September 4, 1912.

65. *Oklahoma Pioneer*, June 15, 1912.

66. Ibid., March 23, 1912.

67. Ibid., October 1912. The *Pioneer* was reduced to a monthly schedule by this date.

68. Ibid., November 1912.

69. Ibid

Local socialists and "nigger equality"   ———— 4

In his standard work on the Socialist party of America, historian David Shannon concluded that most Socialists and most Negroes were disinclined to bear the additional stigma implied by the color each was known for. Shannon points out that the major Socialist newspaper in the Plains states, *The Appeal to Reason*, reassured doubting whites that Socialist reforms would not result in social equality for Negroes. Victor Berger, the leader of Milwaukee Socialists, frankly stated his belief in the inferiority of Negroes.[1] However, America's leading Socialist, Eugene Debs, argued for the full political and economic equality of Negroes but stopped short of endorsing close social contact between black and white. "Social equality, forsooth!" Debs scoffed. "Is the black man pressing his claims for social recognition upon his white burden-bearer? . . . Has the Negro any greater desire, or is there any reason why he should have, for social intercourse with the white man than the white man has for social relations with the Negro? This phase of the Negro question is pure fraud and serves to mask the real issue, which is not social equality, but economic freedom."[2] Shannon argued that the Socialists, by avoiding the touchy issue of social contact between white and black, offered little that was attractive or helpful to Negroes, who suffered special forms of discrimination and oppression.[3]

What happened in Oklahoma when men who called themselves Socialists saw men working in the fields who were black? Did the Socialists include these black workers in their version of the working class? Political commentators in Oklahoma, especially Democrats, frequently observed that the white tenants of Oklahoma were the heirs of southern tradition with its rigid standards of racial separation. Although only 8 percent of the population of the state was classified as Negro in 1910, many white Oklahomans apparently believed that unrestricted voting would attract large numbers of Negroes from southern states where they were legally denied the vote. The editors of *Harlow's Weekly* in Oklahoma City, sober and restrained in their language but no less determined than other Oklahoma spokesmen to see Negroes socially confined and effectively shorn of their political rights, argued that racial subordination was not properly

a party question it is chiefly a social one; and most republicans in Oklahoma are no fonder of negroes than are democrats. The only element that will be unified against such action will be the socialist party and it is extremely doubtful whether even this party can maintain its strength on such an issue. A very large percentage of the recent growth of this party has been among the small farmers in the southern part of the state, who, before they became Socialists—and since—were white men, who upon such an issue will be more influenced by their racial feelings, inherited through generations of southern ancestors than by the highly theoretic considerations which influence the leaders of the Party.[4]

Where *Harlow's* was cautious and ponderous, local Democratic newspapers were pithy and vehement. Mincing no words, the editor of the *Hollis Post-Herald* in southwestern Oklahoma insisted that "Gene Debs, Ameringer and the whole socialist bunch may preach it as political expedient and practice it from choice but they will never make thinking people believe that economic determinism made the Negro's skin black, or that it causes the Negro when he sweats to smell like a peck of mashed green bugs."[5] If the number of envenomed comments on Socialist sympathy for the Negro is an indication of the political value of the issue, the Democrats apparently believed that they had their own mint. Their newspapers reverberate with praise of lynchings, ridicule of Negroes who joined the Socialist party, abuse of "nigger-loving" Socialists, mock sympathy for the poor tenant who unwittingly got involved with a gang of "nigger-lovers."[6] Democrats especially tried to stir up local resentment of the state leaders of the Socialist party. Oscar Ameringer, whose widow said that he was always "right as rain" in the defense of

Negro rights, was the *bête noire* of the Oklahoma racist.[7] The *Caddo Herald* informed his would-be supporters:

> If any democrat should say that the negroes and socialists belong to the same class, he would incur the keenest resentment of all the socialists in the country. That is exactly what Oscar Ameringer, the leading Socialist of Oklahoma, declared in a campaign circular sent out during the fight on the grandfather clause in 1910. To quote him accurately: "We are for the negro because he belongs to our class. We dig with him in the same ditch drink with him out of the same cup, and eat with him out of the same dinner pail." By quoting Ameringer we do not charge that socialists and negroes are of the same class. We simply quote what a leading socialist has admitted.[8]

It was uphill work for state Socialist leaders like Ameringer, Patrick Nagle, and John G. Wills, each of whom was firmly committed to inclusion of the Negro in the working class and defense of his political rights. Ameringer wrote the official ballot argument against the Democratic-inspired grandfather clause intended to disfranchise Negro voters in 1910. After approval of the amendment by the state's voters, Ameringer still maintained that "the negro is part of the working class and we stand for the whole of it."[9] At the same time Patrick Nagle was broadcasting instructions to Negroes concerning how they might approach the polls and attempt to vote in the November 1910 election in spite of the passage of the grandfather clause. He suggested that Negroes go early and unarmed to the polls, try to avoid altercations with Democrats, and swear out warrants before the local justices should election officials deny them the right to vote. Nagle advised blacks who needed help to seek out a "red card Socialist. If he is a southern man it will make no difference with him. Cumbie, the socialist nominee for governor, fought four years in the Confederate army." Nagle explained that Socialists stood by the Negro simply because he was a worker, not because of religious, humanitarian, or constitutional convictions.[10] He concluded with brave defiance: "Here we take our stand and from this rock we will never be shaken."[11]

Although Nagle and Ameringer never were shaken from their position and were able to leave their imprint upon their party's formal pronouncements on race, other Socialists responded with ambiguous mixtures of condescension and sympathy. Many local Socialists, especially in south-western Oklahoma, openly expressed their prejudices toward the Negro and their desire to make Jim Crow part of the Socialist platform.

Some of the local hostility that flowed into the campaign to "decentralize" the party and in particular to reduce the influence of Ameringer and the *Pioneer* group had its origins in dispute over the merit of opposing the grandfather clause in 1910.[12] Patrick Nagle may not have given Negro voters good advice when he claimed in 1910 that they could depend upon ex-Confederate Cumbie for defense of their voting rights, for in 1911 the ex-Confederate was sounding much like an unregenerate southern patriot. To inspire Socialists he set the following ditty to the tune of "Dixie":

> See the poor white girl of "sweet sixteen"
> In the cotton field with the burley "coon"
> As she toils, the sun it broils
> In Democratic Dixie
> Then see the mob as they roast that "coon"
> For the brutal crime that was done
> Are you surprised to learn
> Of the bonfires down in Dixie.[13]

For Cumbie and other local Socialists in southern Oklahoma, socialism would keep exploiting landlords from sending white families into the fields with black laborers. Cumbie was much like Tom Hickey of the *Halletsville Rebel*, a Socialist with a revolutionary and syndicalist reputation whose racial attitudes, in Donald Graham's view, were "much more southern than Socialist."[14] Hickey likened the Texas Socialists to the earlier southern rebels and claimed that the decentralizing "radicals" in the Texas and Oklahoma movements were the "New Rebels of the New South."[15]

To illustrate the dilemma facing white men whose Socialist ideology was less colored with southern "patriotism," we may look at the mixed feelings of a man named Marvin Brown, who edited the *Industrial Democrat* of Oklahoma City. Rivals to Ameringer and the *Pioneer*, Brown and his associates were expelled from the Oklahoma branch in

1910 for allegedly for taking bribes to deviate from party policy. Brown and his friends were restored to the party in 1913 after the *Pioneer* had collapsed and Ameringer had been expelled. Yet even though he was an opponent of Ameringer and indeed was later to become an anti-Catholic writer for the *Menace*, Brown was prepared to sympathize with the Negro to a degree. Commenting upon the national "display of race prejudice" that followed the Johnson-Jeffries prize fight in 1910, Brown concluded that "surely the Negro has been more sinned against than sinning."[16] The grandfather clause in his view would only intensify the Negroes' hatred of whites and "still further jeopardize the safety of our mothers, wives and sisters."[17] Those who hoped that Oklahoma would follow the example of Mississippi in race relations were reminded that Mississippi had five rapes to Oklahoma's one. The "rape complex" made it almost impossible for the Oklahoma Socialist to imagine any solution other than social separation. "Looked at from the social side," Brown wrote, "it is perfectly plain that the Negro can never expect to reach a position of equality with the whites,"[18] so he would be unable to reach "the full degree of development of which he is capable." Brown believed that there was "an instinct implanted by nature for the preservation of race purity" that impelled the whites to separate themselves from blacks. Where there was social contact, "freedom of marriage" would be admitted as a consequence. But social separation could not be complete either, and one race would be "permanently socially inferior to the other," with injury to both. Here Brown had clear insight into the results. "The one will become domineering and regardless of the rights and susceptibilities of the other, and the other either cringing, subservient, or hopelessly menial, or discontented, turbulent, and a source of constant unrest and friction, as is the case today," he concluded.[19]

Marvin Brown confronted the American dilemma and the Oklahoma Socialist's problem. He knew it all too well.

We cannot, under our system, or under the theories of human rights for which we have always stood, with justice or fairness deny to any man the exercise of full political rights on account of his color and yet a majority of the negroes in this country are denied the right of suffrage or of any voice or participation in the government for the maintenance of which they are taxed.[20]

Brown threw up his hands, likening the plight of the Negro in America to the persecuted Jews of Russia, but he did not suggest that the Negroes had anywhere to go. In another article he decided that political and economic equality would not force social intercourse and intermarriage. He called for a ''square deal'' for Negroes and opposed the grandfather clause. Of the Oklahoma City Labor Day parade in 1910 he gave a rhapsodic report:

> In the line of march there was no ''Jim Crow'' division, for scattered through the long line of march were the negro hod-carriers and members of other crafts, all of which brings to mind the fact that in the class struggle there can be no division of labor on account of race, color, or previous condition of servitude, but that the workers of the world must unite and march to victory under one common banner.[21]

Not long after Brown's newspaper collapsed, he was expelled from the party, and he disappeared from the history of Oklahoma socialism. But he left an acidulous postscript on the race question in one of the last issues of his paper:

> Why then are we better than niggers? It is because we are always honorable, just, fair, and kind. It is because we never oppress the poor. . . . It is because we treat women with courtesy and consideration and never drive them to prostitution in order to secure the means of life. It is because we give special honor to those who serve us by digging coal and raising cotton and corn and wheat, and supply them with all the best there is in life instead of robbing these workers and leaving them in poverty. In short it is our innumerable virtues that makes us so much better than the ''nigger''. Rah for us![22]

Except for the painful twists and turns of the frustrated Marvin Brown and the firm demands of Ameringer and Nagle for proletarian unity, the historian finds no strong evidence of the diverging attitudes of Socialist leaders and followers until 1912, when the flattering possibility of Oklahoma City becoming the site for the Socialist party's national convention raised disturbing questions for the party's followers. An article canvassing Oklahoma City's prospects as a convention site suggested that it might be tactful for the delegates, should they indeed meet in

Oklahoma City, to take a more "practical" and less "utopian" stand on the "Negro question."[23] It mentioned the Socialist party's "Unity resolutions" of 1901, which set a high standard of egalitarian, interracial cooperation for members. As reprinted in the *Oklahoma Pioneer*, the soon-to-be controversial sections of the resolutions read:

> . . . that the only line of division which exists in fact is that between the producers and the owners of the world—between capitalism and labor. And be it further
>
> Resolved that we, the American Socialist party, invite the negro to membership and fellowship with us in the world movement for economic emancipation by which equal liberty and opportunity shall be secured to every man and fraternity become the order of the world.[24]

Within two weeks of the appearance of this report a southwestern Oklahoma Socialist lecturer and leader wrote to the *Pioneer* suggesting that if the conversion of one Negro to socialism offended and drove away ten white workers then workers of both colors were injured. But he made it plain that he did not wish to have fellowship with Negroes. He had lived among them, he claimed, and he wanted no more of "that kind of life." His recommendation to Oklahoma's Socialists: if they wanted socialism, then Oklahomans would have to "adopt a resolution declaring for segregation of the negro and let him work out his own destiny."[25] Such a tactic would deprive the Democrats of one of their favorite cudgels for beating Socialists.

Between February 10, when this letter from H. H. Stallard appeared, and April 20, 1912, a number of Socialists wrote the *Pioneer* to give Stallard thorough political and ideological chastisement. A black Socialist from Cogar, Oklahoma, said that this "Brutus" was race rather than class conscious and would betray the principles of international socialism. He concluded, "The voters thus secured would bring with them their prejudice and disregard for human rights so characteristic of this part of our beloved country."[26] John G. Wills, one of the party's major ideologists, argued that socialism could not be achieved through segregation or decentralization, thus linking Stallard's "decentralist" preferences with his attempt to hitch a Jim Crow car to the Socialist party. If the party had lost 10,000 votes in 1910, as Stallard claimed, then they were votes well lost to a Socialist party in Wills' view. Local Wilburton, composed of the miners of that eastern Oklahoma locality, moved that Stallard be suspended from the lecture circuit, citing his letter of February 10 as good cause. Another correspondent depicted Stallard as the unfortunate and hideous product of that "cess pool of hell" known as capitalism. The April 20 issue of the *Pioneer* carried Stallard's rejoinder to this cascade of criticism. Although lambasted more than any other Socialist in recent memory, he still confessed amazement at the existence of the unity resolutions and challenged his critics to state whether an elected Socialist government would be mandated to repeal the state laws providing for segregated schools and forbidding miscegenation.[27]

Stallard got much the worst of the rhetorical battle in the *Pioneer*, the scourge of local heterodoxy, and his views never received any formal recognition in the state platform. The article dealing with the "Negro question" in the 1912 state program reflected the impassioned commitments of its author, Patrick Nagle. His themes were once again the swift evolution of the Negroes from slavery through serfdom to the working class; their brutal victimization by the Democratic party in the South; their right to no longer be "driven in terror from the homes of their childhood and the graves of their murdered dead"; and the necessity and justice of according the "black section of the working class" every political and economic right to be enjoyed by white workers in the "coming civilization" of socialism. Even Patrick Nagle, however, had to draw the line somewhere; and, as usual, "social equality" was the demarcation that would help the Socialists retain some credibility with voters whose intestinal fear and loathing of the Negro made them proof against the argument for unity. Denying that "social equality" was entailed by proletarian unity, the platform stated evasively that

> social equality in this sense does not exist among whites—the plutocrat and proletarian do not meet as social equals. We call attention to the fact that a condition of affairs which they pretend to fear and dread under Socialism now exists in this state under Democratic rule—and we proclaim that at this hour the daughters of the working class, through poverty, are compelled to work with negroes in hotels, restaurants, laundries and other places of public employment. And further, the white working man is compelled to

work with the black working man upon the same jobs in the city and [to] compete as tenant farmers for the land throughout the state.[28]

Socialists had always contended that collective experience deriving from a common social existence would exert pressure upon the consciousness of men, pushing them toward the understanding that their labor was being unjustly appropriated. Understanding their own collective situation and interests, workingmen would struggle to expropriate their employers. Obviously Socialists in Oklahoma found it impossible to tell white men who worked for wages that socialism would bring the races closer together rather than separate them still further. Oscar Ameringer might say that white and black workingmen would dig in the same ditch and drink from the same cup, but for all of his familiarity with Oklahoma's working people he was never really an Oklahoma Socialist. The Socialists of Oklahoma provide one more instance of southern reform sentiment and southern racial prejudice existing simultaneously in the same minds.

The search for a policy on race consistent with socialist theory and inoffensive to white prejudice led Socialist leaders down a tortuous and bootless path. The 1912 platform was approved, and its statement on race was reaffirmed by the 1914 platform, although it is significant to note that the reaffirmation did not include a restatement of the actual policy. It was simply too embarrassing and damaging.

Once Ameringer and his associates were expelled for opposing local autonomy, the party's followers in the country districts felt less constrained to vent their feelings. The Sentinel *Sword of Truth* suggested in the fall of 1913 that the Socialist party's stands in favor of "negro equality" had been "a sweet morsel for some of our opponents."[29] In the same period, the *Social Democrat* was addressing the racial issue with the moral ferocity and spirit of retaliation characteristic of the local Socialists. An unsigned article stated:

No Socialist wants social equality between the races . . . but all claim that the natural resources are the gift of God, and for the use of all mankind not a favored few, or a favored color. But Democrats and clergy scorn our dreams, our ideals, our visions, and hopes of future justice.

The South has ever been brutally Democratic, and we do not

charge that Democrats believe in social equality, but we would like
for Democrats to explain who is responsible for the thousands of half
breed negroes that are found all over the South. They cannot be
charged up to Socialists.[30]

The same newspaper could respect Patrick Nagle for his passion on the
question but did not tell its readers, as the *Pioneer* once did, what Nagle
was advocating. "If you don't believe the Kingfisher (N) eagle can
scream, you should have heard him discuss the status of the colored
workers. It was a fine effort, Pat," the *Social Democrat* said in cryptic
conclusion.[31]

In considering local expression, we have already noted J. T. Cumbie's
"Socialist Dixie", with its complaints against the capitalist Democracy
for forcing poor whites to mix or compete with black workers in the
fields. This was an immediate issue for the *Otter Valley Socialist* in
1915. Editor Rhodyback was tolerant on religious issues but not on the
race problem. He complained that local landlords were importing black
labor and admonished them in his headline to "give white men the work
first."[32] There was nothing to be gained in asserting proletarian unity
when the white laborers were local residents and the black were transient
harvest hands who could not vote. Workers though they were, the blacks
got little sympathy from Rhodyback. He claimed that

> fully two-thirds of the pickers in the country are negroes and are
> largely a very undesirable element come from the black district of
> . . . Fort Worth, Dallas, and Oklahoma City.
>
> At one time there was excuse for hiring this element, but when
> there are many white families that need the work and especially in a
> county where the people are supposed to oppose negro labor, the
> work should be given to white people. . . .
>
> From all over the country comes reports of shooting and killing
> scrapes, committed or caused by this element. Three negroes have
> been killed in the county alone in the last two weeks.[33]

When faced with Negroes, the Socialists regarded their appearance with
the same distaste as Democrats. Transient white laborers probably would
have been resented if they took jobs away from local people, but not as

much as Negroes were resented in a county "supposed to oppose negro labor." Ironically the Democrats, no doubt for their own selfish reasons, would at least hire Negroes who needed work. But then Democrats only claimed to be businessmen anyway.

One Socialist letter writer in southwest Oklahoma claimed that the "SOCIALIST PARTY has nothing to do with the race question, but Socialism will solve it."[34] He suggested that the races mingled with each other only because "the whites live among the others to exploit them; and by their exploitation have caused uneasiness among the others, who in turn drift out among the whites, thinking thereby to better their condition."[35] All races, he suggested, but especially the Negro, were taught that the inferior black race had to look to whites for advancement and comfort. Socialism would solve the problem, he argued, because "the whites will not be able to exploit the Negro so he will have no desire to live among them and will naturally move to the place best suited for him."[36] The suitable place turned out to be localities in the South "where the Negroes and bull-frogs thrive exceedingly well, but a white man can hardly live in, and the only reason he is there is on account of our insane economical condition." He believed that the adaptability "of one race in certain occupations over all other races will help cause separation of them also." He signed himself, "Yours for Socialism."[37] One may doubt that this solution impressed Negroes, Democrats, or proletarian Socialist leaders like Ameringer and John G. Wills. But one is impressed by the transmogrified character of local socialism. Promised full social value for his labor by the state platform, the Negro, if he was listening at all, found the local Socialists eager to send him back to the steaming plantations.

Local Socialist response to Democratic cries of "nigger-lover" was predictably southern and nonsocialist. The Socialists claimed that the Democrats were much the greater practitioners of "Nigger Equality". Doggerel set to popular tunes carried the message:

> I went down to the Solid South
> To see the sights by looking
> And there I saw the yaller boys
> As thick as maggots working
> This by-product of Democrats
> Some were the sons of teachers

> Some were the sons of Congressmen
> And some the offspring of preachers
> Donkey Noodle Democrat
> Increasing yellow stock, sir . . . [38]

The genre was popular. The following week another writer tried to surpass his comrade by describing how the "Real Infidel" passed the grandfather clause, advised the poor to accept their lot, cut the price when the farmer brought his cotton to market, visited booze and bawdy houses, chased Negro women into the woods, and fathered yellow children:

> And when I pointed to that child
> And asked him to explain
> He threw his head up in the air
> And almost split his brain.
> Infidel! Infidel!
> You vile disgrace to hell!
> You "yellow" negro's papa, sir
> Tis *you* that's infidel.[39]

Fascination with the Negro's libidinous nature and scorn for the progeny of interracial sexual union had long been one of the basic subliminal themes in American social life. Its appearance intact in the conscious expressions of local Socialists should make us wary of any suggestion that socialist ideas had altered the mentality of the rank and file.

Yet socialism, when combined with traditional notions of Christian charity, could push a local editor toward an unorthodox formulation of a sensitive problem. The editor of the *Sledge Hammer* was even prepared to counter the intense antagonism associated with the "rape complex." He seemed to recognize that the inferiority of the black man required a social explanation and special measures of reform. A news-service story appearing in his paper prompted his attempt to define his own Socialist convictions on the "Negro problem." The headline supplied with the news story read:

> Black Brute Lynched at Anadarko
> Oklahoma Mob of Nearly One Thousand Hangs

> Ben Simmons 18 year old negro
> Killed Susie Church Sixteen year old Girl . . .

Instead of condoning the fury of the crowd seeking revenge for an alleged rape-murder, the editor of the *Sledge Hammer* questioned the reaction of the crowd and thereby raised questions about the implanted caste system itself:

> For the information of our socialist readers we wish to state that we disclaim all responsibility for the writeup of the lynching at Anadarko, appearing in this issue. We are using the ready-print service of the Western Newspaper Union, but thought we had arrangements made whereby no such objectionable matter would appear in our columns. The crime with which the negro was charged, and of which he was possibly guilty, was diabolical in the extreme, but so was the crime of the mob.
>
> One crime does not excuse another crime. The socialists everywhere stand for law and order, and are unalterably opposed to mob violence. These lynchings are a discrace [sic] to the state, and the widespread publicity of the horrible details of the savage orgies attending them will work an incalculable injury to the country. For the mob maddened by the sight of an atrocious and revolting crime, with the hot blood of indignation running riot in their veins, some shadow of excuse may be found; but for the sensation monger who panders to the basest passions of a morbid and depraved section of society, by rehearsing the gruesome and soul sickening details of the torture of a human being, brutal monster though he may be, by a mob of frenzied savages, there is no shadow nor semblence of excuse. If such things must be, in the name of our so-called christian civilization, spare the public the sickening soul-harrowing details. Socialists are working to bring about an era of peace and good-will—to establish a sane and scientific system of society under which human monsters—the victims of evil environments—will cease to be born.[40]

This convoluted passage is assuredly strange matter to appear in a country newspaper in Oklahoma, especially in a county where the black population exceeded 35 percent. The editor, while looking apprehensively over his shoulder at the rage of whites, mustered all of his eloquence to condemn the ritualized reenactment of the white man's dominance over the specter of the potent black man. He knew that his argument would be unusual and unpopular in his neighborhood but his "Socialism" and his Christian humanity required him to condemn the depravity of the lynch mob. He seemed to be working his way to the conclusion that social advantage should constrain people from committing the crimes produced by social disadvantage. Socialism then becomes the necessary condition in which men could find social happiness.

The pressures against the limited charity of this position were strong. When the news service again supplied a story of a grisly lynching, the editor published no disavowal. When it appeared that landlords were attempting to evict large numbers of white tenants and to replace them with new families, the *Sledge Hammer* observed that the first group to arrive varied in color "from jet black to light mulatto."[41] He argued that if the imported blacks were able to regain their suffrage, the local Democratic oligarchy soon would be replaced by a Republican oligarchy, the "biggest hog" being shoved aside by a bigger one. But worse than this, the necessities of capitalism would perpetuate the disgraceful conditions that placed poor white girls in the midst of Negroes in the cotton fields, giving the lie to the Democrats' boast that Okfuskee County had been made "a white man's county."[42] One can almost feel the palpable strain of trying to be a Socialist in the spirit of the party's resolutions and yet at the same time feeling revulsion at the sight of black males working near white girls. One of the strongest taboos in his society simply was the sense of the matter to him, but official Socialist doctrine enjoined him to condemn equally the exploitation of both races. It must have seemed thankless and unrewarding, especially when he knew that the Negroes would be very likely to vote Republican anyway.

In contrast with southern Oklahoma Socialists, whose concerns were shaped by southern standards, the writers for the *Sledge Hammer* condemned southern sectionalism. The "slavocrats" taught the yeoman farmer "to love the institution of human slavery, and to hate . . . any who might deny that it was a divine institution," with the result that "thousands of working people died in battle in defense of negro slavery who were never able to own a blind mule."[43]

In the North, according to the *Sledge Hammer*, capitalism had produced free laborers, merchants, and farmers who had battled for human rights during the Civil War. But the Republican party, once the champion of free labor, had now become the political tool of the monopolies. It was the destiny of the Socialist party to abolish wage slavery just as the Republicans had earlier abolished chattel slavery. The Socialists would lead free working people into a higher form of social life. As a *Sledge Hammer* writer suggested,

> the Socialists (who are the new abolitionists) denounce slavery in any of its forms as an unmitigated curse to both master and slave, a blight upon society and good morals, and a "covenent with death and an agreement with hell."[44]

Invoking the spirit of William Lloyd Garrison and portraying Oklahoma's Socialists as new abolitionists instead of new rebels, the Okemah Socialists could reasonably be termed egalitarians on political and economic issues (strictly defined). Their understanding of industrial development more closely approximated the party leadership's teachings on class conflict.

These local Socialists, living among people whose racial fears were deep and volatile, did not face unique difficulties. Halfway around the world, a young Socialist agitator in another provincial setting spent much of his time trying to unify the oil workers of the Baku fields in the Russian Caucasus. There, too, religious, ethnic, and national antagonisms, exacerbated by the provocateurs of the Czar's secret police, made it difficult for Joseph Stalin to win converts to socialism.

But what a great difference in the basic social situation! The political system in the United States offered working white men in the South the choice of voting for Democratic candidates who promised them reform *and* strict segregation of Negroes. In Oklahoma the governing party offered whites, during the course of basically democratic elections that would have bedazzled the young Stalin and his Baku comrades, policies that would keep the "black brute" in his place.

One possible measure of the effect of socialist ideas on the minds of those voting for the Socialist party may be found in the division of votes on Democratic proposals to disfranchise Negroes in 1910 and 1916. In 1910 the Democrats had proposed a literacy test with an attached grandfather clause to exempt illiterate whites. In 1916 the Democrats produced a straightforward literacy test to replace the grandfather clause lately invalidated by the Supreme Court of the United States. In both instances the Democrats gave profuse assurances to white voters that they did not intend to disfranchise a single white man.

The Socialist state leaders pointed to experience in other southern states where Democrats had used literacy or poll taxes to disfranchise poor whites. In 1916 the Socialists were able to couple opposition to the literacy test with support for their own initiative petition for a "Fair Election Law". The practices of local Democratic election registrars and precinct officials had been so scandalous in some cases that the Republican party had volunteered its support for the Socialist initiative. This rare instance of fusion was provoked by the Democrats' open contempt for fair elections:

> If we were a registrar under the new election law (here a universal registration act passed by the Democratic legislature), we don't know any decent white republican that we would dislike to register, but believe that a socialist or a negro would have a healthy chase to find us. We don't think that a man who repudiates the stars and stripes and chooses, instead, the red flag is recognized by the constitution as a citizen worthy of the ballot, an [sic] as to the crime of disfranchising the "shine" so often referred to by our republican friends(?), we think the crime was committed in their enfranchisement.[45]

What did happen when southern white men were called upon to vote for or against measures designed to prevent the Negro's participation in politics? Surprisingly, there were significant degrees of correlation in both southern and northern Oklahoma. Recent students have found correlations ranging between $+.37$ and $+.82$ in southern and eastern Oklahoma counties—correlations that tend to vary inversely with the percentage of Negro population. Most significantly, Socialists in Major County, a Republican stronghold in northwest Oklahoma, voted more strongly against the grandfather clause than did the traditional Republican defenders of Negro political rights.[46]

These results are susceptible to no definitive explanation. It may be that Socialist propaganda in 1910 had effectively exploited poor whites' fears of voting restrictions. Perhaps these fears, combined with a basic sense of fair play, did move southern white men to vote against a measure disfranchising Negroes; 106,222 voters had opposed enactment of the grandfather clause (135,443 had favored it). The Republican vote in the concurrent primary was 84,158. Professor Green's judgment is certainly reasonable: "Clearly, members of other parties also voted against the clause. Most of these additional negative votes undoubtedly came from the Socialists who endorsed 'unrestricted suffrage' in an intraparty referendum held in the Spring rather than from Democrats whose leaders initiated the measure and insisted that support for their proposal be made a test of party loyalty."[47]

Perhaps it was true, as segregationist Socialists were to argue in 1912, that Socialist opposition to disfranchisement had cost the party 10,000 votes. The Socialist vote in November 1910 was 27,800.[48] The gap between the 22,000 non-Republican votes and the November Socialist vote was thus slightly less than 6,000. Perhaps Socialist voters in November had stayed home in August or had voted in favor of the grandfather clause amendment. From what the historian can know of racial attitudes in southern Oklahoma many voters must have felt the strong cross-pressure of attraction to the Socialist party and dislike of the Negro. The Democratic party's total primary vote in August was 122,000, and its November gubernatorial vote was 119,000. Because the vote for disfranchisement of Negroes in August was more than 135,000, it is a plausible surmise that some Republicans and some Socialists had voted in favor of disfranchisement. The Republican vote for governor in November was 99,000, an increase of 15,000 over the party's primary vote in August.[49] Since the grandfather clause was the most salient issue in August 1910, it may have been the cause of the fluctuation in the Socialist and Republican votes between August and November 1910. The only established fact is the positive statistical correlation between the Socialist vote in November and votes against the grandfather clause in August.[50] Such correlations, while significant in considering aggregate behavior, tell nothing about individual motivation.

In 1916, after six more years of Socialist agitation and advance, the party once again opposed a Democratic-sponsored literacy test. Graham found strong correlations between the Socialist vote in 1914 and opposition to the literacy test amendment in August 1916. These correlations ranged from +.75 and +.72 in Marshall and Beckham, the Socialists' "banner" counties, down to +.26 in Pontotoc, also a strong Socialist county.[51] Even in Kiowa County, the home of H. H. Stallard and the *Otter Valley Socialist* segregationists, a correlation of + .62 appeared. In Okfuskee County, the home of the *Sledge Hammer* and its "new abolitionists," the correlation between the Socialist vote and negative votes on the literacy test was + .69. Unlike the previous four counties mentioned, Okfuskee County had a large Negro population. Here the strength of correlation did not vary significantly with the level of Negro population.[52]

The Socialists heavily emphasized the threat posed by this straight literacy test to the suffrage of all the working poor. With the Democrats having acquired a reputation for chicanery in the administration of electoral procedures, the statewide vote of 133,100 to 91,600 against the literacy test may be seen as part of a general dissatisfaction with the Democratic administration. No less than eight other amendments were defeated by greater margins than appeared in the literacy test vote. And the "Fair Election Law" jointly sponsored by the Socialists and Republicans to provide for local election boards of three members (one from each party) almost passed, to the astonishment of the Democrats. But the state constitution provided that amendments initiated by the people, as distinguished from legislative initiation, had to obtain a majority of votes cast during the election. Thus 152,054 votes, one more than one-half of the total number of ballots issued, were required. Even at that, the Socialists and Republicans claimed that wholesale fraud by Democrats (tearing off the stubs of *unused* ballots to increase the *total* of ballots used) had insured the defeat of the "Fair Election Law."[53]

Taken as part of general hostility to Democratic corruption and dissimulation, the Socialist votes against the literacy test and for "fair play" in elections do not stand out from similar votes cast by members of the other parties. Donald Graham has argued that these votes indicate that "Socialist ideology, as Sooners interpreted it, was all the more sincere in subordinating race to class. Mere political advantage played no major role in their dramatic resistance to disfranchisement."[54] One caveat is necessary here: white men who were Socialists believed their own rights to be in jeopardy, especially when left to the tender mercies of Democratic registrars and election officials. In defending their own rights Socialist voters did by necessity defend the political rights of Negroes. Some would have been happy to know this; many others were probably appalled.

Repeated expressions of prejudice against Negroes in the local Socialist press must temper, if not controvert, any assertion that the Socialist ideology of proletarian unity, as pronounced by a few party leaders, significantly altered the traditional attitudes and social mores of white southerners in Oklahoma. It would be an optimistic socialist historian who would expect that ideas taught by a kind of catechism would supplant the saturating racial notions available to the Oklahomans from the time in their childhood when they began to understand serious speech. The pessimistic socialist historian must recognize that racial feeling has undercut class consciousness many times in American experience. It is significant that all of the Socialist spokesmen who defended the Negro as a worker and a human being were either outsiders who had moved to Oklahoma or were conscious proponents of the northern Civil War traditions. Oscar Ameringer had lived many years in the North. John G. Wills was a Scotsman who had been a blacklisted (American Railroad Union) striker in 1894. Patrick Nagle had come from Indiana. These leaders perceived the contradictions imposed upon the movement by the intensely racial perceptions of their followers. As confirmed socialists in the Marxian tradition they felt no ambivalence on the issue. Marvin Brown and the writers of the *Sledge Hammer* reveal two-sided feelings that pulled their socialism apart. There is genuine pathos, if not tragedy, in their political lives; they felt contradictions but could not surmount them. All of these spokesmen learned that they could "talk" socialism to Oklahoma audiences but could not persuade most white Socialists and most Negroes to regard each other as brothers in a common struggle against oppression. At that juncture history had prepared each to see the other as an oppressive and threatening specter.

NOTES

1. David Shannon, *The Socialist Party of America: A History* (Chicago; 1967), 50-53.

2. Ronald Radosh, *Debs* (Englewood Cliffs, N. J., 1971), 62. The quotation is from Debs' article in the November 1903 issue of *International Socialist Review*.

3. Shannon, *Socialist Party*, 50-53.

4. *Harlow's Weekly* (Oklahoma City), July 3, 1915.

5. Quoted in Donald R. Graham, "Red, White and Black: An Interpretation of Ethnic and Racial Attitudes of Agrarian Radicals in Texas and Oklahoma, 1880-1920" (Master's thesis, University of Regina, 1973), 151.

6. For an introduction, see *Ada Star-Democrat*, February 4, 1916; *Johnston County Capital-Democrat*, May 18, 1916, June 23, 1921; *Kingston Messenger*, October 20, 1916; *Marshall County News-Democrat*, October 23, 1914, April 30, September 2, 1915, April 26, June 27, 1916.

7. Interview with Freda Hogan Ameringer, Oklahoma City, February 16, 1968.

8. Quoted in *Marshall County News-Democrat*, December 28, 1911.

9. *Oklahoma Pioneer*, October 22, 1910, as quoted in James R. Green, "Socialism, and the Southwestern Class Struggle" (Ph.D. diss., Yale University, 1972), 97-98.

10. Nagle's manifesto to the Negro voter appears in the *Oklahoma Pioneer*, November 5, 1910. The quoted portion appears in Graham, "Red, White, and Black," 293. Graham's excellent research yields the information on which the argument of this chapter will stand.

11. Ibid.

12. Green, "Socialism, and the Southwestern Class Struggle," 108.

13. *New Century* (Sulphur), August 25, 1911, quoted in Graham, "Red, White, and Black," 237.

14. Ibid., 165.

15. Ibid., 124-165.

16. *Industrial Democrat* (Oklahoma City), July 23, 1910.

17. Ibid., July 16, 1910.

18. Ibid., June 25, 1910.

19. Ibid.

20. Ibid.

21. Ibid., September 10, 1910.

22. Ibid.

23. *Oklahoma Pioneer*, January 27, 1912.

24. Quoted in Graham, "Red, White, and Black," Appendix C.

25. Ibid., 222.

26. Ibid., 223. Letter from John B. Porter to the *Oklahoma Pioneer*, March 2, 1912.

27. Ibid., 222-228. For this summary of the controversy I am entirely indebted to Donald Graham's careful research, which he undertook while studying with me at the University of Saskatchewan, Regina Campus (now University of Regina).

28. *Oklahoma Pioneer*, August 17, 1912.

29. *Sword of Truth*, (Sentinel), October 29, 1913.

30. *Social Democrat* (Oklahoma City), October 1, 1913.

31. Ibid., December 31, 1913.

32. *Otter Valley Socialist*, November 24, 1915.

33. Ibid.

34. *Social Democrat* (Sayre), May 1, 1912.

35. Ibid.

36. Ibid.

37. Ibid.

38. *Otter Valley Socialist*, May 10, 1916, quoted in Graham, "Red, White, and Black," 233.

39. *Otter Valley Socialist*, May 17, 1916.

40. *Sledge Hammer*, (Okemah), June 19, 1913.

41. Ibid., August 7, 14, 1913, quoted in Graham, "Red, White, and Black," 236.

42. Ibid., November 24, 1915, quoted in Graham, "Red, White, and Black," 237.

43. Ibid., August 13, 1914, quoted in Graham, "Red, White, and Black," 342.

44. Ibid., August 6, 1914, quoted in Graham, "Red, White, and Black," 344.

45. *Clinton Chronicle* quoted in *Harlow's Weekly*, March 4, 1916; quoted in Graham, "Red, White, and Black," 315.

46. Graham, "Red, White, and Black," 289-290. I supplied Graham with some of the precinct voting data used as the basis for his calculations.

47. Green, "Socialism and the Southwestern Class Struggle," 95.

48. Oliver Benson, et al., *Oklahoma Votes 1907-1962* (Norman, 1964), 73.

49. Ibid., 71-73.

50. Graham, "Red, White, and Black," 289-290. Precinct results on the grandfather clause were available for only nine counties, as Graham and I discovered during an expedition to Oklahoma City.

51. Ibid., 325.

52. Ibid., 324.

53. Ibid., 332-335. Previously Democrats had used the total vote for presidential electors to determine the total vote. But in 1916 they were uncertain that the criterion would produce enough "silent" votes. Hence they adopted the "ballots issued" criterion.

54. Ibid., 336.

Governor Robert L. Williams and his faction: successful democrats and businessmen in small-town Oklahoma

The Democratic party, with battalions of loyal voters in southern Oklahoma rendering it dependable support, enjoyed perennial dominance in the state government in the first decade after statehood. Most of the southern counties produced Democratic majorities above 55 percent and, in many instances, above 60 percent. Oklahoma, in the the phrase of the political scientist, was a "modified one-party state," with only a few safely Republican counties along the Kansas border impervious to the Democracy's appeal to southern pride and tradition.[1] Who were these Democrats, what did they believe, and what did they hope to achieve in Oklahoma?

Thousands upon thousands of southern men—from the central and Deep South and from the adjacent states of Missouri, Arkansas, and Texas—had moved into this belated frontier.[2] Some had come to seek new business and professional opportunities in the growing towns; many more sought fresh soil on which to grow "'cawn' n' cotton." No doubt purpose and energy varied widely among the migrants. There were men who merely drifted in as if blown ahead of the southerly winds. Younger men with professional training who settled in the towns often improved their economic and social condition, achieving prestige and influence in

Oklahoma denied to all but a few young men in the older communities of their home states.

William H. "Alfalfa Bill" Murray, destined to become the president of the Oklahoma Constitutional Convention, first speaker of the Oklahoma House, and a congressman for three terms, had been a fairly typical young migrant. He had done some editing, politicking, and legal work in different Texas towns, and, though he certainly had not been a "failure," he had to borrow the fare required for a trip to the Indian Territory, where he hoped to establish himself as a professional man. After settling in Tishomingo at the age of twenty-eight, Murray quickly became an associate in a law firm, married into the Chickasaw tribe (one of the "Five Civilized Nations"), and entered local politics. It was Murray's good fortune that his patron and father-in-law was elected governor of the tribe. Thereafter Murray derived what was by local standards a substantial income doing legal work on complicated tribal land cases.[3]

Even more successful as a leader of Democrats, though less colorful than Alfalfa Bill, was an aggressive lawyer and businessman from Durant, Robert Lee Williams, who was elected chief justice of the state supreme court in 1908 and governor in 1914. After teaching school and graduating from a small college in Alabama, young Williams arrived in Durant, Indian Territory, where he would pit his skill and luck against other ambitious young men. Within a few years, Williams had established his reputation in the Durant area, enjoying a large income for legal services rendered to the MK&T railroad as well as to local and outside businessmen. He helped to organize and then retained substantial holdings in local banks, a cotton-oil company, an insurance company, and a real-estate firm. Before he had been in Oklahoma a decade, he had acquired large tracts of farm land, including nearly 3,000 prime acres located near Caddo in Bryan County.[4]

By force of personality and ability, both Murray and Williams emerged from the obscurity of small-town life to become leading state politicians. Obviously more successful than the many other local notables who remained obscure, these leaders were nonetheless representative of the social types who were Democratic activists engaged in battle with the Socialists during the 1910s. In a sample of 185 leaders in seven counties, there were 131 men who had arrived in Oklahoma between the ages of thirteen and thirty. This number would rise to 148 out of 185 if the upper age limit were raised to thirty-five. In a slightly different sample, drawn from the same counties, fully 149 out of 205 leaders had arrived, as did Murray and Williams, in the period of the great rush between 1889 and 1903.[5] Similar samples reveal the disproportionate number of business and professional men among Democratic leaders (see Table 2). The counties in these samples were among the most rural in the state; hence, the overrepresentation of middle-class townsmen and the underrepresentation of country people in the Democracy's leadership is even more striking and politically significant.

TABLE 2

Occupations of Democratic Political Leaders, 1912-1930
(seven county sample)

Lawyers	33	Physicians	10
Farmers	30	Public officials	9
Merchants	20	Insurance	4
Bankers	18	Teachers	4
Realtors	11	Other	27

Political commentators from the three competing parties agreed on one point: the Democrats, being substantial property holders in the small towns and rural areas, were generally hostile to the abolition of large, speculative landholdings and to the reform of bank lending practices. A Republican editor in Washita County pointed to a county seat "ring," alleging that most of the local Democratic leaders were financially interested in banks and loan companies and would be unlikely to support candidates advocating strict control of state bank interest rates.[6] These opposition cries might be dismissed as politically cynical, but those who scoff must at the same time explain away the frank admission of the progressive journal, *Harlow's Weekly,* that very important Democratic leaders were privileged property owners. "Governor Williams himself," the *Weekly* noted, "is not in sympathy with legislation to modify the present tenant system in Oklahoma, though he is in sympathy with anti-usury legislation. A number of the most influential members of the present legislature are also large landowners and consequently identified with the present tenant system."[7]

Yet even progressive Democrats would not wish to admit too much, at least not when talking about the governor. Unable to persuade Governor Williams to become a land reformer and unwilling to dismiss the leader of Democrats as a benighted reactionary, *Harlow's Weekly* contrived to present him as an ideal landlord, different from those who would exploit tenants. "Interest is naturally increased," said Harlow's, "when one sees the governor of the state . . . full of resolution to establish here a great modern farm. . . . His 1800 acres is in reality eleven farms combined into one, worked by eleven sets of tenants."[8] Writing as if Williams' efforts were a minor epic in the history of American agriculture, *Harlow's* editors reported that the governor encouraged good farming methods and provided better living quarters and more farm improvements than usually seen in southern Oklahoma. The tenants reportedly like the governor "to a degree approaching affection."[9]

Williams' career affords insight into both the opportunities enjoyed and the problems encountered by the propertied townsmen. Although Williams like to think of himself as a latter-day version of the noble plantation owner, his values and behavior were conventionally capitalistic and acquisitive. He exemplified the spirit of dutiful enterprise undertaken in pursuit of personal achievement. His actions were governed less by the sentiments of noblesse oblige than by the demands of the marketplace and the pressures of political ambition. It will be more useful to study Williams, a state politician, than the national politicians—Senators Owen and Gore and Congressman Murray. Williams and his followers were typical of the local Democrats who met and defeated the Socialists.

Along with his followers, Williams possessed a conventional social wisdom that both "explained" and justified his rise to commanding positions. In 1908, only a few months after his election to the supreme court, he described Oklahoma as a "magnificent country for a young man with integrity, determination, and an unconquerable will." Distinction could be achieved "more rapidly than in an old country."[10] But the paths along which young men might stride toward success had to be kept free of barriers erected by "great financial interests." Newly successful Oklahomans like Williams revered the Bryans who made their own way and distrusted the Tafts who were raised in the "lap of luxury" and who were unsympathetic "with the great masses of the plain people."[11] In perplexity and anger Williams and his political colleagues attributed Bryan's defeat in 1908 to an unfortunate popular tendency to neglect moderate reformers during prosperous times.[12] He was a perplexed "progressive."

While running his own race to a successful and—by local standards—prosperous conclusion, Williams was sometimes obliged to kick dust in the faces of those who fell behind. To a tenant whose work he had previously praised Williams wrote that another man wished to rent a larger parcel of land, including the land and house previously rented by the praiseworthy but now luckless tenant. "Of course I hate mighty bad to lose you, but I couldn't afford to let the opportunity to go by to rent 125 acreas of land with the house," explained Williams.[13] With the landlord keeping a careful balance sheet and the tenant expecting a living from his efforts, painful recrimination and mutual exasperation could follow hard upon reversals for either party to the contract. For example, Williams asked a tenant named A. S. Wheeler to move because he had attempted to sell oats and timber belonging to Williams and had given Williams a bad check as well. Williams claimed not to have received a cent from the farm in three years.[14] When a tenant fell into debt, he could only beg indulgence from his landlord; he had no friendly bankers to help him through the straits. Tenant J. L. Brock asked Williams if he could have the same land for the following year so that he could try to "pay out." He begged Williams not to take his team.[15]

The landlord could take away, but he could also give, especially if he were a politician in the midst of a hot campaign for governor in the summer of 1914, when cotton prices plunged following the outbreak of war in Europe. At this time Williams, with no other political or business alternatives, took care to accommodate the "common man." He advised one of his tenants that "the boys" should not become "blue". For the duration of the depression, Williams instructed, "we will arrange to plant and raise feed and get stock so that we will all live and come out alright."[16] A year later, when some tenants asked for better housing, Williams reaffirmed his good intentions but pleaded hard times. "You know I am just so hard up I am not able to build much of a house anywhere but hold these three boys in tow and we will find out," he replied to a minister who had written on behalf of the tenants.[17]

Like any effective politician, Williams had to help others so that he could help himself. Even when he was a sitting justice on the supreme court he was not at all embarrassed to intervene on behalf of reliably Democratic and deserving farmers. He could offer the officeholder's usual selection of favors, from the trivial to the weighty, in order to secure the gratitude of voters in doubtful constituencies. When Senator Thomas P. Gore requested the names of farmers to whom he might send free "improved" cotton seed, Williams recommended a Blue, Oklahoma, man who had good land and, "in addition to this, heretofore the Socialists have been strong about Blue and this party in a good Arkansas Democrat . . . he is a good farmer and he will cultivate them well and it will make a good display and will help out the local Democracy in that township."[18]

But favors more valuable than cotton seed were available for distribution to the common man. Williams asked his partner in the First National Bank of Bennington if he knew of "two or three good Democrats" who would like to obtain loans from the school land fund and who could show adequate title and security. That the loans were also undeniably intended to enhance the reputation of the Democratic party for providing largesse can be discerned in Williams' suggestion that his partner should look for likely recipients "up about Matoy, and one in there about Caddo, and one in about Jackson, and one down about Wade. Get them scattered over the country; it will do some good."[19] To a Matoy man Williams was blunt: "Of course the money is here to loan, and we want to help our friends and the members of our party. This is strictly confidential."[20] In another letter asking for strict confidence, Williams told an Aylesworth, Oklahoma, man that no more than two or three state loans could be given in any one precinct. "It has to be scattered over the state," Williams reminded him.[21] And Chief Justice Williams followed up his efforts by asking the state school land commissioner about the progress of two loan applications from his home county; he hoped that "everything possible should be done to expedite these applications."[22] When seeking fertile fields in which to sow seeds for a political harvest, Williams was careful to stress that the would-be recipients had to possess clear title to land that was sufficiently valuable to constitute ample security for a loan. He was not proposing that public funds be loaned to legally unqualified borrowers, but if there were two potential borrowers who were equally qualified he clearly and predictably favored, supported, and even solicited the applications of "good democrats." The virtues and rewards of fidelity to the party of Jefferson and Jackson would not be lost upon discontented voters who were listening to the Socialists.

Democratic leaders gave much less accommodating treatment to those whose political opinions and activities placed them beyond the bounds of respectability and the possibility of redemption. In these cases intimidation was substituted for the sweetmeats of reward. In 1915 the governor asked the cashier of a Caddo, Oklahoma, bank if he knew anything about the reputation of one A. Owens, a farmer who wished to rent some land from Williams. Besides wanting to know if Owens was an honest man and good worker Williams inquired into Owens' political affiliation, adding that a "man's politics don't preclude me from renting to him."[23] In reply the bank cashier reported that Owens' previous landlord was dissatisfied with his "cultivation" and that Owens was a "socilist [sic]."[24] A Caddo hardware merchant began his reply with the information that Owens was a Socialist (underlined in pencil by either the writer or recipient) and "sum what of a soar head; I wouldn't feel safe in recommending him as a renter."[25] A bank president volunteered the judgment that Owens was both "pretty sorry" and "a Socialist."[26] The correspondence does not reveal whether the governor rented to the sorry Socialist farmer, but it does cast strong light upon class relations in southern Oklahoma. Socialists in these districts frequently alleged that landlords, upon discovering political apostasy among the tenants, conspired to "rent them out." This correspondence would seem to lend support to the Socialist allegation.

To the extent that the Socialist party made fundamental attacks upon the political and economic interests of the businessmen and landlords of Oklahoma, it was only natural for the local elites to wage political war in defense of what they regarded as their rights, interests, and achievements. Democrats not only passed discreet letters among themselves to facilitate discrimination against Socialist voters; sometimes they even proclaimed their intention to harrass political dissidents and openly expressed satisfaction when measures like the Universal Voter Registration Act of 1916 subjected intrepid Socialist registrants to public exposure. In Marshall County, where the Socialists had won 41 percent of the vote in 1914, the *News-Democrat* chortled that "there has been 113 Socialists leave Marshall County since the registration which blows up the Socialist party so far as winning any of the county offices is concerned."[27]

Because the Democrats believed that the Socialists were not legitimate participants in American political life, they could easily persuade themselves that any Socialist, even one who displayed prowess in cultivation, was a sorehead worthy only of expulsion. A Socialist was worse than even a Republican. Reporting that a local Socialist editor had complained about Republicans crossing over to vote for Democrats, the *Kingston Messenger* argued that "Americans stand together against a common enemy. Socialism is against American institutions. . . . It saps the foundation of our political, social, moral life."[28] In 1914, when it appeared that the Socialists might win a plurality in Marshall County, the *Messenger* beseeched Democrats to remain faithful in spite of economic hardship and party factionalism. "If the Republicans want to vote for a Republican," conceded the anxious editor, "that is their privilege but it is not the honest thing for a Democrat to knife his own party nominee to give aid to a Republican . . . especially when such aid can only result in benefit to a candidate who is arrayed against both the . . . parties—a result which would not be of any credit to the country."[29]

It was a commonplace of the day and the region that "radicals" were resentful of the success earned by better men than themselves. A Democratic editor argued that an enterprising middle class would frustrate Socialist hopes in Oklahoma no less than in the nation itself. "These people who do things and prosper," the editor believed, "create the wealth and build up the country through their energy and ability, and then only, the Socialists come along and tell us how to . . . reduce mankind to a common level."[30]

Thinking well of themselves, the local notables found it hard to understand why country people thought ill of them. They believed that their lives, full of disciplined striving, should have been imitated by tenant farmers. The *Caddo Herald* complained that the tenants gathered in the hundreds to hear Gene Debs tell them that they were downtrodden when they should have been listening to their banker's advice on how to save money, diversify crops, attend church, and send their children to school. And, the *Herald* regretfully observed, "the same banks, merchants, and professional men whom the socialists so loudly abuse, will be called on almost every day this winter to feed and clothe some poor kumrid's child, and they'll do it."[31] When the *Madill Socialist-Herald* argued that tenants did not need landlords to tell them how to work, the *Kingston Messenger* was almost frantic in asserting that the landlord had an essential role in providing land for renters to work. "Renters make landlords and not landlords renters," said the *Messenger,* ignoring the widely acknowledged facts of land speculation and concentration of ownership in southeastern Oklahoma.[32] Land rent was only the owner's reward for "giving someone else a chance to live."[33] To accuse the landlord of being a profit-making speculator was to play with a dangerous "class prejudice."

Indeed the cultural perceptions of the property-seeking townsmen seemed to emerge from social and sexual fears similar to those that have been found at the core of racism.[34] Democratic spokesmen frequently accused the Socialists and their poor white constituency of lewd and perverse behavior. When a case of statutory rape was reported to the authorities in Marshall County, a Democratic editor alleged that "all the parties concerned" were Socialists and rhetorically questioned the origins of "such depravity."[35] Editors also saw wife beating, murder, and suicide as predicable results when the doctrines of socialism inflamed weak minds.[36] If not always lethal or degenerate, then Socialists were ill mannered and vulgar, according to Democratic townspeople. The *Marshall County News-Democrat* characterized a local Socialist spokesman as a "great big squabby specimen of humanity chock full of vulgarity and profanity, and obscene anecdotes."[37] Socialism seemed to embody filth, laziness, and blackness, everything that decent white people believed themselves not to be. "If they were sincere in their actions," said the *News-Democrat*, "they would apologize to the Democratic Party of Oklahoma . . . and clean up otherwise by paying all their debts, rents, etc. . . . As long as the Socialists teach negro equality, and cater to the black trash, instead of listening to the men who have made our great nation, they may expect to be ignored by all refined and sensible people."[38]

The multiple anxieties of the business-professionals are nowhere better illustrated than in the comments of the locally acclaimed editor of the *Johnston County Capital-Democrat*, W. C. "Rube" Geers, who scorned Socialist voters as thieves and "bellyachers" who believed that "there should be no bottom rail in the fence, but all the rails should be on top. A socialist is a goose that wants a new mate every spring, and had as soon have a black one as a white one. He persuades himself that he has been robbed by the rich when he never had enough to buy a negroe's supper."[39] There was no bottom rail in the fence to let the striving citizen know where he stood: it was this fear that nagged the townsmen. They needed the "nigger" and the poor tenant farmer to prove to themselves that they had not failed in the "new state."

The religious experience of townspeople confirmed their belief in their own moral superiority and increased the social and cultural distance separating them from the tenants in the countryside. In the towns the Baptist, Methodists, and the Disciples of Christ attracted the bulk of the worshippers. The educated ministers of these churches delivered a message that flattered their audiences, emphasizing the middle-class virtues of thrift, sobriety, and personal responsibility for one's standing in this world. Because the churches, like other social institutions in a town, were expected to ''pull together'' in an effort to ''boost'' their town as the best place in which to live and raise Christian families, differences over doctrine and liturgy were, if not forgotten, somewhat de-emphasized. ''Booster'' religion consecrated the ''success'' of its participants, encouraged scorn for country people, and thus intensified conflicting social perceptions.[40]

Why was this? Most tenants did not attend church as often as townspeople because they were generally too rootless and too poor to support neighborhood churches. And they avoided town churches because, according to the report of the Presbyterian Home Mission, the town churches were dominated by ''merchants, middlemen, and agents, bankers and landlords—and the farmer thinks of these people as different from himself.''[41] When they sought religion, tenants went to revival encampments and schoolhouse meetings in which intense emotion and apocalyptic vision found expression. Consequently tenants were more likely to be found in the more radical Protestant sects that accentuated the need for doctrinal purity and scorned the physical luxury and theological .compromises of the town booster's church. Although conservative in theology and strict in maintaining biblical tenets, the ''holiness'' preachers often conveyed to their rural flock a feeling of resentment against corruption in town life and religion and provided poor, workworn rural people with an optimistic vision of a better day coming. The rural style of religion, with its emotional spasms and convulsive conversions, seemed alternately risible and divisive to the condescending townsmen.

But even the preacher's soothing praise could not close the fissures of self-doubt and anxiety that were opened by competitive life in these new towns. Sermons could not increase a man's income in spite of the claims of preachers. And when prices for the staple crops fell, the florid eloquence of the booster, employed so often to exorcise the specter of socialism, was deflated as rapidly as prices.

So the propertied townsmen sometimes found themselves sorely pressed by the mundane and unavoidable demands of creditors. Opportunities for new entries into business enterprise probably declined after the first decade of settlement. Even a firm believer in "unconquerable will" was beginning to advise fellow professionals that Oklahoma was overcrowded. "It is hard to form a partnership in this new country now, so many lawyers are coming in," wrote Robert L. Williams.[42] When the collapse of the cotton market chilled the marrow of business life throughout the South in 1914, Williams was even gloomier, and he bluntly discouraged a Mississippi lawyer who inquired about opportunities in Oklahoma:

I would not think about moving to Texas or Oklahoma, except in an exceptional case. The bar is crowded in both of these states, and just a few men are making big money; and my experience is that very few men, after they are forty-five years old go to a new country and find it satisfactory, unless they carry money there to make investments and gets [sic] quickly aligned with business enterprises. There are not many openings in either one of these states. We always hear about the man that succeeds, but not about the man that fails. . . . Mississippi and Louisiana represent just as good fields as the West does now.[43]

Another lawyer wrote to Williams from Mississippi that he had left Oklahoma because he could not meet expenses from the proceeds of his practice. He inquired whether anyone needed a law clerk or stenographer, though it is not clear from the letter whether he was offering his own services or those of his former employees.[44] Williams' correspondence yields a picture of Oklahoma prospects that varies considerably with the public optimism of the booster.

The high politicians and their associates could ease the burden of debt they bore by using various devices unavailable to the tenant farmers who had to "pay out" at the end of a year or live at the sufferance of the landlord. Williams thanked P. A. Norris of Ada, Oklahoma, for a loan allowing him to refinance his debts "so as to cut out my indebtedness bearing a high rate of interest."[45] Only six weeks before Williams had received a letter from a mortgage company in Oklahoma City that informed him of interest due on six loans for a total of $26,000, which were secured by 1,475 acres of land in Bryan County.[46]

Some of Williams' banking associates, lacking the prestige and wherewithal to get new loans to cover their debts, had to content themselves with "insiders' " loans. This practice, however, stirred the governor's wrath. To the president of the First National Bank of Bennington Williams wrote, "The indebtedness of J. W. Lloyd, $3,680.95, with no security, and Lewis T. Martin, $5,282.20, secured by only $110 worth of collateral notes, is absolutely not justified and especially is this so when they are active officers of the bank; and, so I request, as a stockholder, that this indebtedness be reduced. They ought not to have a line of credit, where no security is offered, above $1,500 each. . . . I am sure that all their lands are encumbered and that everything they have is in equities. No bank can live and prosper that has big loans to its active officers no better secured than this."[47] Williams would hardly allow his own investments to be jeopardized by corrupt practice, but he was nonetheless indulgent of his fellow speculators, if they were to be reproved by permitting them "only" $1,500 credit against their debts. Many a tenant in southern Oklahoma would have appreciated as much. And there were methods of propping up a sagging investment. In a letter marked "personal" Governor Williams had previously informed the president of the troubled Bennington Bank that the state land commissioners had given the bank a deposit of $10,000.[48]

If business activity could be so problematical for Governor Williams, then how much more uncertain and frustrating it must have been for men with less power and influence. What did these bank officers say in the privacy of their homes after being reproved by Williams? They were no less ambitious, no less avid for gain than the Murrays and Williamses, but for lack of luck or skill they did not acquire the means and influence to achieve a really secure feeling of success. Probably not very many returned to their point of origin like the downhearted Mississippi lawyer who bemoaned his fate to Williams. Those who remained in the struggle to "make it" must have felt themselves on the desperate edge of a morass, with the peril of slipping or sinking only too real. They would be "failures" in the "new country" where any man worth his salt ought surely to succeed. Thus they were always in danger of being humiliated by their own belief in the possibility of "making it."

Not all Oklahoma businessmen had to worry about financial difficulty or failure. In Oklahoma City a small number of mercantile and financial men served as the new state's version of the big bourgeoisie. The two leading publishers in the state, E. K. Gaylord of the *Daily Oklahoman* and Victor Harlow of *Harlow's Weekly*, were closely linked to these businessmen and, by virtue of the statewide circulation of their publications, could make a strong claim themselves for the leadership of "responsible" business opinion. Gaylord and Harlow prided themselves on taking the "long view" of the state's needs. They feared that Oklahoma's impoverished countryside and its reputation for agrarian radicalism would make investors wary of providing capital and would keep Oklahoma City from becoming a major center of trade. The boosters who envisaged Oklahoma City in successful rivalry with Dallas, Wichita, Kansas City, and St. Louis were more willing to seek aid from large business interests, including the big meatpackers and the railroads.

By 1915 both *Harlow's* and the *Daily Oklahoman* were saying that the days of strict and "punitive" regulation were past in Oklahoma and attempts would be increasingly made to induce capital to enter the state and develop its resources. *Harlow's* noted that Governor Williams had warmly invited capital and had promised that the state would protect the interests of investors. At the governor's conference in 1916, Williams saw government as "nothing but one great business enterprise to be administered according to business sense and business judgment under the promptings of an honest and humane heart."[49] Now even the Bryanites had left rhetoric about the "producers" and the "parasites" to the Oklahoma Socialists. Wilson was in the White House and Williams was in the state house and the business of Oklahomans was to be business. The *Daily Oklahoman* was pleased to observe that the 1915 legislature was much less "radical" than its predecessors and had done nothing to cause complaint from business interests.[50]

But the spokesmen of the "public interest" in Oklahoma City found the small-town and rural Democrats distressingly inflexible on the issue of land reform. Shortly before the 1914 election the editor of the *Daily Oklahoman* had asked his readers to ponder the implications of federal census figures revealing that a majority of the state's farmers were tenants. "This condition is due in large part to the Indian Land problem on the east side of the state," the editor argued. Title to this land passed "largely into the hands of non-resident owners who place tenants upon the same and hold it as a speculative proposition."[51] With the Socialists winning from 25 to 35 percent of the vote across southern Oklahoma in 1914, both *Harlow's* and the *Daily Oklahoman* expressed tactful but clearly increasing dissatisfaction with the Williams administration's seeming indifference to tenancy. While the governor directed his political energies to the task of disfranchising black voters in 1915 and 1916, the *Daily Oklahoman* felt constrained to suggest that 60,000 Socialist voters were a more serious threat than were 40,000 Negroes to the continued ascendancy of the Democratic party.[52] *Harlow's* found Democratic complacency astonishing. "Socialism, I.W.W. . . . these are flaming warning signals which no wise statesman will overlook and which no shrewd politician can afford to ignore," *Harlow's* admonished.[53] But in early 1916 *Harlow's* dolefully reported that land speculators had purchased large acreages of Chickasaw and Choctaw lands at government sales in eastern counties. The result was that the "tenant system" seemed "to be fixed upon that section to an extent that it can hardly be broken loose."[54]

Singled out for special praise were those Democratic notables who promoted land reform by argument or example. J. B. A. Robertson, already campaigning for the gubernatorial nomination, which he would eventually secure in 1918, received *Harlow's* commendation during the fall of 1916 for proposing a graduated land tax, a limitation upon the amount of land one individual could hold, and a program to promote farm home ownership. *Harlow's* was especially eager to report Senator Robert L. Owen's announcement that he intended to sell his large landholdings in small, individual parcels. Both Owen and Governor Williams had been pilloried by the Socialists as landlords who received unearned benefits from the tenant system. It was *Harlow's* suspicion that Owen's decision portended a rupture with the state Democrats on the land issue. The weekly noted that Governor Williams had said nothing in response to Owen's announcement.[55]

The "progressive" land reformers found their best hopes persistently disappointed. The *Farmer-Stockman* lamented that there had not even been a serious discussion of the tenancy question, which was, in the editor's view, "vital to the state's prosperity."[56] Proposals for a graduated land tax and antidiscrimination provisions to protect farmers co-ops were given lip service and legislative burial. And *Harlow's*, after quoting with approval a *Tulsa Times* editorial that accused eastern

Oklahoma landlords of fastening a heavy yoke upon the neck of the tenantry, then gave what was coming to be its perennial explanation of legislative inaction: "The landlord, the banker, the merchant and all other property owners are vocal in their demands for selfish legislation when the legislature is in session, and in many instances the benefits they obtain through legislation are accompanied by further inroads upon their less fortunate fellow citizens."[57] Much of the same explanation was given by a defeated Republican candidate for governor, Horace G. McKeever, who agreed with the land reformers among the Democrats that politicians with vested interests would be unlikely to vote for reform because they could not bring themselves to "relinquish their profit which they make off of the tenant farmer."[58] *Harlow's* had published McKeever's comments at the beginning of the 1919 legislature in an attempt to lend an appearance of bipartisan urgency to the issue.

In their response to the country people, the Democratic townsmen could hardly separate their view of the "white trash" from their own self-perceptions and self-portraits. The rage of the hustling entrepreneur at his own failings fueled his rage at the slatternly tenantry. The view into the lives of Robert L. Williams and his associates gives us a rudimentary comprehension of the "new" men who sought opportunity in the old American way. The Oklahoma businessmen were desperate to achieve some distinction in communities praised as "classless" by their boosters—communities that were actually fissured with competing anxieties about material self-advancement and social esteem. Williams' accomplishments posed an almost painful problem for his associates and neighbors: they had to explain to themselves why they had not achieved Williams' standing. Why did Williams' associates have to endure his stinging rebuke for using "insider's advantages" in their banks when the great leader himself obviously operated on the inside to secure his own advantage and that of his party and friends? Unable to deny that Williams deserved his distinction, his neighbors and associates had to admit that they had not "made" themselves equally successful. Yet they also believed that they were decent church-going and business-minded folk who deserved respect. They could not help but feel somewhat diminished when Williams, from his loftier station, tendered his respect and issued his commands. In their turn, they demanded gratitude and respect from the ragged country dwellers who were thought to need the "intelligent" help and kind charity of townspeople. For the same reason—to bolster their own self-esteem—they scorned the "nigger", the "nigger-loving" socialist, and the tenant whose mind was warped beyond redemption by the perverse "class" doctrines of socialism. The morally corrupt and politically dangerous could not be made to render even grudging respect; they were fit only to be driven from decent society.

In the terms of the day most of the Oklahoma Democrats would easily qualify as progressives of the Bryan and Wilson varieties. As small businessmen in the hinterland, they were deeply suspicious of eastern corporate business. As southern Democrats they were fearful of the federal power exercised by Republican "tools" of the interests. As aspirants to middle-class decency, they feared the sullen hostility of the local lower class.

The Oklahoma progressives, more than their counterparts elsewhere, were identified in their own locale as the "vested interests," the "machine," or the "court house ring." They held the decisive portions of power and property in this rural society, and they had to defend their interests against what must be regarded as a politically aroused, landless, rural, laboring class. The Socialist party, with its vigorous organization and incessant agitation, dramatized the discontents of the tenants and small farmers, focused those discontents upon business enterprises, and threatened to arrest the entrepreneurial and speculative activities that conferred advantage and prestige upon middle-class Democrats.

NOTES

1. Oliver Benson et al., *Oklahoma Votes, 1907-1962*, (Norman, 1964), 19-14, 35, 38.

2. U.S. Department of Commerce, Bureau of the Census, *Census of the United States Taken in the year 1910*, vol. 3, *Population* (Washington, D.C., 1913), 461.

3. Keith L. Bryant, Jr., *Alfalfa Bill Murray* (Norman; 1968), 3-44.

4. Edward Everett Dale and James D. Morrison, *Pioneer Judge: The Life of Robert Lee Williams* (Cedar Rapids; 1958), 68-69, 84-85, 94-95, 97-98, 146, 229.

5. Rex F. Harlow and Victor E. Harlow, eds., *Makers of Government in Oklahoma* (Oklahoma City; 1930). In 1929 the Harlows decided to compile lists of political leaders in the state. They made their selections on the basis of local reputation. In order to insure that the leaders were present in Oklahoma during the

1910s, I included only persons who had arrived in Oklahoma prior to 1912 and who had been born prior to 1889. It is possible that they did not enjoy the same measures of esteem in the 1910s as in 1930, but they were present as mature men in the earlier period. The seven counties to which I referred in the text were Major, Roger Mills, Beckham, and Kiowa in the west; and Marshall, Johnston, and Pontotoc in the east.

6. *Cordell Herald-Sentinel*, October 19, 1916.

7. *Harlow's Weekly* (Oklahoma City), October 30, 1915.

8. Ibid., October 2, 1915.

9. Ibid.

10. Williams to Dr. W. F. McGhee, February 11, 1908, Robert L. Williams Papers, Oklahoma Historical Society.

11. Williams to W. N. Green, September 28, 1908, Williams Papers.

12. J. B. A. Robertson to Williams, November 7, 1908, and Williams to George S. Ramsey, November 5, 1908, Williams Papers.

13. Williams to George W. Grant, August 27, 1908, Williams Papers.

14. Williams to A. S. Wheeler, August 7, 1908, Williams Papers.

15. J. L. Brock to Williams, August 5, 1907, Williams Papers.

16. Williams to Ed Overcast, August 27, 1914, Williams Papers.

17. Williams to Rev. T. P. Levins, October 4, 1915, Williams Papers.

18. Williams to T. P. Gore, March 10, 1908, Williams Papers.

19. Williams to W. O. Byrd, November 5, 1908; for other offers of help to Democrats, see Williams letters to Frank Standifer, November 7, 1908; to Eugene Wolverton, November 7, 1908; and to G. W. Phillips, November 5, 1908: Williams Papers.

20. Williams to W. H. Cummings, November 7, 1908, Williams Papers.

21. Williams to J. Frank Adams, November 7, 1908, Williams Papers.

22. Williams to Ed O. Cassiday, November 5, 1908, Williams Papers.

23. Williams to Arthur Manning, September 28, 1915, Williams Papers.

24. Arthur Manning to Williams, September 29, 1915, Williams Papers.

25. Jack Moore to Williams, September 29, 1915, Williams Papers.

26. F. R. Semple to Williams, September 29, 1915, Williams Papers.

27. *Marshall County News-Democrat*, October 19, 1916.

28. *Kingston Messenger*, November 16, 1912.

29. Ibid., October 24, 1914.

30. *Marshall County News-Democrat*, June 15, 1916.

31. *Caddo Herald* quoted in *Kingston Messenger*, October 23, 1915.

32. *Kingston Messenger*, October 6, 1916.

33. Ibid.

34. I am thinking here of the brilliant explorations of this theme to be found in

Winthrop Jordan, *White over Black* (Chapel Hill, N.C., 1968), and James Baldwin, *The Fire Next Time* (New York; 1963).

35. *Marshall County News-Democrat*, July 6, 1916.

36. *Ada Evening News* article reprinted in the *Kingston Messenger*, October 5, 1912; *Ada Star-Democrat*, October 27, 1916.

37. *Marshall County News-Democrat*, January 14, 1910.

38. Ibid., May 25, 1916.

39. *Johnston County Capital-Democrat*, May 25, 1916.

40. For these insights into southwestern religious life and its relation to the political conflicts under study, I am indebted to James R. Green, who lent me his unpublished manuscripts on social structure and social institutions in the Southwest. Some of the same material appears in James R. Green, "Socialism and the Southwestern Class Struggle" (Ph.D. diss., Yale University, 1972), 254-255.

41. Cited in ibid., 255.

42. Williams to J. P. Clayton, February 28, 1910, Williams Papers.

43. Williams to Sam Whitman, Jr., January 29, 1915, Williams Papers.

44. Andrew Wood to Williams, September 26, 1914, Williams Papers.

45. Williams to P. A. Norris, February 26, 1916, Williams Papers.

46. Gum Bros. Real Estate Mortgage Loans to Williams, January 6, 1916, Williams Papers.

47. Williams to E. F. Rines, February 16, 1916, Williams Papers. It could be argued that Williams was approving "signature" loans for persons of reputation and property in the community. The small-town banker could well have a reasonable expectation that the loans would be repaid. On these counts the tenant farmer would not qualify. But that is precisely the point: the work energies of the tenantry were given low valuations in the local marketplaces. The "other" class received the social and economic advantages of market society.

48. Williams to E. F. Rines, January 5, 1916, Williams Papers.

49. Dale and Morrison, *Pioneer Judge*, 246-247.

50. *Harlow's Weekly*, January 1, April 3, May 1, 1915; *Daily Oklahoman* (Oklahoma City) quoted in *Harlow's Weekly*, April 3, 1915.

51. *Daily Oklahoman*, October 21, 1914.

52. *Daily Oklahoman*, quoted in the *Kingston Messenger*, November 6, 1915.

53. *Harlow's Weekly*, December 11, 1915.

54. Ibid., January 22, 1916.

55. Ibid., September 13, October 18, 25, 1916.

56. *Oklahoma Farmer-Stockman* (Oklahoma City), March 25, 1917.

57. *Harlow's Weekly*, December 12, 1917.

58. Ibid., January 8, 1919.

Years of decline and ———————6
disruption, 1916-1918

The Socialist vote in 1916 had receded from the protest-swollen total of 21 percent in 1914, but it is significant that the party's supporters did not all rush headlong to the Democrats, whose strong electoral campaign was based upon President Wilson's reputation as a progressive, a friend of the farmer, and a statesman of peace. The Socialists polled slightly more than 15 percent of the statewide vote in 1916, nearly equal to the 16 percent that Debs had attracted in 1912. There were still twenty-two counties, mostly in the cotton and wheat areas, in which the Socialists polled at least 20 percent of the vote. As ususal, their percentages in the country precincts were much higher, generally ranging from 33 to 50 percent.[1]

With farm prices beginning to make startling leaps upward from their 1913-1915 levels, the Democrats had been happily predicting the demise of socialism in the autumn of 1916. An editor from Beckham County reported ''good attendance'' at the Socialist summer encampment of 1916 but observed that ''the enthusiasm did not seem to be as great as in former days.'' A taste of prosperity had had a healthy effect upon farmers:

> Someway with wheat way up and hogs way up and cattle way up and cream way up and eggs way up and everything else way up, they do not have the heart to talk hard times. Many of them are better off financially than the capitalist whom they have been talking about.[2]

After a long, hard look through the pages of Socialist newspapers, the local reader would find the occasional backhanded admission that individual gains were causing political problems. A "red carder" complained about laziness in Local Pleasant View:

> Don't think because some of you have automobiles, electric lights, bath tubs, and bank accounts that you are out of the rut. . . . You may have gotten out of the rut of poverty, but have plunged into a deeper and more rotten rut, the rut of selfishness.[3]

Having challenged the Democrats to reveal how they would try to defeat socialism when "the good crop argument is knocked into a cocked hat next fall," the local Socialists were themselves forced to explain an unhappy turn of political events.[4] The *Otter Valley Socialist* attributed the reduced Socialist vote to the increase in cotton prices and to Wilson's policy of avoiding American involvement in the Great War.[5] L. K. Rhodyback argued that the voters had been fooled by the capitalists, who would soon charge higher prices for the goods that farmers required, effectively draining away the increased earnings on their crops. What would happen to the farmers, he warned, when the current prosperity ended?[6] State secretary H. M. Sinclair suggested that the shrinkage of the Socialist vote resulted largely from the departure of those who had cast ballots of "protest" in the depression year of 1914. In his opinion the 1916 results revealed how many votes had been cast in a truly class-conscious spirit.[7] The Rev. O. E. Enfield found cause for optimism in what he took to be a process of winnowing: he wanted to see only "Socialists" in the movement, not a motley crowd of disgruntled Democrats and their useless "votes".[8] Although disappointed that their vote had not grown as it had in every previous election since 1907, the Socialists of Oklahoma were not politically exhausted. They had retained a core of rural support and had maintained an effective organization. In another two years, however, they were to experience an electoral disaster flowing directly from their opposition to a national war effort and a rural prosperity in full gallop.

In the 1918 election the Socialist percentage of 4 percent was lower than in any other election since statehood, when the party organization was embryonic. In both the total number of votes and in percentage, the Socialist decline was steeply disproportionate when compared with the Democratic and Republican percentages that year. The voter turnout was unusally low in 1918, and all parties polled a smaller vote than they had previously, but the Socialists polled a far smaller vote. Marshall and Beckham Counties, where the Socialists had been within striking distance of majorities in 1914, now recorded a 7 percent Socialist vote. In the six strongest Socialist precincts in Marshall County, the rate of decline from 1916 to 1918 ranged between 88 and 93 percent. Moreover, the Socialist votes do not reappear in the major party columns. Some of the most vigorous political participants in prior years simply did not cast votes. Contrast these results with those in the six strongest Democratic precincts in Marshall County where the rate of decline was between 20 and 30 percent in four precincts, and 41 percent and 51 percent in the remaining two precincts. Beckham County, on the western border of the state, also followed this curious electoral pattern. In their six strongest precincts, the Socialists suffered losses that, in all but one precinct, ranged between 83 and 100 percent. In Hext precinct, the loss was "only" 57 percent. In Beckham County's strongest Democratic precincts, the decline in total vote ranged between 37 and 66 percent at four boxes, while the Democrats increased their vote by 43 and 62 percent in the other two boxes.[9]

Where the presumed national honor of the United States was involved, American Socialists were no less vulnerable than German Socialists in 1914 to charges that their patriotism was tepid and insufficient. American Socialists, from Eugene Debs down to obscure street-corner speakers, criticized the nation's foreign policy when it seemed to foster oppression and exploitation abroad. As early as December 1914 the Socialists of Oklahoma, relying upon good Socialist doctrine, resolved that the war in Europe was "the offspring of capitalism" and condemned the slaughter of "our brothers and comrades." The Oklahoma Socialist Convention recommended urgent action by locals to help the national party "go on record in favor of Comrade Allen Benson's proposed constitutional amendment concerning declaration of war." Benson wished to ensure that a national referendum would allow the people to vote for or against direct participation in the war. Finally, the Oklahoma men advised their distant European brethren to guard against the "duplicity" of American capitalists who would try to bring "great numbers of European unfortunates to this country to still further increase the competition for the means of life and thus to more easily exploit the workers of America."[10] In the minds of many Oklahoma Socialists, capitalist rivalry and duplicity would remain the basic explanation of the cause of the Great War. Naturally this belief made the war itself and any preparations to take part illegitimate and oppressive in their eyes. They denounced the postmaster general's "arbitrary rulings" that infringed citizens' rights.

The most controversial resolution passed by the Oklahoma Socialists addressed the issue that had exposed the myth of "proletarian unity" in Europe:

IN EVENT OF WAR. Since the European socialist movement has been nearly destroyed because of unpreparedness to meet the crisis, and since the militarists of the United States are bending every effort to involve our nation in war, and since in such event, we the working class may find ourselves in a position similar to that of our European comrades at the beginning of the present war, be it therefore

RESOLVED; that if war is declared, the socialists of Oklahoma shall refuse to enlist; but if forced to enter military service to murder fellow workers, we shall choose to die fighting the enemies of humanity within our own ranks rather than to perish fighting our fellow workers. We further pledge ourselves to use our influence to the end that all toilers shall refuse to work for the master class during such war. [11]

Recommending that the national executive prepare a political plan against the event of a war declaration, the assembled Socialists of Oklahoma concluded their audacious appeal for resistance and awaited the storm.

Opponents of socialism were soon confirmed in their belief that Socialists were potentially disloyal and dangerous rebels. In convention a year later Oklahoma's Socialists declared "preparedness a menace to the working class." [12] Socialist representatives in the Oklahoma legislature presented a resolution condemning military appropriations. Eighteen members of the other parties joined the five Socialist legislators in a losing effort, twenty-three to sixty-five. [13]

Democratic politicians in Oklahoma and Texas, however, were encountering increasing popular resentment of preparedness. The most notable victim of this hostility was Congressman William H. "Alfalfa Bill" Murray. Practically alone among Oklahoma Democrats in his strong support of President Wilson's foreign policies and programs for war preparations, he was defeated in his southern Oklahoma district by a popular Democratic state legislator from Ada in Pontotoc County, Tom McKeown, who had sharply criticized President Wilson's defense and farm policies.[14]

In the summer of 1916 when Mexican politics in general and Pancho Villa's raids in particular were causing President Wilson so much vexation, the issue was being hotly discussed in the dusty towns of the Southwest. The *Kingston Messenger*, always fiercely anti-Socialist, reported that a local Socialist had claimed that he would join the Mexican army if war were declared on Mexico. According to the report, the Socialist "had no sooner made this remark than one of the bystanders called for a rope. . . . Such a man does not deserve the protection of the American government and ought to be transported to the firing line and turned over to the greasers."[15] In a similar incident, a Socialist editor had been driven from his home for having expressed the hope that any American who invaded Mexico would be buried there. A Democratic editor, pushed beyond restraint, recommended that "such lying reprobates and degenerate libertines should all be driven from the American continent. All honor to the good people of Wewoka. Repeat the trick, boys, every time you are disgraced by such heathenish apes."[16]

Despite the threat of violence, some Socialists persisted in signing articles condemning the proposed use of American arms to chastise Mexicans and to bolster the Allied powers. Chris Imke of Shattuck, Oklahoma, believed the campaign for "preparedness" to be a capitalist fraud calculated to induce working people to throw away their lives in defense of "the big ranches of Hearst and the oil wells of Rockefeller and the mines of Guggenheims." Workers would be fighting "to gain more land, more oil wells, and more mines for those who have already robbed the United States of its natural resources."[17] Without fear that its courage would be questioned, the *Ellis County Socialist* reported approvingly that "Comrade S. V. Luellen says he is a peace at any price crank and that's the dope for your tank. If you take it each day, 'twould be better for the U.S.A."[18] That loyalty would soon be a contentious issue was virtually granted. After O. E. Enfield had spoken against militarism, the *Ellis County Socialist* praised him as a man who "will not mislead the good and loyal citizen, the man who wants peace and does not want to fight for it. We have a very strong peace sentiment in our country but we want to make it much stronger than it is."[19] The Socialists had seen some straws in the gathering winds, but they could neither predict nor comprehend the full fury of persecution that would descend upon their movement after President Wilson delivered his war message.

The Oklahoma Council of Defense, appointed by the Democratic state administration and comprised of so-called leading citizens, encouraged popular suspicion of "dangerous" political attitudes after American entry into World War I. In a message obviously concerned with the Socialist party, which was widely published in Oklahoma newspapers, the state Council of Defense warned that "here and there in Oklahoma are those who still maintain secretly that American young men are being sent to the trenches of France at the call of American dollars, that the draft is but the beginning of oppression of the poor man by a military machine, that the Liberty Loan was a scheme by which moneyed interests of the country worked to obtain the poor man's coin, that this is a useless war, a fight that was none of our affair."[20] Local Councils of Defense responded quickly and vigorously to this call for vigilance and control. In an official history of the Council of Defense, *Sooners in the War,* the local councils proudly pointed to their most effective and noteworthy actions during the war. The Beckham County chairman reported that his group had gathered twenty cars full of men and had treated a Socialist speaker "to a dose of tar and so forth." No one knew who did it, he chortled, but "from that day on our difficulties were slight, besides converting a few with religious scruples and a few Redflaggers."[21] The council in Choctaw County was pleased to report that "the application of a few courses of yellow paint, posting of slacker bulletins, and spankings administered with a heavy 'two-handed' strap have been most expedient and efficacious remedies."[22] Schoolteachers who asserted that the war was being fought for the benefit of the rich were removed from their classrooms by the wrathful Council of Defense in Dewey County. Both the Dewey and Ellis county councils claimed credit for securing evidence to convict western Oklahoma Socialist leaders (an "undesirable element" in their phrase) of sedition. The Dewey patriots noted that one of the convicted Socialists had "for years been a local soap box orator who was in the habit of ridiculing the government and all its activities."[23]

Anyone who doubts that officially sanctioned wartime compulsions provided the Democrats with a unique opportunity to destroy their Socialist opponents need only look at the process at work in Beckham County

where the Socialist vote between 1910 and 1916 was the second highest
in Oklahoma. Here the Socialists had won 40 percent of the vote and had
elected a state representative in 1914—a result that both stupefied and
mortified the local Democratic party.[24] The suppression of Socialists can
be followed in detail in the correspondence of Sam Williams, a leading
businessman and Democrat who served as secretary of the Council of
Defense. Explaining one of his problems to the state council, Williams
wrote that a recalcitrant local resident had delivered an

> unpatriotic talk to our gin office last fall and he has been nominated
> by the Socialist fraternity for the office of county weigher. I am sure
> that a letter from you to the effect that his seeking office under the
> Government he had vilified would hardly comport with the dignity
> of the people that he is a resident among will have the desired effect
> of causing his name to be withdrawn and of shutting his mouth at
> least during the term of the war.[25]

The chairman of the local Liberty Loan campaign wrote to Williams
concerning a woman in a rural district who had refused to pledge because
she would not pay money "to murder" anyone. "She is a Socialist of the
rankest," reported the Liberty Loan salesman, and "she has a good farm
and no mortgage against it." He suggested that the council "look after"
this case.[26]

Resentment smouldered in the rural areas of Beckham County,
prompting Sam Williams to report to the state council that something
would have to be done about numerous "slackers" who disrupted Liberty Loan meetings with defiant declamations that they would go to jail
before paying.[27] Williams implored the state council "to make some
show out here among these slackers." He feared that future loan drives
and Red Cross appeals "will simply fall down bad, as all the work so far
has been done by a few men in each district and they swear that if the
Government don't get behind them and make the slackers come through
this time that they will not lead and take the abuse any longer."[28]
Williams reminded the council that Beckham County had fallen so low as
to have elected Socialists to office, implying that the radical tendencies of
the voters presented special problems to those crusading for total support
of the American war effort.

Numerous letters from rural districts in the county complained that the solicitors of Liberty Loans were laying a heavy hand upon tenants and poor people generally, making them bear a burden that properly belonged on the backs of nonresident landowners.[29] One such complaint came from Hext, where the Socialists had polled a majority vote more than once.[30] From Mayfield, Oklahoma, came an expression of grievance, which, in style and substance, was typical. The writer reported on a "Thrift Stamp" meeting at Friendship schoolhouse in which

> poor people that did not own any property at all and did not have a dollar to there [sic] name was Bull Dozed and made to pay as much as men that was worth 10 to 15 teen tousand [sic] Dollars.
>
> One old man 84 yeers [sic] old without any money or property of any kind was forced to sign the card for 45 dollars or Be called a slacker.[31]

Apparently the exactions of the county council were so onerous in one neighborhood that the distressed residents complained directly to the Oklahoma War Savings Commission. The commissioners then informed Williams that he had been accused of forcing people to pledge more than their means would allow and reminded him that the Treasury Department would not support any local council that demanded excessive contributions.[32]

That conflicts occurred between town businessmen hustling war bonds and farm folk suspicious of the businessmen after years of haggling over prices and politics is not surprising. Conflict undoubtedly occurred as well in areas where the Socialists were not especially strong simply because hostility—or at least suspicion—flourished between farmers and tradesmen. In areas where politics was confined almost wholly to the activities of the two major parties one can find town merchants complaining bitterly about disloyal farm customers who purchased with cash from mail-order catalogs while requesting credit from the merchant. But the chronic town-farm conflict was greatly intensified in areas where the farmers, perhaps poorer than most, perhaps burdened by the weight of tenancy, lent their support to political movements that proposed to restrict sharply or even to eliminate precisely such business interests as Sam Williams' cotton gins. To someone in Williams' place, it would seem only natural that the malcontents who had previously seized every chance to accuse him of taking his profit out of the farmer's hide would now undermine the country that provided opportunities for business success to able and worthy men like himself.

Claims for their own worthy citizenship and impeccable patriotism were usually the first—and by no means hypocritical—resort of local leaders who were accused of overbearing behavior. When he replied to the inquiry concerning his methods of soliciting Liberty Loans, Sam Williams suggested that his intentions were being misconstrued and that the state officials should be wary of the allegation because "this particular district is a Socialist stronghold which accounts for the letter to you."[33] How satisfying that reply must have been to the man who made it—to be able to reaffirm that one's actions were in harmony with the highest national purposes and that complaints from bums and malcontents need not be credited by good Americans. Making "patriotic" demands and accusations gave the Democrats a profound psychological —and political—advantage over the country folk who had stubbornly supported the Socialist party for nearly a decade.

More than any other event, the rebellion of hard-pressed tenant farmers in east-central Oklahoma against enforcement of the draft law in early August 1917 provided clinching proof, so far as Democrats were concerned, that the Socialist party was a sink of evil and disloyalty that had to be cleaned out. This uprising of tenants, known as the Green Corn Rebellion, was centered in an area where the Socialist party had always polled a strong vote.[34] Consequently it would give Democrats the opportunity to level accusations of insurrections and treason at the political organization that indeed had tried for so long to organize poor tenant farmers for *political* action. No one realized more quickly than the Socialist leaders that the Green Corn Rebellion could only portend disaster for their party. H. M. Sinclair, still the party's state secretary, issued a statement denying any connection whatsoever between Socialist party policy and the rebellion. He reminded the voters that the party had pleaded with them in 1916 to vote Socialist and prevent war. Because Socialist warnings had gone unheeded, Sinclair argued, his party should not be blamed for desperate conditions that it had proposed to remedy. He then reaffirmed that the Socialist party would "continue the fight for working class emancipation along political lines" and invited people "to join with us and by intelligent action pave the way for a better day."[35]

Such disclaimers afforded the Socialists as much protection as a rickety shack in the midst of an Oklahoma tornado. *Harlow's Weekly* suggested that the locale of the rebellion had seen much Socialist activity in the past few years, indicating a connection between socialism and the rebellion. Socialism, it argued, had the same goals as the organized groups that led the uprising.[36] Local editors in Pontotoc, Hughes, and Seminole counties were not included to make even crude distinctions. The editor of the *Ada Star-Democrat* pointed to well-known Socialists, some of whom had been candidates for local office in 1916, among the arrested Green Corn rebels.[37] His conclusion was that if law-abiding and patriotic citizens tolerated "this revolutionary and anarchistical movement" any longer, they would be as foolish as the "Royalist France" that had allowed Rousseau "to write the bloodiest page in all history."[38]

Down in Marshall County, the editor of the *Kingston Messenger* always quick to observe each new instance of Socialist wickedness, saw the Green Corn Rebellion as the culmination of four years' agitation. "Responsible citizens," he wrote,

remember that shortly after the outbreak of the war (1914), when cotton prices were low and transportation costs high, tenant cotton farmers esserted that when they ran out of food and money they would go get it if it was not furnished them. Socialist agitators since have constantly preached a reign of anarchy. . . . Just now Oklahoma is reaping the harvest of Socialistic seed sowing, and the consequences that the *Messenger* has heretofore pointed as sure to result is now being realized.

His conclusion was that the "mad Mob" had to be put down and its leaders given the punishment traitors deserve.[39]

In the aftermath of the Green Corn Rebellion, the Socialists endured unofficial demands that they prove their loyalty and, in some instances, suffered official exclusion from privileges that should have rightfully been theirs. Or so *Harlow's Weekly* implied when it reported H. M. Sinclair's request that one Socialist jury commissioner be appointed in every southern Oklahoma county where the Socialists received a significant minority of the vote. Although *Harlow's* admitted that the Socialists had a case, it quoted with approval the reply of a state district judge in Pontotoc County who refused the Socialist request on the grounds that they held "revolutionary views" and stood "indicted at the bar of public opinion of insubordination to their government." Their participation in judicial proceedings, the judge argued, would ''outrage the state of mind possessed by the patriotic citizenship of this locality.''[40]

The public outrage against the Socialists was apparently bipartisan. The Republican party's state executive decided, shortly after the Green Corn Rebellion, not to press the suit that Republicans and Socialists had brought against the state election board's decision that the electoral reform initiative, itself jointly sponsored by Republicans and Socialists, had failed to pass in the November 1916 election. After sharp debate, a majority of the Republican executive had concluded that it was more disadvantageous to cooperate with ''un-American'' Socialists than to give up an election law reform that would give the Democrats less opportunity to manipulate ballot counts.[41]

When his social and political advantages and the virtue of his nation appeared to come under challenge from an ''un-American'' source, the town-dwelling, middle-class Oklahoman put on the armor of ''Americanism'' and went forth to fight his very real social and political opponents. No one expressed the nationalist litany better than the editor of the *Ada Star-Democrat* and no one more clearly exemplified the frantic response of the Americanist who felt that the virtues of America were threatened by the political vices and iniquities of Europe. ''Autocracy,'' wrote the earnest editor,

is government of, for and by class. Democracy means equal rights, and equal protection in enjoyment of common rights and privileges. It means equal opportunity not only in self-government, but for self-advancement. . . . It means freedom of thought, speech, and action, with due consideration of the rights of others and security of persons and property from the aggression of individuals or nations.[42]

And how did the editor propose to apply this undeniably liberal and generous creed? The following week he suggested that all those voters in Wisconsin who would support a Socialist state senator for reelection after he had already been expelled by the legislature should be rounded up and shipped to Germany. The state and national governments, he argued, had been too lenient with the Victor Bergers who had ''abused'' their right of freedom of speech to the point where they should be tried and hung.[43]

In this illiberal and intolerant atmosphere Socialists struggled to keep their ideals in print, their newspapers in circulation, their local organizations intact, their voters informed and unintimidated. Only in a few areas can we even follow that struggle in any meaningful detail, for the local newspapers did their patriotic best to keep news of activity they considered disloyal off their pages. Most Democratic editors were pleased to publish reports of Socialists convicted of sedition and perhaps an occasional cryptic comment on the decline of Socialist activity. "Where, oh where has the Socialist Party gone?" the *Madill Record* gloated in the spring of 1918.[44]

Where indeed? What Democrats were doing to the Socialist party organization in Marshall County during the war years has been obscured by an almost complete absence of evidence. However, there are a few counties in western Oklahoma—Beckham, Roger Mills, Kiowa, Major —where the Socialists had strong organization, persistent support, and two newspapers that stated their case. With the two Socialist newspapers we can draw a fairly clear and detailed picture of the political and intellectual response of grass-roots Socialists to the war crisis.

Long before the United States had entered World War I, the *Otter Valley Socialist* had sharply criticized the "preparedness" campaign of 1916. The OVS (as its readers sometimes called it) contended that the strongest proponents of war preparations were jingoists, firebrands, and munitions makers who displayed great ardor when the nation's honor was mentioned but who would step aside when the war came and allow the sons of "farmers" and "hill-billies" to man the front lines.[45] Once the United States had joined the fighting, both the OVS and the *Strong City Herald* drummed their insistent message that rich men and their big businessess starved workers in peacetime and then conscripted them to sacrifice their lives "for the dirty dollars of Wall Street."[46] The OVS alleged that the police chief of Oklahoma City, federal agents, and packing plant operators had conspired to arrest a union organizer for sedition, which prompted the Socialist paper to comment: "Sure, Mike, these dollar pa(y)triots would like to discredit this organizer as it means about 2 or 3 thousand dollars a day to the packers to keep an open shop."[47]

In October 1917 the Socialist local of Roll, Oklahoma, addressed an open letter, published in the *Strong City Herald,* to the President of the United States. An extended recitation of political and economic grievances, the statement of the Roll Socialists was an effective critique not only of recently implemented war policies but of the failure of fifteen years of "progressivism" to reduce social inequalities. The Roll Socialists insisted that the

> reason for the dissatisfaction of the working class is an economic one. . . . The immense bond issues, the unparalleled profits, the arrogance of the federal officials of every type, and the prosecution of every man who dares to raise his voice in protest, breeds dissatisfaction and discontent. In short, the economic security of the rich and the economic insecurity of the poor, the ability of the rich to enjoy leisure and vacation vs. the necessity for ceaseless labor by the worker, luxury vs. squalor, palaces vs. hovels, social caste amd many other things are the real and actual cause of the protest, which the big daily papers deliberately term disloyalty, traitorous, and pro-German.[48]

And the Roll men added their own specific grievance: the President, they said, had controlled the price of wheat and had cut their income by a third while allowing mine and mill owners to pile up profits. The OVS had made a similar point but suggested that the problem of exploitation was international and consequently the people in both American and Europe could not hope to improve their conditions unless they overthrew "their Kaiser and Kings in Europe and the Monied Plutocrats of America."[49] They tactfully added the suggestion that Wilson's reward would be "great" if only he would improve the lot of the common farmer and laborer.

No one defended the freedom of "speak, publish, and assemble" more consistently than the isolated, vulnerable, and increasingly beleaguered Plains Socialists. They condemned "pseudo-patriots" who whipped up mob violence, "brainless fanatics" who harassed German-Americans, and local authorities who jailed war critics exercising their First Amendment rights.[50]

Laboring under official suspicion and the constant threat of vigilante terrorism, which was sometimes inspired by the local authorities, the Socialists began to show signs of weariness and resignation toward the end of 1917. The editor of the OVS had already been involved in a dispute with his draft board—a dispute, he alleged, that grew out of his attacks upon President Wilson's policies. The U.S. Solicitor had requested copies of the OVS so that the government could scrutinize its contents for seditious statements.[51] By November 1917 the OVS lamented that the jails were full of outspoken critics of the war and advised its readers to say nothing that could somehow be construed as interference with the nation's war program.[52] Six months later—and shortly before his printing plant was consumed by a fire of unknown origin—the editor of the OVS sadly suggested that "new anti-sedition law . . . is undoubtedly the most drastic piece of legislation since the Blue Laws, or even the ancient code of Hammurabi." It seemed to him "quite useless to expect reasonableness during the present crisis and it behooves each and all to remain silent upon the matters of war for, regardless of your good intention, you will be misjudged and ill-abused if your opinions are a [sic] variance with the now established ideas on the war."[53]

By the late spring of 1918, both of the southwestern Oklahoma Socialist papers had begun to give prominent space to local and national leaders who advocated the abandonment of the St. Louis platform opposing the war.[54] Sharp opposition to the war did not entirely disappear from Socialist pages, however. For example, readers found alongside a Socialist's proposal to support President Wilson a letter from O. E. Enfield, soon to stand trial on a charge of sedition. He advised Socialists to remember that "we hate evil principles, not evil men . . . let us remember that we have hydra-headed industrial kaisers at home who wrong us and rob us; let us fight them by a campaign of education and shell their trenches with volleys of enlightened ballots in every election till victory is ours."[55] The Roger Mills County Socialists, expressing themselves in the columns of the *Strong City Herald,* were far less bold. They carefully balanced their profession of loyalty to socialist principles with one to "our country." While calling for an end to the exploitation of labor and farmers, they pledged in the same breath to give "total support" to the nation's effort to destroy "Prussianism."[56]

Socialists recognized that all the stirring editorials and manifestos published in their newspapers would mean little if they did not organize voters to support their criticism of inequalities in the American social order. Organizing a base of opposition did not seem to Socialists to be an impossible and futile endeavor. Despite repercussions from the Green Corn Rebellion, there were modestly encouraging developments as late as September 1917. The Democratic senator from Oklahoma, Thomas P. Gore, had begun to oppose President Wilson's policies on conscription and agriculture. The Oklahoma Farmers' Union, not a Socialist organization but nonetheless a militant defender of the small farmers' economic interest, had endorsed Gore's opposition to the administration. Both the *Strong City Herald* and the *Otter Valley Socialist* saw this as a heartening sign of underlying rural opposition to the war, and the OVS noted that even the respected Democratic political magazine, *Harlow's Weekly*, had conceded that a majority of Oklahoma farmers were opposed to the war.[57]

Socialists tried mightily to organize that sentiment. Local Roll in Roger Mills County claimed to be adding new members at each bimonthly meeting in August and September 1917. Local Roll's secretary reported that not "all of them have lost their head over this war score" and that all who were "interested in permanane [sic] peace and real democracy are invited."[58] Two weeks later the Roll spokesman, still seeking to kindle spirited resistance, argued that "organization is power. We must support our press and persecuted comrads [sic] . . . if we are to win and save America from militarism, we must not be discouraged at anything."[59] It was an earnest and admirable plea, but it apparently received no echo elsewhere in the state. Where a dozen locals had flourished in the county between 1914 and 1916, there now seemed to be only Roll.

Over in Kiowa County the *Otter Valley Socialist* was no less concerned to organize opposition. Having learned that a group of county officials, bankers, and merchants had sent a well-publicized letter to Senator Gore demanding that he resign, the OVS encouraged circulation of a petition praising Gore's opposition to American war efforts and claimed that farmers had signed in large numbers throughout the country.[60] In November 1917 the OVS exhorted its readers to attend an "old-time rally" on a Saturday afternoon, perhaps hoping to revive the fervent Socialist encampments of earlier years.[61] As winter began the Socialists of Kiowa County were encountering fear, reluctance, and apathy among their former supporters. The OVS editor, hailing the return of H. H. Stallard from the Far West, called upon readers to help "wake the Oklahoma movement up from its sleep." Stallard advised his would-be audience not to be afraid of vigilante interference at the meetings, for he intended to speak on the topic, "Can We Beat the Kaiser?" His argument would conclude that the United States could win the war only if it socialized industry. Whatever it proved about the efficacy of public ownership, the lecturer's caution and his topic gave evidence of local Socialist accommodation to increasing political and social pressure.[62]

The year 1918 saw a winter with no spring for the Socialist party in Oklahoma. The OVS declared that the party was in severe straits and could even be supplanted by the Non-Partisan League if individual Socialists did not return to their tasks. Stallard said that it was discouraging to find only a few locals where little more than a year previously there had been 160. Having returned to Oklahoma to help establish a statewide Socialist daily, he found "socialists with hundreds of dollars worth of wild cat oil and mining stock, and little or no stock in the *Oklahoma Leader.*"[63] Steadily improving wartime agricultural prices and the alluring possibility of oil riches probably did provide additional inducement to farmers to leave the dangers and scant rewards of Socialist activity to those few who were willing to endure abuse, to risk jail, or to live with the threat of death so that they might defend their ideals.

In the summer and fall of 1918, the scattered remnants of the once-proud Socialist party did obeisance to demands for national unity. The *Oklahoma Leader*, published in Milwaukee with an editorial page for Oklahoma, noted the presence of Oklahoma Socialists at the war front in France whenever Democrats stigmatized the Socialists as disloyal.[64] The *Leader* stressed that Socialists were reported serving on the Council of Defense in Craig County, speaking for the Council of Defense in Beckham County, and rendering support to the Red Cross in Love County.[65] The proposed Oklahoma Socialist platform for 1918 delicately called for the end of autocracy and aristocracy; for collectivism and democracy *after* the war; and for a tax upon war profiteers. It also called for an end to "race hatred and mob rule," though it specified no culprits. The state executive committee of the party warned the membership not to engage in discussions of the war because it feared that "farmers and workingmen without skill in the selection of words with a fine shade of meaning under the espionage law as now enforced would invite themselves into the penitentiary."[66]

Within the party leadership there apparently were differing tendencies even where all recognized the necessity of caution. "Heck" Sinclair, always the organizer, admonished Socialist sympathizers to select committeemen and revive their locals. He acknowledged the chilling effect of "indictments, arrest, and mobs" on Socialist political activity but still urged sympathizers to take heart. "The fact that you are holding out," he argued, "is pleasing to the opposition and distressing to your friends who are doing their part in this great struggle . . . there is no danger of your getting in bad by standing up for humanity."[67]

Practical experience, however, clearly suggested that a Socialist stand for humanity would plunge its proponents into serious trouble. No one knew this lesson better than the Major County Socialists, who had faced prolonged harassment from a fervent nationalist who edited the local Democratic paper and headed the Council of Defense.[68] Major County Socialists made their professions of loyalty unmistakable during the 1918 campaign. They proclaimed that "the quickest and best way" for their "beloved country" to get out of the war was "to win". This declaration to the voters then proceeded with an act of political tightrope walking. Reaffirming their adherence to the principles of "International Socialism," Socialists pledged, at the same time, support "to our President in the consummation of his war aims and peace measures."[69] They could scarcely be faulted for favoring freedom of speech, press, assembly, and religious belief, though the latter had become controversial in Major County, where Mennonite residents adhered to their church's traditional peace testimony. Opposition to "lynching, mob-rule, and intimidation" was carefully balanced with opposition to "sabotage." They recommended prosecution of persons "whose language, influence, or overt acts prove him to be intentionally disloyal to our country and its democratic institutions" and of persons who violated "the lawful rights of our citizens" (the war resister and the persecuting vigilante).[70] A Socialist who took over the editorship of a local paper in mid-October of 1918 urged "loyalty and harmony at home and for active cooperation in every way possible to make the world safe for democracy."[71] That much of this was expedient acquiescence for the duration of the war can be seen in the change of tone in the Socialist editor's comments barely two months later—after the armistice had been signed: "Universal compulsory military training is the program of organized greed and it is sure a strong organization in this country. It would seem that the idea that great military preparedness is a guarantee of peace would be somewhat shattered by recent events."[72]

Known acts of physical intimidation were relatively few in number, but they undoubtedly served as examples of what might happen to active socialists.[73] With governments from the national to the local level providing sanction for virtually compulsory community programs to support the war effort, the local elites and their followers in the towns used the opportunity not only to inflict physical punishment upon dissenters but more importantly to apply social and psychological pressure to citizens who would feel genuine distress if they felt themselves disloyal to America. As noted earlier, whatever the Democrats might say about the supposedly alien and vicious character of socialism, the impoverished farmers of Oklahoma believed the party's state program promised fulfillment of their undeniably American hope for land of their own and a decent living from it. To be told that their support for socialism was tantamount to disloyalty to their nation in a period of grave crisis must have nourished doubts in the minds of all but the most committed Socialists. Those who spoke out to "save America from militarism" (as they put it) ended up in jail, and the remainder, beset by doubts and fears, fell silent or else muffled their socialism in heavy patriotic wraps as the deepest of political winters descended upon them.

Having struggled through the worst of times, the Socialists hoped that the end of the war would bring better days, perhaps even the rebirth of the expansive prewar movement. It was a forlorn hope. In November 1920, after two years of the most arduous attempts to reorganize the locals and rekindle the old enthusiasm, the party managed to gather in only 5 percent of the statewide vote for Eugene Debs, the now imprisoned presidential candidate. In only eight counties (mostly in the western part of the state) did the Socialists drum up more than 10 percent of the vote.[74]

If we were to seek a more precise date for the death of the Socialist party of Oklahoma, we could settle for February 14, 1920. In an issue of the *Oklahoma Leader* which appeared on that day, H. M. Sinclair, back in his old job as party secretary, announced that the party's locals had ceased to function, requiring all party memberships to be held "at large" thereafter.[75] The eager participation that had once made the locals fearsome in the eyes of their opponents was now gone. All of the anger, passion, intelligence, and sheer bravery that the country people had brought to the local meetings had evaporated in the wartime atmosphere of national patriotism and heady prosperity.

It was not for want of effort on the part of the old leaders that resuscitation failed to revive the party. In late 1918, an old friend and comrade had returned to Oklahoma, had found himself welcomed back into the ranks, and would remain in the state until his death in 1943. He lent his superb organizational and agitational talents to the party that had expelled him in 1913. Oscar Ameringer brought with him a plan that, at first glance, seemed to be outrageously removed from the current political reality in Oklahoma. He proposed to found a new statewide socialist newspaper, unaffiliated with the party and receptive to the propaganda mounted by any Socialist. The plan would have been quixotic but for the help promised and received from Victor Berger's *Milwaukee Leader.*[76]

From the scattered localities where socialism had once flourished, many of the old leaders reappeared—to serve on county committees, to run for local office, to sell *Leader* subscriptions and bonds.[77] Now there would once again be the good news of the Socialist gospel. The secretary-treasurer wrote in early 1919:

> For some time you have had little or no news from your state office. This was not the wishes of those handling the work, but we felt "No news is better than bad news," and you were not asked to listen to griefs which we endeavored to carry faithfully for the party.[78]

Thus the spring of 1919 was more than the mere warming of the weather to the Socialists. Local Chickasha implored its fellow locals to pay off the state office indebtedness and to pay the salary (months in arrears) owing to the secretary-treasurer, who had worked diligently with little recompense.[79] There was a report that the Socialists were finally "breaking into one of the old strongholds, Choctow County,"[80] but this was the only mention of any success in penetrating the southern cotton districts. O. E. Enfield, though not yet out of jail, was back in print, celebrating the advance of the plans to turn the *Leader*, already published as a weekly, into a big daily:

> The Oklahoma Socialists, after two years of mob rule, after having been dictated to and domineered by pay-triotic Councils of Defense, are ready to install a paper for themselves. In spite of three years' drought, in spite of Democratic gag rule, in spite of all opposition, the Oklahoma Socialists are putting two hundred thousand dollars into a daily.[81]

It was impossible to intimidate Enfield.

But the cotton districts would not come back, possibly because cotton prices remained generally high, falling sharply only in 1921.[82] A report on the condition of the "daily" *Leader* in October 1919 suggested that the southern counties were still not doing their share. They were bluntly told not to wait until someone was sent to collect their subscriptions.[83] In April 1920 the manager of the *Leader* reported that 7,000 Socialists had contributed to its operation; he wished to know where the remainder of the 50,000 prewar Socialist voters had put their money.[84] It was in this period that a delusive myth of 50,000 Socialists in Oklahoma took hold, both sustaining and bedevilling the ebbing life of the Socialist party. The myth prompted the remaining activists to believe that just the right key would turn the latch that would release the fearful voters. More exhortation was attempted:

> There are still some old-time comrades who are "skeered" and holding back in their activities for the cause.
> To those we have but pity.
> They told us that the powers that be would not let us function as a party, but we are functioning notwithstanding.[85]

There were good reasons for people to be fearful of association with radicalism. Ameringer recalled that the "Green Corn Rebellion and the Red scares frightened the very lives out of our supporters. People who had given us hundreds of dollars for launching our paper were afraid of having it delivered to their homes, afraid of being marked Reds."[86]

The 1920 platform was recognizably and vigorously socialist with its call for the full socialization of all major industry, for land titles that would be based upon use and occupancy, and for a novel form of political representation by occupation instead of by geographical district. In addition, the Socialists called for the restoration of political and civil liberty, national amnesty for political prisoners (mentioning Cumbie and Enfield of Oklahoma), and higher wages for railroad workers.[87]

Socialism, however, had become an exercise in futility in postwar Oklahoma, as elsewhere in the country. After the 1920 election, the *Leader*, attempting to explain the low Socialist vote, argued lamely that potential Socialist sympathizers were so disgusted with the wartime tyranny of the national and state Democratic administrations that they had voted Republican to insure the ouster of the tyrants.[88] Less than two years would elapse after the debacle of 1920 before Ameringer's political intelligence would guide him toward a new kind of political insurgency.

His *Leader* would become, to the chagrin and resentment of perennial Socialists like O. E. Enfield, the champion of farmer-labor insurgency within the Democratic party. And most Oklahoma Socialists would follow Ameringer along the path to the politics of "reform".

It cannot be argued that *either* repression or prosperity killed the Socialist party of Oklahoma; *both* did. Repression frightened away many who had struggled, fitfully and desperately, to apply the ideas of socialism to their lives. Only the most committed local and State leaders remained to take the party's ship through a stormy and treacherous passage. Until 1916 the "starved-out farmers" had believed that they had "a protest coming."[89] The protest was primarily against conditions perceived as short term and unnatural in their lack of reward. If the small farmers had not aspired to achieve individual profitable operations and had sought a transformation of their mode of production, they would have had good reason to return to the Socialist party when it was once again relatively safe to do so. But, as one hostile observer noted, farmers, "instead of abandoning their farms in search of work in the cities, are riding in automobiles to town for the purpose of conferring with income tax collectors. . . . Socialism is being neglected by the farmers as a result of this prosperity."[90]

It was not merely a question of the farmers leaving the Socialist party; they had to have somewhere to go. They did; they went back home to America. Prosperity gave them the opportunity to feel "American" again, to be successful in private acquisition and possession, to leave behind the departure from orthodox belief that had separated them from the myth of America. They could leave behind the feelings of rage felt toward others and toward themselves when they had raised the red flag to symbolize their protest. That collective act had taken them too far from their origins and desires. Their next agrarian protest against "conditions" would be more consonant with the traditions of the American countryside.

NOTES

1. I have drawn my voting statistics from Oliver Benson, et al., *Oklahoma Votes, 1907-1962* (Norman, 1964), and from the Election Board Archives, State Capitol Building, Oklahoma City. Where Benson and his colleagues lumped the Socialist vote together with such splinter party votes as the Progressives and

Prohibitionists, I have checked to see whether the percentages for the splinter parties comprised the significant part of the total of Benson's "third-party" column. In both 1912 and 1916, the percentages Benson recorded are basically the Socialist vote. The other parties in the combined third-party column received less than 1 percent of the statewide vote. Thus the 16 percent recorded for "other parties" in 1916 (Benson, *Oklahoma Votes*, 63) contained a 15.4 percent vote for the Socialists and 0.6 percent for the others.

2. *Elk City News*, quoted in *Roger Mills Sentinel* (Cheyenne) August 24, 1916.

3. *Ellis County Socialist*, July 20, 1916.

4. *Otter Valley Socialist*, January 26, 1916.

5. Ibid., November 16, 1916.

6. Ibid., December 21, 1916.

7. *Harlow's Weekly*, December 6, 1916.

8. *Otter Valley Socialist*, January 4, 1917.

9. See the appendix to this book for precinct data on the abrupt decline of the Socialist party vote in Marshall and Beckham counties in 1918.

10. *Proceedings of the Socialist State Convention*, December 29-31, 1914, 13.

11. Ibid., 14.

12. *Appeal to Reason* (Girard, Kansas), January 8, 1916, quoted in James R. Green, "Socialism and the Southwestern Class Struggle" (Ph.D. diss., Yale University, 1972), 357.

13. Ibid.

14. Ibid., 358.

15. *Kingston Messenger*, July 14, 1916.

16. *Marshall County News-Democrat*, June 22, 1916.

17. *Ellis County Socialist*, October 19, 1916.

18. Ibid., April 27, 1916.

19. Ibid.

20. *Roger Mills Sentinel*, June 12, 1917.

21. Oklahoma Councils of Defense, *Sooners in the War* (n.p., n.d.), 28. A copy of this report is available in the Library of the Oklahoma Historical Society.

22. Ibid., 32.

23. Ibid., 37.

24. The editors of the *Cheyenne* (Roger Mills County) *Star* and the *Sayre* (Beckham County) *Standard* exchanged friendly jibes over the fact that both counties had elected Socialists as state representatives. *Cheyenne Star*, November 28, 1914.

25. Sam Williams to J. M. Aydelotte, May 21, 1918, Sam Williams Papers, Western History Collection, University of Oklahoma Library.

26. J. K. Breckinridge to Sam Williams, June 29, 1918, Sam Williams Papers.

27. Sam Williams to George W. Barnes, June 30, 1918, Sam Williams Papers.

28. Ibid.

29. G. M. England to Sam Williams, June 29, 1918; D. C. Cummings and W. A. Mayfield to Sam Williams, June 28, 1918; Thirteen men of Hext district to Sam Williams, July 1, 1918; H. W. Davis to Sam Williams, June 30, 1918: Sam Williams Papers.

30. Thirteen men of Hext district to Sam Williams, July 1, 1918, Sam Williams Papers.

31. G. M. England to Sam Williams, June 29, 1918, Sam Williams Papers.

32. W.M. Morris to Sam Williams, September 18, 1918, Sam Williams Papers.

33. Sam Williams to W. M. Morris, September 20, 1918, Sam Williams Papers. He conceded, however, that the loan quotas had been reduced after severe drought had ruined the county's crop.

34. See chapter 7 below.

35. *Strong City Herald*, August 23, 1917.

36. *Harlow's Weekly*, August 15, 1917.

37. *Ada Star-Democrat*, April 24, 1917.

38. Ibid., August 10, 1917.

39. *Kingston Messenger*, August 10, 1917.

40. *Harlow's Weekly*, December 12, 1917.

41. Ibid., November 7, 1917.

42. *Ada Star-Democrat*, May 4, 1917.

43. Ibid., May 11, 1917.

44. *Madill Record*, March 7, 1918.

45. *Otter Valley Socialist*, March 8, 1916.

46. Ibid., April 26, 1917 (article by O. E. Enfield). See also ibid., May 24, August 2, November 29, 1917; see *Strong City Herald*, March 29, April 26, August 30, September 6, 1917 (extensive coverage of Senator LaFollette's proposal to "conscript wealth").

47. *Otter Valley Socialist*, December 6, 1917.

48. *Strong City Herald,* October 11, 1917.

49. *Otter Valley Socialist*, June 7, 1917.

50. Ibid., March 29, May 31, August 9, November 15, 22, 1917; Strong City *Herald*, July 5, August 16, 30, September 20, 27, 1917, March 14, April 18, 1918 (criticism of local Democratic newspaper for approving the tarring and feathering of a Socialist organizer in an adjoining county).

51. *Otter Valley Socialist*, June 14, 28, August 23, 1917.

52. Ibid., November 15, 1917.

53. Ibid., May 9, 1918; *Oklahoma Leader*, May 23, 1918, for description of the fire.

54. *Otter Valley Socialist*, May 9, 16, 1918; *Strong City Herald*, May 9, 30, June 6, 13, 1918.

55. *Otter Valley Socialist*, May 16, 1918.

56. *Strong City Herald*, May 9, 1918.

57. Ibid., August 30, 1917; *Otter Valley Socialist*, September 6, 1917; *Harlow's Weekly*, August 29, 1917. *Harlow's* and most Oklahoma editors were flabbergasted that the state Farmers' Union would support Senator Gore's opposition to President Wilson's agricultural and defense policies.

58. *Strong City Herald*, September 6, 1917.

59. Ibid., September 20, 1917.

60. *Otter Valley Socialist*, September 27, 1917.

61. Ibid., November 8, 1917.

62. Ibid., December 20, 1917. H. H. Stallard had in the past taken opportunistic positions that clashed with party principles. He called for Socialist support of Jim Crow legislation in 1911 and was roundly criticized for pandering to prejudice. In the spring of 1918, he was to join those Socialists who called for a repudiation of the St. Louis platform. *Strong City Herald*, May 30, 1918.

63. *Otter Valley Socialist*, January 31, 1918.

64. *Oklahoma Leader*, June 6, 13, 20, July 25, 1918.

65. Ibid., July 11, 18, 25, 1918.

66. Ibid., August 22, 1918.

67. Ibid.

68. See editor and local Council of Defense leader Ivan Williams's attacks on Socialists in the *Fairview Leader*, October 4, 11, 1917, January 4, August 15, 1918.

69. *Cleo Springs Chieftan* [sic] October 18, 1918.

70. Ibid.

71. Ibid.

72. Ibid., December 20, 1918.

73. For other instances of vigilante repression of radicals and opponents of American involvement, see H. C. Peterson and Gilbert C. Fite, *Opponents of War 1917-1918* (Madison, 1957), 40-41 and 171-176.

74. Benson, et al., *Oklahoma Votes*, 63.

75. *Oklahoma Leader*, February 14, 1920.

76. Oscar Ameringer, *If You Don't Weaken: The Autobiography of Oscar Ameringer* (1940; reprint ed., Westport, Conn., 1969), 358-366.

77. *Oklahoma Leader*, April 5, May 10, July 19, August 16, October 18, November 22, 1919, February 14, 28, May 8, June 12, September 30, October 22, 1920.

78. Ibid., January 30, 1919.

79. Ibid., May 3, 1919.

80. Ibid., May 10, 1919.

81. Ibid., July 26, 1919.

82. Ibid., October 18, 1919. The average yearly price for Oklahoma cotton for eight consecutive years beginning in 1913 was as follows: 1913—11.6 (cents per pound); 1914—9.6; 1915—8.8; 1916—13.3; 1917—21.1; 1918—27.9; 1919—29.0; 1920—28.1; 1921—10.9. The prices of agricultural commodities are available in Trimble R. Hedges and K. D. Blood, "Oklahoma Farm Price Statistics, 1910-38," *Agricultural Experiment Station Bulletin No. 238* (December 1939): 24.

83. *Oklahoma Leader*, October 18, 1919.

84. Ibid., April 3, 1920.

85. Ibid., June 12, 1920.

86. Ameringer, *If You Don't Weaken*, 361-362.

87. *Oklahoma Leader*, February 14, 21, 1920.

88. Ibid., November 7, 1920.

89. Ibid., July 30, 1926. A former Socialist made this comment during the course of an interview he gave while seeking the Democratic nomination for governor in 1926.

90. *Harlow's Weekly*, January 2, 1918.

The green corn rebellion — 7

In the impotence and desperation of the tenant farmers of eastern Oklahoma lay seeds of rage and rebellion. Many had lost their hopes for a "home," as they understood the term; yet they were unable or unwilling to migrate. They would move from one farm to another, from one county to the next, but they would not migrate from the cotton country. It was an ironical result of the millennarian excitement and rhetorical violence of some Socialist agitation that it revived the hopes of the traditional husbandmen and reinforced their conservative desire to stay on the land. Trapped in a particular system of exploitation and lacking in the experience of collective political action, the southwestern tenants had required an avenging Jehovah to legitimize communal defense of their neighborly way of life, of the virtues that were inseparable from the producer's activities. They found whatever community they had in the figure of a Christ who would give them succor, bind up their wounds, and encourage them to save their "Social Souls". In this case Jehovah's wrath and Christ's mercy were mixed with the idea of class war brought to the tenants by Marxian Socialists from the city. The novel system of ideas was absorbed into an American evangelical Protestant emphasis upon equality in the sight of God that was coeval with Marxism, if incongruent with the materialist idea of class war in this world.

When the Socialist party resolved that its members should refuse to serve the "militarists" and die "fighting the enemies of Humanity" in their own country, some of the tenants took the advice literally. When distant Europe's troubles were officially declared to be America's own and when federal and state authorities prepared to enforce the 1917 Conscription Act in Oklahoma, country people rebelled. On August 3,

1917, an ill-organized band of country rebels met a well-armed posse along the banks of the South Canadian River between Seminole, Pontotoc, and Hughes counties. The country rebels did not know that their plans had been largely betrayed by an informer in their own ranks. Catching sight of the advancing townsmen, the country people fired a few desultory shots and fled in disorder. This was the pathetic end of their overt resistance to the incursions of outside political authority.

In seeking the origins of the Green Corn Rebellion (so-called because the rebels had supposedly planned to march across the country, eating "green corn" along the way, eventually to join thousands of other working men who would overthrow "Big Slick" Woodrow Wilson and repeal the draft act), we must go back a few years to discover the social atmosphere that encouraged rebellion. As early as 1912, one can find the odd Socialist dissatisfied with the progress of political agitation. A report in the *Oklahoma Pioneer* described a meeting at McLoud, a town on the South Canadian River:

> The crowds were fairly good when the Social gospel was expounded from "Genesis to Revolution." The speakers remained most of the time within the realm of comprehensibility . . . one speaker was ruled down by the Chairman for saying: "Use your ballots is [sic] you can and your bullets if you must."[1]

When calls for armed revolution drifted in from the country districts, Socialist leaders interested in change through gradual means were predictably alarmed. The specter of night riders roaming the roads and tracks of eastern Oklahoma would give the local capitalists ample justification for training their own guns upon the countryside. They would use the excuse of violence to disrupt and suppress the legitimate political activities of the Socialist party. Socialist leaders quite wisely wished to avoid provocation. The *Boswell Submarine* even suggested that Democrats themselves may have fabricated "Socialist" appeals to violence in order to provoke popular antagonism. This was the editor's surmise when it was reported from Seminole County that a circular had appeared, warning voters to "get wise" or "get killed" because the majority of workers wanted their bread and meat.[2] This was obviously the "fraudulent" trick of some "desperate donk," the editor argued, because the Socialist philosophy would not countenance such acts.

It may well be true, however, that some of the tenant farmers in Seminole County received a different message from socialism. The year 1914 was a desperate time for the cotton tenants of Oklahoma, with the market price reduced to six cents per pound by the disruption of the European market. Probably no one will ever know what was said among the tenants in the scrub-oak woods and ravines of southern Seminole County, but we do know that three years later the Green Corn Rebellion occurred in that locale.

It was after the defeat of the Socialist party in 1914, when so many hopes had been raised by coal miner Fred Holt's proletarian campaign, that signs of frustration became more visible in the country neighborhoods. The 1914 election showed very clearly that Socialists might win majorities in numerous country precincts, but they still had difficulty gaining more than a third of any countywide vote because of the overwhelming anti-Socialist vote in the towns.

The general crisis of 1914, coupled with growing anger over high loan charges, probably inspired the organization of the Working Class Union (WCU), whose meetings were secret and whose activities came to include night riding, whipping, and dynamiting. WCU actions were concentrated in the South Canadian River valley from Seminole County across to Sequoyah County on the Arkansas border. As James R. Green writes, "The dirt farmers of eastern Oklahoma and the Arkansas Ozarks insisted on regulating their own lives even if it meant resorting to violence to preserve archaic cultural traditions."[3] They gathered in "committees" in the time-honored tradition of the southern hill country to chastise irregular behavior in the community. Although they might constrain one of their own from stealing another's cattle, their enforcement of informal social judgments did not reach effectively beyond country neighborhoods. Rural people could not regulate the legal demands imposed upon them by town businessmen.

According to Green, Socialists were able to expand the tenant farmers' outlook so that their violent actions amounted to something more than "primitive" banditry and "prepolitical" resistance to changing market forces. Socialists supposedly enlarged the legitimizing belief in natural rights and local freedom that animated the farmers. Committing himself to the proposition that the Socialist-voting tenants were *becoming* secular, modern, and revolutionary in outlook, Green concludes that the WCU, heavily influenced by the IWW, made its members think more like proletarians than peasants.[4] But he sharply qualifies the force of the assertion by saying that the overall setting and character of the rebellion does not amount to a genuine "red rising."

In analyzing these puzzling phenomena, the historian faces almost crippling difficulties. What furtive evidence can be found of the mentality (or mentalities?) that developed in meetings around flickering fires in the woods? What was the quality of the actions that seemed to ensue?

In early 1915 the USDA county agent working in Checotah wrote to the director of extension at Oklahoma A&M to advise that it was useful for agents from adjoining counties to discuss common problems. "For instance I heard a great deal of this Working Mens Union in some of my neighboring counties while at the short course," he reported. "I understand that they have pursued some very drastic measures to make their presence known in various localities." It is perhaps fitting that one of those paragons of modern commercial agriculture, the county agent, should give one of the earliest warnings of the new form of radicalism.[5] Before the year was out, county agents and county elites whom they served had encountered violent resistance when they tried to help farmers make "progress." In October and November of 1915 nightriders set off explosives placed beside cattle-dipping vats in Sequoyah, Muskogee, and Pontotoc counties. Stock owners had protested that the liquid mixture, intended to kill the cattle ticks that spread the virulent Texas fever, had been improperly mixed in numerous instances, proving lethal not only to the ticks but to the cattle themselves.[6] Significantly, owners of small herds were reported to have protested more vehemently because they were less able to withstand losses. Big herds owned by large capitalistic operations had supposedly carried the disease into the Canadian River valley from Texas. *Harlow's Weekly*, from its vantage point in Oklahoma City, said that only the "prejudiced and the uninformed" attributed the death of cattle to the poisonous dip instead of the disease.[7] Such was the judgment of the Oklahoma City businessman and editor when informed that country people, rightly or wrongly, believed that their livelihoods were being irresponsibly jeopardized.

When an owner refused to have his stock dipped, as did two men from Lula (Pontotoc County), the sheriff was empowered to dip the cattle, charge the owner $1 per head, and obtain fees for the distance traveled to perform his duty. The cattle were to be held until payments were made or else sold under sheriff's orders for the amount of the charges.[8] The USDA agent for Pontotoc County warned that if the dipping program was delayed and disrupted, a special quarantine might be placed around the county to prevent the movement of cattle in or out.[9] A man from Vanoss, who identified himself as a Jeffersonian Democrat and a law-abiding citizen, advocated public protest to stop the enforcement of the "tyranni- cal" dipping law.[10] Other men still preferred stealth and direct action. In early November still another dipping vat was blasted in the night.[11]

Pontotoc County authorities persuaded themselves that the Socialists had some part in the "outrages" against public order. The newspapers printed letters purportedly written and delivered by the vat bombers. One addressed to the county attorney said:

> If u dont go dam slow trying to catch the ones that blue up the vats and burnt barns ul git what Malone and Gilmor got and worse. Ur to dam smart.
>
> Commite.[12]

The *Star-Democrat* stated flatly that the "anarchists" should be lynched. Then it was the editor's turn. He claimed to have received a letter by the same hand:

> u cant blow hot and cold and git by if u and ur paper dont shut up on dipping ul git what u dont want.
>
> Commite.[13]

The *Ada Weekly News* commented that those who burned the barns of County Commissioners Gilmore and Malone were condemned by the "better element" who were the "great majority" in Pontotoc County. Governor Robert L. Williams, it noted, had offered a reward of $200 for each instance of barn burning. The *Weekly News* itself had been threatened, according to its own claim:

> Editor Evening Paper
> Your paper accuses the socolists burning up those barns. We did and we will blow up your office by January 1st.
> You watch. Our plans are complete. You think this is a goke. Watch & c.
>
> Red Flag.[14]

Whether these threatening letters were genuine or only heavy-handed, humorous fabrications intended to mock the poor education of country people, they do amply reflect the hostility felt by one side *or* the other in these local social struggles. It is not impossible to imagine that the townsmen could have indulged in fabrication to inflame feeling against the Socialists. But it is also easily imaginable that the angry country people would resort to violence against intruding public authorities.

In an editorial on dipping the *Ada Star-Democrat* drew the moral for the towns:

It merely afforded an excuse for the same old lawless bunch to howl.

Last year they made things hideous on account of the low price of cotton, but as all products of the farm are selling on the market at exceptionally high prices, all labor profitably employed, nobody idle by the professional deadbeat. . . . They seized on the cow dip as an excuse to make themselves famous. But a change has come over the country. Their party went to the bow-wows last year. . . . Men who have been misled into it are quitting it. Good business men no longer want their trade, banks will not loan them money, farm owners will not rent them land.[15]

This comment hints that the militant townsmen were not employing business criteria to the exclusion of any other when dealing with country people. Political affiliation and social feeling affected business relations. Country people were stigmatized as thieves and thugs. The sheriff of Pontotoc County prohibited the Socialists from using the county court-house for their public meetings. The *Star-Democrat* pronounced him "eminently correct":

Nobody has a legal, historical, or moral right to use a public-owned place as a hot-bed of crime. It might be a mistake to lay recent nightrider crimes in this connty [sic] at the door of the socialist party. There is one thing unmistakable and that is such acts of violence as above referred to are simply crystallized socialist senti-ment that has been prevalent for several years, and has been preached and advocated on every street corner in this town. Only last Saturday—we are reliably informed—one of their speakers declared at the court house that the democrats had stolen the election in this county and that the socialists would have the next election if they had to take it at the point of a gun.[16]

Try as they would to be "fair," the townsmen simply could not help but suspect the Socialists because the idea of socialism itself seemed illegitimate and criminal. "Crystallized socialist sentiment that has been prevalent for several years"—the phrase says a good deal about the mentality of the local elites now fearful of rural criminality and something about the persistent actuality of an emboldening radicalism in the country. Town leaders were probably correct in attributing the "villainies" to the "socialism" of the country. Socialism easily flowed into the notions of "natural rights" and Christian election with which the country people were deeply imbued. This confluence of justifying feelings and attitudes could have moved the impoverished tenant farmer, under the pressure of increasing frustration, to launch violent attacks upon people who gave him no respect.

Local Socialists in other parts of the state noted the charges and countercharges hurled by town and country in Pontotoc County. Apprehensive about the potential damage to the political movement, the *Otter Valley Socialist* professed itself unacquainted with the conditions in the eastern counties. "Undoubtedly the farmers must feel that they are justified but we fear that such methods can only bring disaster to their cause," the *Otter Valley Socialist* editor warned. He believed that the use of horsewhipping and death threats would make the tenant farmers "outlaws before the eyes of the people living away from there" and would call down retributive legal sanctions upon the rural folk. But most worrisome were the reports that "some few Socialists are participating in such methods." As a Socialist the editor could only regret these reports, "for one of our cardinal principles is that we must win at the ballot box and all other methods are boomerangs. Nowhere can they find any endorsement of such principles in our philosophy."[17] If this western Oklahoma Socialist could not quite comprehend the depth of the eastern tenant's anger, he did know his enemies well enough. He predicted that should one Socialist be associated with night-riding vandals and assailants, it would be widely publicized by Democrats, "notwithstanding many of these same people who condemn these farmers endorse the work of the Ku Klux Klan."[18]

Hostilities intensified on the east side. Unknown night prowlers had allegedly fired a shotgun blast at the kitchen window of the Pontotoc county attorney. In his statement the prosecutor carefully abstained from accusing Socialist party leaders of the offense but did allege that there ''is a secret inner circle whose purposes are not benign and whose objects are not pacific who are directly or indirectly connected with these outrages or actively encourage and rejoice in their commission.''[19] However, the accusation partially withheld was made soon enough:

> From this same cowardly gang, there now arises the hysterical cry, that the shooting of Tuesday night was part of a concocted plan on the part of the officials and two or three newspapers to wreck the Socialist party by pulling off a fake attempted assassination and that the threatening letters received by them were self-written and part of the same scheme.[20]

Now townsmen were as much convinced of the existence of a Socialist conspiracy as Socialists were persuaded that bankers, merchants, and landlords comprised a conspiracy of ''parasites.'' If conspiracy is construed as one group taking hidden action against another, then both sides were almost surely conspiring. The landlord's ''blacklist'' and the tenant's nocturnal revenge produced a full measure of secret plotting and open hatred.

Townsmen long subjected to rhetorical political attacks were convinced that the Socialists' oft-proclaimed revolution would soon begin in their locale. Like the Socialists they seemed to have little understanding of the requirements for revolution beyond Pontotoc County and eastern Oklahoma. It was enough to know that revolution impended in their home county. The *Ada Star-Democrat* believed that the attempted assassination of the county attorney had finally ''awakened the law-abiding citizens of this county to the effects of the revolutionary teachings of the itenerant [sic] agitators, who have with impunity verbally assaulted every honorable business man in the city.''[21] Honor and success had been disparaged. ''In their appeals, on street corners, to ignorance, viciousness, and prejudice they have denounced the merchant, the banker, and the professional men as robbers, thieves, and grafters.''[22] At bottom the "revolution" threatening the townsmen really menaced their expectations of improvement and their self-esteem as much as it menaced their physical well-being and material interests.

Agrarian hostility toward the bankers of eastern Oklahoma was so strong in 1915 and 1916 that insurance companies had actually cancelled policies protecting banks against loss from robbery. The companies reportedly believed that too many people considered it fair to rob a bank. Store lootings and robberies had greatly increased in the eastern part of Oklahoma since the depression of 1914.[23] A famous train robber, Henry Starr, who was known for his kindness among the hill people of eastern Oklahoma, gave an engaging apology for his bank robberies by suggesting that some of the bankers he had victimized were in the "robbery business, too."[24]

Throughout 1916 the Socialist party carried on its agitation along electoral lines, while the militant agrarians of eastern Oklahoma, an indeterminate number of whom were members of the still shadowy Working Class Union, carried out sporadic violent attacks upon their perceived enemies. The *Daily Oklahoman*, disturbed by social conditions that created sentiment for socialism, reported in February that eleven night riders, including a deputy sheriff, had been arrested in Sequoyah County for beating a farmer who had refused to join the WCU. The next day 2,000 men marched in Sallisaw to protest the harassment of a county judge who had resigned his office to give legal help to the WCU in its campaign against usury.[25] When this news reached the editor of the *Ada Star Democrat*, he sputtered that a county full of cutthroats should either be abolished or attached to Mexico.[26] *Harlow's Weekly* reported twenty-five WCU farmers marching through the streets of Muskogee to demonstrate support for the resigned judge, who had been subjected to disbarment proceedings in Sequoyah County because his financial accounts were alleged to have been irregular during his tenure in office.[27] Within a few weeks a saddened Democrat state legislator from LeFlore County wrote to Governor Williams to thank him for offering a reward for the capture of unknown men who had bombed his mill and engine, causing him a "total loss of 700." Unable to stand the loss, he would nonetheless be consoled if the episode led to the destruction of "this bunch of anarchist [sic] who denounced our State Government with all her moral and Religious Institutions."[28] Later in the year he wrote the governor to report new clues in the case and to request a renewal of the reward. His letter anxiously conveys information given by a WCU member turned informant:

> On yesterday one Dr. Winegarden, a Socialist and W.C.U. came to my home and volunteered to . . . make an affidavit as to the parties that blew up my Engine and gin mill. He says parties are still at Milton; all except one, the one who furnished the Dynamite. . . . You remember on the adjournment of the Legislature, I reached home . . . and on Thursday night following the W.C.U. held a meeting at the school house where they planned to blow up my mill and engine. He says they agreed to do that, that night; then he went home and in about 1 1/2 or 2 hours the mill was blown up. He says he has heard them talk about the matter since, on two occasions, and tell how they trimbled [sic] when they set off the last shot. . . . Winegarden says he will stay with me if I will put up the $200.00 reward we offered. . . . I feel sure you will help me with what I ask, if you could only realize the situation in this section. If I get a clue to the starting point, I think we will be able to uncover one of the dirtiest bunches of anarchist [sic] that has ever invaded a country.
>
> It is deplorable to know that we have organizations in our midst that pose as the Working Class Union, who will meet in some secret place, at an hour when all is slumber, and perfect their plans to take your life or destroy your property.[29]

More than all the newspaper reports, this remarkable document probably gives us a view of events and feelings as they really were during those tense days: night riders conspiring to attack their enemies and trembling (with a vague sense of thrill and satisfaction?) at the power of their work, a guilt-ridden or reward-seeking informant looking over his shoulder at his past; an enterpriser and solid citizen angry and bewildered at the infestation of snakes in his garden.

The towns raised the banner of suppression and struck hard at the open political activities of Socialists. In May 1916 *Harlow's Weekly*, unable to report any noteworthy accomplishments on the part of the authorities hunting the WCU, was able to tell its readers that socialism seemed to be declining in the southern counties. The reason: Democratic landlords and bankers had begun an "open boycott" against the Socialists. "In fact," *Harlow's* continued, "in certain communities the bitterness against the socialists has reached the stage that it is a serious handicap to be known as one. In Johnston County the Democrats drove many of them to cover by announcing that every man's name who registered as a socialist would be published."[30] *Harlow's* seemed to ignore the possibility that the suppression of political activity in broad daylight might drive more men into the covert and nocturnal politics of the deed.

In August 1916 there were renewed reports of minatory action by night riders—action quickly attributed to the WCU by the townsmen. The WCU allegedly posted notices with skull and crossbones advising laggard farmers that they had thirty days to join "voluntarily."[31] Dipping vats were dynamited and barns once again set afire in Pontotoc County.[32]

Warning notices appeared for the first time on the west side of the state. Near Cordell in Washita County posted notices stated:

Warning to landlords Any man that rents his land for more than one third and [doesn't?] pay his part of thrashing grain where renter furnishes seed or rents for money rent will get his land seeded to Johnson grass and his houses and barns burned or tries to dodge this by working big bodies himself.

And any renter agrees to give more will be looked after in a way that will not be pleasant to him. Any gin or thrasher that gins or thrashes on land that fails to heed this warning will also be burned. . . . We mean business.[33]

It was unusual for such threats to be made in western Oklahoma where lower rates of farm tenancy seemed to make political and social relations somewhat less bitter and abrasive. The notice does call attention to the new practice (in 1915 and 1916) of landlords of asking for more than one-third of grain crops as rent, thus violating the expectations of renters. Competition among renters for the best lands had made landlords ready to raise rents. The warning itself alludes to division and competition among renters. Some renters, perhaps the more able and less debt-ridden ones, were obviously trying to make "progress" in a way that displeased the traditional renting community.

The threat of such disruptions of the customary patterns of renting and the incursions of "improvers" like the county agents may provide the best clue to the origins of agrarian violence in 1916 and of full-scale local rebellion in 1917. There is little enough evidence available with which to attempt close social identification of the violence-prone agrarians of the WCU. "Renters" is the only frequent occupational identification. Sequoyah County was the only locale where the WCU seemed strong or bold enough to hold open public demonstrations. The legislator from adjoining LeFlore County who was pursuing the bombers of his mill through most of 1916 expressed his fear of their ability to retaliate. But in 1917 there was to be little rebellious activity in the Arkansas border counties.

The Green Corn Rebellion developed at the adjoining borders of Pontotoc, Seminole, and Hughes counties. Pontotoc was the locale where the authorities were most militant in attacking the legitimate political activities of Socialist country people. They expelled the Socialists from the courthouse in Ada. They hurled stern defiance at the night riders. Unlike the harassed and half-intimidated officials of Sequoyah County, they blacklisted Socialists and yielded nothing to the countryside. In both Pontotoc and Hughes counties, the Socialist vote fell significantly between 1914 and 1916 (from 1108 to 791 in Hughes and from 1,277 to 936 in Pontotoc).[34] Coercion combined with the rise of cotton prices undoubtedly affected the votes cast by farmers. But significant minorities still voted Socialist (22 percent in Pontotoc and 19 percent in Hughes). As usual, most of these votes were cast in country precincts.

In analyzing this hazy if not opaque situation, it should be permissible to speculate that the level and intensity of frustration among the country people must have been very high at the end of 1916. Their bombs had not stopped the dipping program. Their party had lost one-fourth of its vote in the election. Party leaders throughout the state were claiming that the Democrats had "counted out" the Socialist- and Republican-sponsored "fair Election Laws," the purpose of which was to make it less hazardous to vote Socialist and to increase the likelihood of one's Socialist vote being counted.[35]

But resentment rebuked and partially suppressed was not resentment eliminated. When the federal government began to draft youth for war in the summer of 1917, the country people believed conscription an invasion of their rights, the war in Europe none of their business. They rebelled to keep their own sons from being taken away from their neighborhood.

Once he has located the area of rebellion, the social historian must surrender any serious hope of discovering direct evidence of the psychology and motivation of the rebels. No documents survive that come to us from the hand of the WCU members. Any conclusions about the mentality of the rebels must be speculative and tentative. *Harlow's Weekly* reported that the WCU had called its followers to arms with this manifesto:

> Now is the time to rebel against this war with Germany boys. Boys, get together and don't go. Rich man's war. Poor man's fight. The war is over with Germany if you don't go and J.P. Morgan and Co. is lost. Their great speculation is the only cause of the war.[36]

A generalized idea of exploitation, simply and even crudely expressed, does appear in this leaflet. The idea descends fairly directly from Gene Debs' attacks upon the capitalists' war and from the Oklahoma Socialist party's appeal to stay at home and fight the "enemies of humanity" wherever they presented themselves.

If we can believe the reporter for the *Oklahoma News,* the "Southeast Oklahoma Revolution" was a rising of the country against the towns. The revolution was to have begun

> first by the burning of bridges and seizure of trains Thursday night, the capture of banks Friday and grand climax at midnight Friday night, when grain elevators, cotton mills, wealthy men's houses, and property of all kinds was to be destroyed.[37]

This report seems somewhat implausible unless one assumes that the rebels were so desperate that they would destroy the facilities that would hold and process their crops even after their "revolution" had succeeded! The reporter also claimed that the WCU's battle cry was "Shoot every man who wears a white shirt." The officers and volunteers chasing the rebels reportedly referred to them as "Rubes."[38]

The descriptions and explanations of the rebellion offered by townsmen and city news reporters were full of condescension and tinged with fear. From Sasakwa, the "staff correspondent" of the *Daily Oklahoman* accurately reflected the attitudes of the self-styled makers of Oklahoma. In his dispatch he wrote:

> Poor farmers, "crackers," ignorant and the prey of anarchistic radicals, have believed in a division of profits with their more industrious neighbors until in some cases all reason has been lost. They have joined the Working Class Union and have come to oppose all government. . . .
>
> One old man, long-bearded and trembling with age, shrieked at the curious bystanders in Sasakwa, after he had been refused permission to leave the town today:
>
> "Tryin' to civilize us with guns: that's the way the government allus does."[39]

One can comprehend the firm confidence and middle-class curiosity of the reporter from the capital city, but how does one fully comprehend the feelings of the bewildered old man? Habituated to the life of tenant farming, he found himself a prisoner of people who had intruded into his locale. He probably cared little about a war in Europe, especially if it was the result of a banker's speculation (he knew about the "interlocked parasites"). He simply wanted to leave town and go home.

Conscription, suddenly thrust upon the old man and his neighbors, threatened to remove able-bodied sons who were needed to pick cotton. An informer testified at the trial of the WCU leaders that H. H. Munson, reputedly a Wobbly organizer, had told meetings that young men would be taken away to war, old men would be forced to work on government farms, and wives left behind would be mistreated. Consequently, according to the government witness, the majority of WCU members had voted in secret meetings "to die at home" and to be buried under their own soil instead of going to Germany to be killed.[40] This testimony, if true, suggests once more the strain of traditional resistance that ran through the rebellion. The men showed a natural disinclination to leave their families, their rented acres, and their clapboard shacks to go into the army or to go to work on "government farms." The historian must seriously question whether these people would have been any more willing to leave "home" in order to work on capitalist bonanza farms or socialist cooperatives.

The *Oklahoma News* claimed that it had an authoritative account of the methods itinerant agitators employed to organize the WCU in eastern Oklahoma. The report implied that misrepresentations were used initially in order to induce farmers to come out to meetings. As the reporter described it:

> They began by instituting "agricultural meetings" in every community. There would be brief discussions of crop diversification . . . and then the organizers would break the gatherings up into groups and talk of doctrines they called "Socialism" and which had to do altogether with the necessary overthrow of the present government.
>
> When enough men had been taught the rudiments of Working Class unionism, a "local" would be formed which thereafter held its meetings secretly, in canyons, deep recesses of the forests, and caves along the river banks. New members were initiated as into the ordinary fraternity order.[41]

There is nothing implausible in the account. Certainly the country people were accustomed to hearing about socialism. The hint of seduction may be the invention of an unbelieving reporter or a captured and cowed rebel. The nature of the secret meetings is unsurprising considering the activities being essayed.

The *Daily Oklahoman* published a "WCU" constitution under a subhead undoubtedly intended to be disparaging: "All Races and Colors." The constitution specified that all members of the "working class" over the age of eighteen, "regardless of race, sex, color, or occupation" could join the WCU. Five applicants were required to form a local; the password was to be given to new members only in closed meetings. Presiding officers were to be newly elected at each meeting and were empowered to decide whether the meeting would be open or closed. "Any means necessary" would be used to better the conditions of the working people.[42] Except for the emphasis upon secrecy and the approval of all necessary means of struggle, the local organization of the WCU seemed to replicate that of the Socialists in their public meetings.

The reported programmatic demands of the WCU also closely paralleled those of the Socialist party. WCU literature proclaimed that workers were being robbed of their "natural rights to the full product of labor."

The first demand encompassed the "total abolition of the crime, disease, and death-producing practice of rent, interest, and profit-taking as iniquities that have been and are now being imposed upon the working class of the world." Then followed familiar Socialist and IWW demands: the eight-hour workday; one day of rest in every seven; public ownership of all utilities; free schools, free texts, and compulsory education; enactment of laws against child labor; sanitary inspection of factories, mines, and homes; introduction of the "imperative mandate" from voters to representatives; prohibitions against the use of injunctions in labor disputes; and ample provision for those injured in industrial accidents and for old people. "In short," the WCU program concluded, "we demand a better, higher, and nobler life. For the attainment of these things we are on the road. Are you with us?"[43]

When the WCU made its only overt attack upon the system, it felt the full force of legitimized repression. The towns had been given a nasty fright. The *Oklahoma News* described one of the first responses of the townspeople to the prisoners:

> The five prisoners, one black, were loaded in the center of a big auto-truck and made to stand. Officers—most of them specially deputized citizens—then sat in a row around the truck, rifles pointed inward at the rioters.[44]

Although the stance of the townsmen may seem rather dramatic, they were engaged in a symbolic ritual of patriotism that was of considerable significance in their lives. They were now purging their communities of moral evil.

The rebels seemed literally strange to their captors. The *Shawnee News-Herald* commented on the "picturesque leaders of the old mountaineer type with long unkempt hair and heavy beards" who wore "flaming red sashes around their wastes [sic]."[45] Anyone who could claim past contact with *these* country people now became an expert in the explanation of their origins and their supposed pathology. The *Oklahoma News* reported that a Pontotoc County judge had taught school in the area of the rebellion and personally knew most of the men in the WCU local in southern Seminole County. The *News* carried these "first-hand" observations:

Utter, crass ignorance, from babyhood up, is Judge Busby's explanation of the ready susceptibility of the Seminole co. renters to the anarchistic teachings of the W.C.U.

Judge Busby was mayor of Konawa before he was 21, and was first president of the Young Men's Democratic League.[46]

The certified expert who diagnosed the source and conditions of infection was prepared to join with his associates and neighbors in an effort to cauterize the diseased tissue in local society. Having endured the Socialists for five years, the citizens were now determined to put an end to the troubles and thus to revitalize their community. A committee of notables would direct the task:

A modern Ku Klux Klan, directed by a committee of 13, whose chairman is R. B. Cain, president of the Farmers' State Bank, Ada, proposes to take the responsibility of eradicating lawlessness from this part of Oklahoma.

"We will keep within the law," the committee said in a brief statement of its plans, but unofficially, members of the committee declare that the W.C.U. will be punished and driven from the county if it must be at the end of the salted wet rope with which the rebellious society punishes members who reveal its secrets.

Close to a score of W.C. unionists brought to Ada were examined by the committee of 13, but according to Chairman Cain, gave little satisfaction.[47]

It is intriguing that the rebels "gave little satisfaction," especially in such an intimidating situation. The historian can only hope to imagine how the rebels felt when brought out of the woods after their rout and delivered at gunpoint into the midst of people who scorned and reviled them. Their experience of life and politics in the countryside must have given them the psychological and political resources necessary to withstand the besetting feelings of fear and hopelessness. According to reports sympathetic to the object of their interrogators, they remained uncooperative and defiant in spite of the imposing reputations of the men opposite them. The reporter described the interrogators more closely:

Cain, besides being head of the Vigilantes, is Chairman of the Pontotoc co. Council of Defense, appointed by Governor Williams. Another significant event closely following the rioting was the organization of the Ada Rifle Club, with W. C. Williams, president; County Judge Orel Busby, vice-president. . . . Among the committee men heading the citizens' volunteer organization, are Representative Robert Wimbish . . . and P. A. Norris, widely known banker and capitalist.[48]

The townsmen had not only the advantages of local reputation, official patriotism, and severe legal sanction on their side; they could confront their captives with incriminating information brought to the county sheriff by a former Socialist who had been attending WCU meetings and who had lately decided that it was his patriotic duty to turn informer.[49] It was altogether a terrifying circumstance for country people—people who had been accustomed all their lives to a social intercourse confined largely to their "neighbors." Now their neighbors could not help them, as the "big men" leaned in and glowered at them.

At this point in the analysis it would probably be fruitful to confront the argument that these were politically minded rebels, "not ignorant night riders or religious fanatics." In one view, the WCU "had a fairly well-defined ideology which had shifted away from Socialism toward anarcho-syndicalism in the course of a violent struggle with property owners and lawmen in the region."[50] Certainly the Green Corn rebels were not "primitive" and "prepolitical" peasantry in the sense developed by Hobsbawm in his illuminating *Primitive Rebels.*[51] The Oklahoma tenants, unlike the country people of Spain, Sicily, and Mexico, had not lived on their land for centuries. They were annually involved in the fluid exchange of land, labor, product, and money characteristic of a full market economy. They rented their land and sold their product as individuals without the constraints of deep communal traditions. Capitalism had long since penetrated the once remote but now settled and productive American frontier.

The formal literature of the WCU, assuming that the reports are reliable, was modern and anticapitalist. It explained the exploitation felt by cotton tenants in their own neighborhood as the result of an exploitative industrial capitalism. It proposed measures to reduce the ability of large property holders to command the labor and determine the reward of the propertyless. In short, the formal program does contain a generalized ideology, which, in its explanatory power, ranges far beyond the local situation of the WCU adherents.

But there is a gap that the historian may not be able to bridge. He cannot easily prove that the local adherents understood the general ideology in the same sense as those who gave it a formal statement. It is probably mistaken to place as much interpretive pressure upon the evidence as Green does when he suggests that the rebels, though "largely illiterates who could not read the Socialist press (or the capitalist press) . . . understood exploitation and imperialism in a fundamental way."[52] Without doubt the tenants felt exploited and also believed that distant wars were no concern of their neighborhood. But the evidence suggests another interpretation: the tenants who rebelled did so only when the outside world of big capitalism and imperialism made drastic incursions into their local neighborhood.

The war initially disrupted the cotton market and the customary ways of the laboring men in the cotton fields. It put the greatest economic and social pressure upon those least able to bear it. The social historian does not belittle the tenants' aspirations by suggesting that they had basically parochial expectations and concerns. These can be seen in the statement of a Green Corn rebel:

We decided we wasn't gonna fight somebody else's war for 'em and we refused to go. We didn't volunteer and we didn't answer the draft. Most of us had wives and kids and we didn't wanna leave them here to do all the work of harvestin' and have us go over to France and fight people we didn't have anything against. We didn't have any bands and uniforms and stuff down there in the sandhills so that crap about the Germans comin' over here when they finished up the English and French didn't go over with us.[53]

It may be that such a statement describes a "fundamental" understanding of exploitation and imperialism. But to say this without more surety misses the point: the rebels were not fundamentally interested in events, let alone relationships, beyond the country neighborhood and the nearby towns where they spent their lives. Customary patterns in their localities would have been satisfactory to them if their work efforts consistently had yielded a good living. The reported cry of the captured old man could be taken as characteristic: "Tryin' to civilize us with guns: that's the way the government allus does." Or consider the difficulty prosecutors experienced in their attempts to induce defendants and witnesses to testify against their neighbors. One WCU man, after a reported suicide attempt, explained that he would rather die than "tell things I knew would be against my neighbors."[54]

What could have been going on in the minds of these rebels who would remain sullen and silent in the presence of their betters? They believed that they had the common right as ordinary men to defend the terrain and govern the morality of the communities where they lived and labored. They had had no parades with "bands and uniforms and stuff." Unlike the townsmen they felt no need to regenerate their communities. They did not know the thrill of martial patriotism that was so important in the ritual of revitalization taking place in the towns. For the rebels local loyalties and fears were most important—loyalty to their own laboring kind and fear of local bankers and landlords who embodied "capitalism." It was the particularistic character of their loyalty that made their minds proof against the appeals of prosecutors and town notables to show their "patriotism."

The government, with its draft law, and the local capitalists, with their plans for agricultural and commercial progress, literally imposed a new conception of civil life upon people accustomed to freedom within their community—cattle-dipping sheriffs and Council of Defense authorities could be damned. They would defend themselves if the Germans came to *their* shores. Like other backward-looking people, they would in future decades know the pain of seeing their neighborhoods eroded and their customs circumscribed by regulations and requirements externally-imposed by governmental and corporate institutions.

The aftermath of the Green Corn Rebellion was predictable. Amid a crescendo of public outrage and abuse, WCU men were put on trial for their actions and Socialists were arraigned in the state's press for their beliefs. According to James R. Green, 266 of the arrested men were released without indictment, "184 were indicted, 150 convicted and about half that number sentenced to prison terms in the fall."[55] The courts inflicted prison sentences upon the leaders, who were considered especially culpable for misleading the ignorant. Among the leaders was none other than J. T. Cumbie, former Confederate, Socialist candidate for governor in 1910, and finally once again a rebel. Other leaders convicted and sentenced were H. H. Munson, H. C. Spence, Roy Crane, and W. L. Benefield. In its reports on the trials, the *Daily Oklahoman* identified Numson as a lead and zinc miner whose family lived at Seneca, Missouri, a few steps across the border. Munson was said to be a "direct actionist I.W.W." who did not believe in political agitation to win reforms. H. C. Spence, thirty-six years old, had a wife and six children and lived with them on a rented farm six miles from Wewoka in Seminole County. Never having attended school, he had been an active Socialist and WCU organizer. Roy Crane was reported to be twenty-six years old, married, and living near Holdenville in Hughes County. He had been educated at Christian Brothers College in St. Joseph, Missouri, but had subsequently become an "anti-Catholic" lecturer and was reputedly the author of two books on "Catholic theology." Bill Benefield ("Captain Bill" with the red sash during the uprising) had lived many years near Sasakwa in Seminole County with his wife and seven children.[56]

It would be fitting to give Bill Benefield the last word on the rebellion. He wrote to the *Oklahoma Leader* in 1921 to thank the Oklahoma radicals who were helping to support his family while he served his term. Unrepentently he said that he hoped that he had done his part so "that the children of this age will enjoy the coming golden age."[57] His was a preeminently decent hope, even if his vision was limited by his vantage point on the South Canadian River in rural Oklahoma.

NOTES

1. *Oklahoma Pioneer* (Oklahoma City), August 17, 1912.
2. *Boswell Submarine*, October 16, 1914.
3. James R. Green, "Socialism and the Southwestern Class Struggle" (Ph.D. diss., Yale University, 1972), 342.
4. Ibid., 379-380.
5. County Agent, USDA, Checotah, to Professor James A. Wilson; Stillwater, January 16, 1915. I found this letter in the files of Governor Robert L. Williams. Professor Wilson apparently thought the report of sufficient concern to pass along to the state's governor.
6. *Harlow's Weekly* (Oklahoma City), September 25, 1915.
7. Ibid.
8. *Ada Weekly News*, October 7, 1915.
9. *Ada Star-Democrat*, October 26, 1915.

10. Ibid., October 29, 1915.

11. Ibid., November 16, 1915.

12. Ibid., December 17, 1915.

13. *Ada Weekly News*, December 23, 1915.

14. Ibid.

15. *Ada Star-Democrat*, December 24, 1915.

16. Ibid., December 28, 1915.

17. *Otter Valley Socialist* (Snyder), January 5, 1916.

18. Ibid.

19. *Ada Star-Democrat*, January 14, 1916.

20. Ibid.

21. Ibid.

22. Ibid.

23. Green, "Socialism and the Southwestern Class Struggle," 344-348.

24. Ibid., 346.

25. *Daily Oklahoman* (Oklahoma City), February 15, 16, 1916.

26. *Ada Star-Democrat*, February 18, 1916.

27. *Harlow's Weekly*, February 26, 1916.

28. T. G. McMahon to Robert L. Williams, March 8, 1916, Robert L. Williams Papers; Oklahoma Historical Society.

29. Ibid., November 3, 1916, Williams Papers.

30. *Harlow's Weekly*, May 20, 1916.

31. Ibid., August 19, 1916.

32. *Ada Star-Democrat*, August 18, September 29, 1916.

33. *Harlow's Weekly*, September 27, 1916.

34. State Election Board, *Directory and Manual of the State of Oklahoma, 1967* (Oklahoma City, 1967), 308, 338.

35. See chapter 4 above, and, especially, Donald R. Graham, "Red, White, and Black: An Interpretation of Ethnic and Racial Attitudes of Agrarian Radicals in Texas and Oklahoma, 1880-1920 (Master's thesis, University of Regina, 1973) 332-335.

36. *Harlow's Weekly*, August 15, 1917.

37. *Oklahoma News* (Oklahoma City), August 4, 6, 1917. The Oklahoma City dailies and *Harlow's Weekly* printed more reports about the rebellion than appeared in the local weeklies. Local editors were fearful that news of one rising would inspire other potential rebels among the country folk. Rumors of new risings were rife. See Green, "Socialism and the Southwestern Class Struggle," 374.

38. This comment conflicts with the memory of a Green Corn participant who stated in a WPA interview in the 1930s that the rebels did not fire upon the

townsmen because there were too many men of their acquaintance in the posses. See Green, "Socialism and the Southwestern Class Struggle," 373.

39. *Daily Oklahoman*, August 5, 1917.

40. Ibid., October 31, 1917.

41. *Oklahoma News*, August 6, 1917.

42. *Daily Oklahoman*, August 8, 1917.

43. Ibid.

44. *Oklahoma News*, August 6, 1917.

45. *Shawnee Daily News-Herald*, August 7, 1917, quoted in Green, "Socialism and the Southwestern Class Struggle," 377.

46. *Oklahoma News*, August 6, 1917.

47. Ibid.

48. Ibid.

49. Sherry Warrick, "Radical Labor in Oklahoma: The Working Class Union," *Chronicles of Oklahoma* 52 (Spring 1974): 189-190.

50. Green, "Socialism and the Southwestern Class Struggle," 379-380.

51. E. J. Hobsbawm, *Primitive Rebels* (New York, 1965), 1-3.

52. Green, "Socialism and the Southwestern Class Struggle," 379. It is curious, especially in the light of his interpretation, that Green readily accepts the frequent assertion (made by the rebels' contemporaries and by earlier students) that the rebels were largely illiterate. In 1910 the rate of illiteracy among white male adults of voting age throughout the state was 4 percent. In the Green Corn counties the rates were as follows: Hughes, 7.4 percent; Seminole, 8.6 percent; and Pontotoc, 6.6 percent. Even if we allow for a higher rate of illiteracy in the country districts and for the possibility that the census-taker's method may not accurately uncover functional literacy, the data by no means force us to conclude that most of the rebels were so lacking in letters that they could read neither the capitalist nor the Socialist press. Percentages of white adult male illiteracy appear in *Thirteenth Census of the United States Taken in the Year 1910*, vol. 3, *Population* (Washington, D.C., 1913), 467-479.

53. Dewitt interview with Walter Strong, Federal Writers' Project, WPA, Western History Collection, University of Oklahoma; quoted in Green, "Socialism and the Southwestern Class Struggle," 378-379, n. 69. By placing the recollections of Walter Strong in a footnote instead of his text, Green accentuates what might be regarded as the more conscious and formally expressed political thought and thereby underestimates the importance of the parochial character of the rebellion. As a clear recollection of rebel motives, the statement deserves to be placed in the text along with formal expressions of ideology.

54. *Shawnee Daily News-Herald*, September 25, 1917, quoted in Green, "Socialism and the Southwestern Class Struggle," 373; n. 55. Again, Green has

dropped a very revealing comment into his notes while accentuating intentional political action and thought in his narrative.

55. Green, ''Socialism and the Southwestern Class Struggle,'' 373.
56. *Daily Oklahoman*, October 31, November 1, 1917.
57. *Oklahoma Leader* (Oklahoma City), January 8, 1921.

Agrarian radicalism ——————8
and the Ku Klux Klan

Corrosive insecurity burdened the lives of townsmen and country people in southern Oklahoma during the early 1920s. Agricultural prices had fallen sharply, incomes were shrinking rapidly, debts were beginning to press.[1] But Oklahoma's recently founded and still underdeveloped settlements had seldom been prosperous, and so the renewed economic pressure in the early 1920's was not a novel experience for the small businessmen and farmers. The novelty lay deeper—in the intense disappointment and futile weariness felt by people who had recently enjoyed the boon of war-induced prosperity, the satisfaction of high public esteem in their localities, and the sense of belonging to a national community of patriotic citizens. Had Oklahomans not been good Americans who sold and bought war bonds, saved wheat, knitted sweaters, hunted slackers, and silenced reds? Had they not rendered full support to their revered Democratic President, Woodrow Wilson? Had they not worked hard for two decades and more building their homes, businesses, churches, and towns?

Yet by 1922 Oklahoma was experiencing political uproar that erupted out of social conflict between the town and the countryside. Townsmen were calling candidates of a new Farmer-Labor Reconstruction League "reds," and the country people delivered their retorts to the town "parasites." In the summer of 1922 the *Oklahoma Leader* reprinted Patrick Nagle's well-traveled manifesto, "The Interlocked Parasites of the Electric Light Towns," thus reviving its trenchant condemnations of the businessmen-landlords who battened upon the "producer."[2] This theme echoed and reechoed through many farmers' meetings between 1921 and 1925. On the other side, a major Democratic speaker, annoyed and distressed by the appearance of "farmer-labor" insurgency within his party, decried the presence of Socialists among the insurgents. "These are the men," he cried, "who cursed Woodrow Wilson; these are the men who derided our constitution and even the declaration of independence while the beloved youth of America stood under alien skies and bared their breasts to the red blasts of war."[3] Insurgents would become accustomed to having the "bloody shirt" waved in their faces.

Radicals in Oklahoma had indeed conceived a new political stratagem for the purpose of redeeming the cotton tenant and other afflicted farmers. Leaders in the former Socialist movement, evangelized by Ameringer and Nagle, supported the effort to organize a coalition of farmers and laborers, which would try to capture the Democratic party in order to obtain relief.[4] The Farmer-Labor Reconstruction League held its first convention in Shawnee in February 1922 and wrote a radical (but not a Socialist) platform calling for a state-owned bank and laws to allow the state and municipalities to take over and operate public utilities. The league favored a gross production tax on all public service corporations, including the railroads. It called for laws to regulate the grading and marketing of farm produce and for a tax exemption of up to $1,000 for heads of families in farm or city homes. The exemption would apply to farm implements, equipment, and the tools of urban workers.

In the same spirit of serving the immediate interests of the "producers," the league also proposed that a minimum price be fixed for basic farm commodities, that co-ops be exempted from federal antitrust laws, and that a national bank guarantee law be enacted. It supported the Plumb plan for government ownership of railroads and called for the government to take over the Muscle Shoals project. The league explicitly opposed the reduction of railway workers' wages as a means of reducing freight rates. Finally, reminiscent of Socialist opposition to American participation in the Great War, it called for a national referendum on any declaration of war, excepting cases of invasion, and it opposed compulsory military training.[5] Oklahoma City's mayor, John C. "Our Jack" Walton, supported by the city Trades Council as reliably prolabor, received the league's endorsement for governor in the Democratic primary.[6]

After a bitter campaign in which farmer-labor candidates were often maligned as reds, Walton won the primary, defeating a Klan-endorsed candidate and a conservative banker in the primary election. Surviving

TABLE 3

Vote for Walton in the Democratic Primary, 1922 (Marshall County)*

Precinct	Percentage	Precinct	Percentage
Lark	75.6	Madill, fourth	23.7
Shay	78.0	Madill, third	13.5
Isom Springs	14.2	Woodville	10.4
Linn	89.0	Madill, second	45.3
McMillan	33.3	Kingston	34.9
Willis	77.6	Aylesworth	40.9

*Six highest and six lowest Socialist-voting precincts, 1910-1916.

some defections in the general election, Walton advanced toward the state house, much to the alarm of conservative opinion in the state. Between 1923 and 1925, the rise of the Ku Klux Klan dominated politics in Oklahoma. After Governor Walton had largely failed to support the leaguers by his earnest but futile attempts to win the favor of conservative Democrats, he suddenly reemerged, amid derisive charges of opportunism, as a "Klan fighter."[7] The nationally publicized "Walton war" on the Klan ensued, with the result that the Klan and conservative non-Klansmen, outraged by Walton's use of martial law to suppress Klan violence in Tulsa and Okmulgee counties, coalesced into a movement to impeach Walton.[8]

In Marshall and Pontotoc counties in southern Oklahoma, the social war over the Klan can be traced in revealing detail, owing to the presence in those locales of stubborn anti-Klan editors who did their best, with the encouragement of local agrarian radicals, to expose Klan activities to the full glare of daylight. The success of the Ku Klux Klan in the small towns and cities of Oklahoma had its origins as much in the specific social and political tensions locally felt as it had in the general suspicions and fears found in southern Protestant culture.[9] There was, of course, plenty of generalized nativism. Oklahoma Klansmen took turns sneering at the "squatty dagos" and "krist killers" in the "foreign" cities of Boston and New York. The editor of the *Madill Record*, noting that Thomas Dixon, author of *The Clansman*, had condemned the modern Klan, suggested that if Dixon "wants to call the squatty dago an equal to his

Anglo-Saxon forefather, he has a right to do so; but in the minds of many, there is quite a difference between the man of spaghetti and the Puritan and Cavalier."[10] The inimitably vulgar "Rube" Geers remarked in his *Johnston County Capital-Democrat* that the "Jews crucified our Savior, and we have even less use for them than we have for a red-card socialist, if possible."[11] The link between aliens and radicals was made by the *Madill Record*'s editor when he claimed that labor troubles, strikes, assassinations "and I.W.W. brawls originate where aliens trade." The lead mines in northeastern Oklahoma had had no labor troubles for years because, he contended, they were worked by "Americans."[12]

These fears of contamination, as might be expected in Oklahoma, sometimes had a tone peculiar to southern latitudes. A former state senator, speaking to a Pontotoc County audience on the merits of the Klan, said that no one was

> more deeply concerned about this movement [KKK] than the big buck negro himself. He wants this social equality with the white man that others are contending for because it means that he will marry the white man's fair daughter. He has long had this desire, and it was greatly augmented by his experience in the recent war.[13]

The impact of the war experience was also noted by the *Madill Record* in the course of a complaint about the encouragement that would-be Negro congressmen allegedly received in districts where the "foreign element" resided. Soldiers would recall how in France, where Negroes sat in the Parliament, "the negro soldiers were treated with absolute equality."[14] A Klan potentate, visiting the town of Ada, bluntly described the usual southern response to the menace of "mongrelization." He claimed, "We southerners know how to treat a negro and treat him right."[15]

There were very few Catholics, Jews, and Negroes in Oklahoma and while they had symbolic importance in some local minds, they could not be an immediate threat. A pro-Klan editor indirectly acknowledged this when he observed that the Klan, "those strange robed figures who are causing Catholics, Wops and Jews to see things at night in the larger cities, appeared in Tupelo."[16] But townspeople had frequently scrutinized and condemned "inferior" people very close to home; they had found the poor white country folk an embarrassing, exasperating, and monotonously present threat to a "moral" community.

The Klan focused town animus and helped to revivify the old Oklahoma desire to catch up with the rest of America. Nothing impresses the historian of Oklahoma society more than the need for approval that the new settlers, especially the more socially ambitious among them, felt as they built their new towns. They became a marginal middle class seeking to wrest for themselves a firm moral respectability in the eyes of their countrymen. But their state's reputation for radicalism, violence, and immorality undermined their aspirations. Wounded by the sneers that said that Oklahomans were people who had fled their crimes and failures elsewhere, the townspeople sought all the more to be the most moral and the most ''American'' of all their countrymen.

In southern Oklahoma it was the tenant farmer who was considered a blight upon the community. Shacks were said to ''disgrace the rolling hills and blackland prairies'' of Marshall County.[17] Tenant life begot Johnson grass, soil mining, and radicalism and would continue to do so until competent farmers owned their own lands and homes.[18] But how were farmers to acquire their homes and why did they not have them already? Although the *Madill Record* seemed at times to be able to view tenancy as a ''social'' problem, it reverted under pressure to the conventional accusations of individual moral failure. At a time when the local Klan faced a formidable challenge from agrarian radical constituencies, the *Record* could find relief from despair only in expressions of contempt. Although Marshall County had some of the ''best people on earth,'' the editor proclaimed, it was also plagued with ''some of the sorriest, dirtiest, most lowdown white trash ever to be assembled spontaneously to steal the breath of life.''[19] With similar lofty scorn a Pontotoc County editor dismissed anti-Klan men as loafers who stood around corners, exhaling ''hot air'' and spitting tobacco juice. ''You know the kind of cattle we have reference to,'' he confided to his upstanding readers.[20]

In all but the Red River counties of southern and southeastern Oklahoma, the Klan swept from success to success, achieving domination in most major cities and towns.[21] The story of Klan activities is familiar and need not be repeated at any length. In promoting their version of moral community life, Klansmen warned and sometimes whipped those alleged to be bootleggers, pimps, prostitutes, and wayward husbands. For example, one advertisement signed ''KKK'' stated, ''Recently a single man and a married man were seen with two married women in a questionable place. If this is not stopped, names of all parties will be published."[22] In Coalgate the local Klan proclaimed that "we oppose socialism and bolshevism. We are 100 per cent Americans. We are for white supremacy. We are for public free schools. Agitators better clear out. . . . Gamblers and bootleggers, hit the hike."[23] To minatory notices of this type some local Klans added well-publicized acts of charity to Protestant churches and to worthy individuals.[24]

It is not the easiest task to uncover the sources of support and opposition to the Klan in those areas where it prevailed completely and where local non-Klan editors were therefore unwilling to make its activities a matter of controversy. This was especially true between 1921 and late 1923, a period in which the Klan made its greatest political gains and which culminated in the impeachment of Governor Walton by a legislature widely acknowledged to have been run by a Klan majority. However, in the southern counties of Oklahoma, it is possible for the historian to follow more closely the growth of the Klan and its opposition simply because there was a constituency in that area antagonistic to the Klan. In Pontotoc and Marshall counties there were two newspapers, the *Ada Morning Bulletin* and the *Marshall County Enterprise*, whose editors endorsed and proclaimed the anti-Klan sentiments of their readers. These newspapers flourished during the days of the "Klan war" precisely because there was significant social support for their attacks on the Klan. And that support came directly from the agrarian radical experience of southern Oklahoma's country people. This country resistance emerged from those longtime suspicions of townsmen as an "upper class" who lived off the labor of "producers." In the southern counties there continued to be, as there had been before the Great War, two versions of public "morality" and the public "interest."

In the towns the Klan made special efforts to enroll local notables, especially public officials and Protestant ministers. Certainly the farmers and editors who opposed the Klan in Marshall and Pontotoc counties did not feel constrained to dispute Klan claims that the "worthiest" citizenship wore the white robes. The pro-Klan editor of the *Allen Democrat* was happy to be able to report that the Protestant ministers of Ada, the county seat, were solidly opposed to the anti-Klan candidates in the 1922 Democratic primary. The pastor of the First Baptist Church of Ada snidely remarked that he had not talked to the Catholic priest and thus could not report his opinion on the Klan.[25] In many instances Klansmen made dramatic visits to Protestant congregations and were often welcomed and praised by the ministers.[26] But not all Protestant congregations were respectful. An anti-Klan judge in Pontotoc County accused Klansmen of "invading" rural churches in the neighborhoods of Egypt and Roff for the purpose of frightening country people, "a large per cent of whom have a very bitter opposition to this dunce-cap regalia."[27]

There is sufficient evidence to indicate that town businessmen and professionals, as well as leading Protestant ministers, showed great enthusiasm for the Klan's moral crusade. The Johnston County Klan claimed a membership "of highest standing, composed of preachers, doctors, lawyers, merchants, in fact men from every walk in life."[28] This was a curiously limited view of the "walks of life" in a county where most men were farmers. In its regular "Klan Kronicles" feature, the *Wapanucka Press* asserted that almost every chamber of commerce man in Atoka County was in the Klan.[29] "Realm No. 71" of Marshall County, organized in November 1921, claimed 475 members of the "best citizenship."[30] Among them (apparently) was District Judge George S. March, who rode proudly at the head of a Klan parade in Madill.[31] The editor of the *Marshall County Enterprise* charged that the leaders of the Madill Chamber of Commerce, who had called for meetings throughout the county to organize a county fair, turned out to be the leaders of the local Klan as well. They "had sidetracked the interests of the county fair for pasture meetings and initiating of American-born citizens into an order for the purpose of 'naturalizing' the joiners."[32] Among the members of a Klan band arrested for murder in Carter County were a Baptist preacher, butcher, stockman, optician, insurance agent, retired rancher, and two oil-field workers.[33] When a Johnston County judge rendered a decision that went against the hopes of the local Klan, the *Capital-Democrat* could not bear to contemplate the affront to the "best people" who had given "conclusive" evidence against two anti-Klan sheriff's deputies who had been involved in a fracas with Klansmen. The editor concluded that the judge had now repudiated his association with "the best class of the county's citizenship and has lined up with the element that has no respect whatever for law and order."[34]

No one knew better than southern Oklahoma Klansmen themselves that the farmers in their area were hostile to the Klan's claims and blandishments. After seeing Jack Walton win the Democratic primary in 1922, the *Stonewall Weekly News* carried the mournful headline, "Truth

Crushed to Earth'' but resolutely avowed that ''we are still for and with the Klan.'' The *Weekly News* explained cryptically that ''politicians conceived the idea that to abuse the klan would prove popular among the residents of the rural districts and with certain people in the towns over the county.''[35] The *Ada Bulletin* had touched off the controversy about the social character of the Klan by observing early in the 1922 primary campaign that farmers and laborers would probably be excluded from the Klan by an oath that required members to maintain the Klan's ''social cast and dignity.''[36] The *Bulletin* explained that ''invisible government'' appealed to those who believed that the ''upper classes'' ought to rule. But the ''great mass of common folks who work for a living'' would demand the right to see their rulers ''face to face.''[37] Rural opposition foiled Klan efforts to capture the Pontotoc Democratic party. In elections for party chairman, the Klan's designee had run ahead in the town of Ada and his supporters were reportedly covered with smiles until the rural returns arrived. Then, according to the *Bulletin* editor, ''the smile began to fade from the faces of the holier-than-thou crowd.''[38] Delighted with the opportunity to mock his enemies, the editor gleefully proclaimed in a bold headline; ''Kluckers Knocked Kerflumix, Kouldn't Kontrol the Korn-fed Kountry Kuses.''[39]

Any defeat for the Klan was sweet solace to a man who had published his paper in the Klan's lair for nearly three years. In June 1922 he had claimed that the Klan had instigated a boycott of the *Bulletin*. Taking heart from his growing subscription list at the time, the *Bulletin*'s editor predicted that his paper would be ''a universal farm organ in Pontotoc County before September.''[40] His brazen contempt for the Klan angered the citizens of Ada. Schoolteachers allegedly asked their pupils not to carry the ''bad'' paper, a gesture that brought from the *Bulletin* editor the bristling rejoinder that his taxes paid their salaries too.[41] And it did not matter to him that there were ''a number of good sisters in Ada who pass the editor of this sheet with averted heads and almost audible sniffs of the atmosphere. . . . We are no worse in the sight of God than we were before the Klan was organized and that fact is all that counts.''[42] Such was the life (self-portrayed) of the beleaguered anti-Klan editor living in the midst of an insecure and now militant town middle class.

Although it is probably impossible to prove conclusively that the *Bulletin* editor represented the characteristic thought of the Pontotoc country people on the issue of the Klan, his success in publishing his paper in the teeth of town disapproval could imply a measure of approval in the countryside. It is therefore important to identify correctly the origins of the editor's opposition to the Klan. Always very firm in denying that he was a "radical," the *Bulletin* man believed that Jack Walton's "farmer-labor" candidacy represented the overthrow of a corrupt "machine" and the restoration of the "true" democratic principles of Jefferson and Jackson.[43] He admonished bankers who saw "bolshevism" in the Farmer-Labor Reconstruction League that "you are up against the people from the 'grass roots' and the 'forks of the creek.' A new era has come . . . we are on the march."[44] But his "new era" definitely did not include socialism. "Stanley J. Clark," the *Bulletin* warned, "is back on the soap boxes declaring that the old Red Card Socialist system is the best and advising the down-trodden farmer to return to it. Stanley J. has tried a good many systems and ought to know which one is the most profitable."[45] An antimonopoly southern Democrat and a devout Protestant who always published a "Bible thought of the day," the *Bulletin* editor opposed the Klan for essentially populist reasons. The sovereignty of the "common man" was his test; both the Socialists and the Klansmen were too peculiar and uncommon to pass.

Another spokesman of agrarian populist opposition to the Klan, the county judge, had also been an uncompromising opponent of the Pontotoc County Socialists before and during the Great War. In 1918 he had declared that to have Socialists sitting on juries would insult the good citizens of the land. In 1922 he attacked the Klan because its oath of loyalty might conflict with the traditional test of good southern citizenship: unswerving commitment to the Democratic party.[46] His opposition to the Klan was inseparable from his opposition to local loan companies and landholders. He was a conventional anti-Catholic. Indeed he believed that the Klan was trying to aid the loan companies by circulating the rumor that he was sympathetic to Catholicism. The Klan, he maintained, knew that his "opposition to Catholicism is as great as theirs." He reaffirmed his fear of the "joining" of church and state and disputed the status of "semi-deity" that (he believed) Catholics accorded to the rulers of the church.[47] He would be outdone by no one in his respect for the traditional family home. Nettled by Klan insinuations that he had shown drunken disrespect to ladies, the county judge replied that "the best mothers in Ada were attending their home duties and that their lives were dominated by the spirit of love rather than the spirit of hatred" and that he could "not understand how extreme hatred could dwell in the same heart where the love of Christ dwelt."[48] Good mothers would not go through the town spitefully stirring up discord among the Lord's following.

The activities of agrarian radicals were reported most extensively in the old Socialist recruiting grounds of Marshall County. During the early 1920s many southern Oklahoma farmers were recruited by an intensely interest-conscious organization reminiscent of the Populist and Socialist movements. The Farm-Labor Union, organized by cotton farmers, was conceived in Bonham, Texas, in late 1920 for the purpose of establishing a regional cooperative cotton marketing agency that would displace middlemen, speculators, and others deemed to be "parasites" on the farmer. It infused farmers with renewed hope and purpose and even a sense of destiny that they had not experienced since the disintegration of the Socialist party.[49]

Membership in the FLU was restricted to those who actually tilled the soil, whether as owners, tenants, or laborers. Judging from the notices of individual local meetings (usually twice a month), the FLU had a wide and active following in Marshall County.[50] The *Marshall County Enterprise* claimed that the FLU held the balance of political power in the county. In both the Democratic primary, which saw Walton nominated, and the special initiative election of 1923 held to decide whether the legislature should be convened to impeach Walton, the rural precincts organized by the FLU split sharply from the towns by their support of Walton. The membership of the FLU had reportedly reached 1,000, not including wives and old men from whom dues were not required. The *Enterprise* stressed that the FLU roster, unlike some others, was open to public examination and its members were proud to be known as such.[51]

Cooperation was an important part of the FLU's program in Marshall County. The local men wished to establish two cooperative general stores at Willis and Enos and discussed the possibilities of erecting a warehouse in Madill. A farmer at Willis said that his community had no special grievance against the town merchants who sold goods at "reasonable" margins of profit, but his neighbors did believe that they could get higher prices for their commodities and purchase their necessaries at lower prices from a co-op.[52]

The FLU locals in southern Oklahoma often expressed sympathy with the aims of industrial workers and identified themselves as members of "organized labor." The Atoka County FLU, one of the first in Oklahoma, recommended that its members buy only union-made goods.[53] The same local resolved that all members who attended Governor-elect Walton's mammoth inaugural barbecue had to be clad in union-made overalls.[54] The state convention of the FLU passed a resolution endorsing a strike of railroad shopcraft workers and voted to give $25 to the Haileyville local of the shopcraft men.[55] In 1923 the president of the state federation of labor addressed the FLU convention, emphasizing the necessity for cooperation between "progressive" farm and labor groups. In its turn the state FLU resolved to send observers to the state labor council.[56]

TABLE 4

Vote Against Calling Legislature for Purpose of Impeachment
(Marshall County), October 1923

Precinct	Percentage	Precinct	Percentage
Lark	97.6	Madill, fourth	23.1
Shay	80.0	Madill, third	24.1
Isom Springs	71.5	Woodville	37.0
Linn	74.5	Madill, second	36.4
McMillan	28.9	Kingston	36.5
Willis	71.5	Aylesworth	20.4

SOURCE: *Madill Record,* October 4, 1923.

This well-politicized farmers' movement perceived the Klan as the major enemy of organized labor, both urban and rural. In October 1923, at the height of the Walton-Klan war, the FLU local at Armstrong in Bryan County proposed a boycott to fight the Klan. Their manifesto, circulated on the streets of Madill, called upon "organized labor and all red blooded Americans who believed in equal rights, social justice, and good government" to begin the boycott of Klan sympathizers. Readers of the circulars were treated to one of the strongest indictments of the Klan ever heard in Oklahoma. And it seems reasonable to say that the indictment drew its strength from the mixture of interest- and class-consciousness that lay beneath so much local political conflict in Oklahoma:

Inasmuch as there is in our midst an organization, the legitimate offspring of the Fascista movement originated in Italy, the purpose of which is to disrupt organized labor and co-operative enterprises; the members of which are avowed open shoppers, and who conceal their identity with a hooded mask, and who resort to mob violence and white cap methods, having no regard for the welfare of society, and who are using the boycott and black list against all who are not affiliated or in sympathy with their organization, namely the Ku Klux Klan.

Therefore, we heartily endorse the resolution made by locals of the F.L.U. of A., the substance of which is to rid ourselves of an exploiter class off our backs and encourage the establishment of co-operative enterprises and thereby establish working class solidarity.

Be it resolved that we refuse to patronize anyone known to be a member of or in sympathy with the Ku Klux Klan, and that this resolution be circulated to and endorsed by all labor organizations, and given general publication. And that a copy of same be sent to Governor J. C. Walton of the state of Oklahoma, and that we appeal to all who have been missled and deceived by propaganda of the K.K.K. who wish to be restored to our confidence and esteem, that they renounce and proclaim the same to the general public.[57]

The pro-Klan *Madill Record* suggested that the "idiots" who proposed the boycott were only preparing themselves for a "move," reminding all concerned that tenant farmers had to do whatever their landlords told them.[58] The FLU response to this threat was characteristic of its politics: a spokesman for the Armstrong local challenged the *Record* editor to debate one of its farmer or renter members, with the audience to decide who was the "idiot."[59]

The agrarian movement was apparently strong enough in Marshall County to permit farmers to feel safe in demonstrating their anti-Klan sentiments in the local lair of the Klan dragon. A week after the boycott controversy, a full-page advertisement signed by Edd Long, president of the county FLU, extended the following invitation to the people of the county: "F.L.U. and Anti-Klux Round-Up at Madill Saturday November 17. . . . This is everybody's meeting. There is a place for you."[60] The day before the "Round-Up" the *Marshall County Enter-*

prise assured readers that "everything will be 100 per cent American, without masks or obligations to the Imperial Gizzard or the Chief Cyclone. . . . The meeting will be strictly in the interests of Americanism and of the men who work for the food they eat and the raiment they wear."[61] After the meeting the *Enterprise* reported that a "large" crowd of "farmers and farmers' wives and sweethearts" had gathered in Madill to find out if anyone besides farmers opposed the Klan.[62]

The organized farmers of Marshall County supported a democratic style of political agitation and asserted a populist, open-ended conception of Americanism that embraced all common men. As early as August 1923, just when Governor Walton was beginning to act against the brutal terrorism of the Klan in Tulsa County, the Marshall County FLU voted to "Condemn All Lawless Acts committed by mobs, either masked or unmasked, in the state of Oklahoma . . . [and] most heartily endorse the action of Governor Jack C. Walton in calling out units of the Oklahoma National Guard to see that the laws of the state are executed and fully enforced."[63] The resolution closed with an invitation to Walton to attend the Marshall County Fair. He did, and there he advised farmers to use their shotguns on any masked visitors to their homes. The *Madill Record* reported with disgust that many in the crowd of 1,000 cheered when Walton promised to pardon anyone convicted of murdering a nocturnal intruder.[64]

Walton's speech tapped the deep resentment of intrusion felt by country people—especially when the intruders were inclined to make self-righteous claims to moral superiority and to scorn the "backwardness" of the tenant farmer. The electric lights, paved streets, and whitewashed houses of the county seat towns seemed, in the eyes of country people, more a product of the farmer's unrewarded labor than of the townsman's worthy exertions. The countryside was less concerned about being modern and fashionable. Socially isolated and impoverished, the country people were less affected by the new trends of mass marketing and the increasing tendency of "up-to-date" Americans to measure their satisfaction in possession and consumption of products.

The belief of the countryside in the equality of "producers" and the uselessness of "parasites" cropped up as much as in prewar days of Socialist insurgency. Some FLU doggerel approached the very effulgence of local agrarianism. The following verse begins with a description of the farmer's trials in raising and selling a crop—hail, flood, drought, and boll weevils. Then follow the characteristic perceptions and preoccupations of southern Oklahoma's aroused producers:

> He's got to pay the taxes and the landlord's per cent;
> Got to pay the interest and dig up the rent;
> And when that's done, he ain't got a dollar,
> And yet the Coo-Coos in town all holler
> Bout "the dear old days spent down on the farm"
> When sweet Maude Miller, so safe from harm,
> Whistled her tune and raked up the hay,
> And chatted with the mocking bird over the way.

Not one to leave the slightest doubt about the identity of the "Coo-Coos in town," the FLU artist made the political moral explicit:

> These Coo-Coos what's singing is the Ku Klux Klan
> A tyin' up the farmer like a sackful of bran!
> These Kukes have gone loco, its affectin' their health,
> They've eaten too much of the farmers wealth!
> We might say it different—there's nothin in a name—
> These Ku Klux are Grafters—they're one and the same!
> We've been a figgerin' from finger to thumb—
> The farmer plants the tree but who gets the Plum?[65]

The planting farmer produces and the grafting Kuke consumes. The town, the Klan, the market, the capitalist, and the middleman are a knot of unitary evils in the mind of the FLU poet. It is the town-dwelling Klansman and merchant, not the farmer, who talks of the sweet idyll down on the farm. The Oklahoma farmer tells us of his bad luck, hard work, high rents, low prices, and paltry returns. To the FLU the market conditions that denied a man a living from his labor had to be wrong and iniquitous. Although the distinction between the producers of the field and the parasites of the marketplace assumed the moral superiority of the cultivator, the particular morality was not exclusive. It encouraged FLU spokesmen to demand a redistribution of power and reward in favor of all common men—farmers and industrial laborers—who worked with their hands. The egalitarian agrarian morality facilitated recognition of the necessity for political action and political alliances to secure a broad measure of social and economic "justice."

For the farmers of Marshall County, the fight against the economic interests identified with the Klan was inseparable from the fight against the Klan's social attitudes. The FLU men found the "open shopper" and the Klansman intolerable. Local businessmen may have acted against the "co-operative" plans and activities of the FLU. The boycott circular suggested that the Klan was trying to disrupt farmers' "union" activity. And when townspeople made themselves Klansmen, with a special duty to apply the scourge to the immoral and the derelict, they turned their attention, as usual, to the countryside. Some country people returned the uncomplimentary looks. A "leading farmer" from the south end of the county reportedly said that floggers and masked men were unwelcome in his neighborhood. The *Enterprise* quoted him as saying, "We do not want any revised edition of the A.P.A. of thirty years ago. We don't give a d——m what a man's religion may be but we do want to know how he stands on the Klan question."[66] The statement is impressive for both its conscious historical memory of an earlier episode of nativist intolerance and for its affirmation of the irrelevance of the religious issues raised by the Klan. Whether the "leading farmer" (who may have been Edd Long, president of the FLU) spoke for many country people is a matter of speculation. When an election did come in which the issues could be tested, the country people did not respond favorably to the nativist, exclusive, and "moral" appeal of the Klan.

Klan intolerance was discussed frequently in the *Marshall County Enterprise*. Although its editor did not always agree with the FLU, he still considered himself a firm friend and spokesman for country people. He flattered his farmer readers with the observation that anti-Klan activities, like everything else worthwhile in Marshall County, had "sprung up among the farmers."[67] His brief editorial paragraphs mocked the foolishness of Klansmen: "It is alleged to have been a Madill Klucker who remarked the other day, that there are over a 'million Jews in America, every dern one of them is a Catholic.' And yet the K.K.K.'s talk about ig-nor-ance."[68] Keeping a zealous watch, the *Enterprise* editor reported the Madill speech of a Klanswoman from Texas. She told how the Klan had given an alleged reprobate " 'a beautiful coat of tar and feathers.' " She shouted that the victim had " 'got what was coming to him. I would like to have been there; I would like to have been there and jabbed feathers into his flesh.' '' When a heckler hooted at her claim that Catholic churches were arsenals and followed his hoot with an offer of $500 for every gun found in a church, the Klanswoman reportedly "tongue-lashed" him and suggested that he must be a "nigger-lover." When the Klan ran things, the lady concluded, people would scoff and say "haw" only when told to.[69] "Woman Orator Spills the Beans," laughed the headline of the *Enterprise*, now persuaded that its argument against the Klan's bigotry had been irrevocably confirmed.

Although obviously opposed to the coercive intolerance of the Klan, the *Enterprise* editor infrequently revealed doubts about people not of his own kind and from his own community. At one point he asked "Honest Anti-Klan Farmers" whether they could stomach a Klan claim that "only" Catholics, Jews, foreigners, bootleggers, crooks, and IWWs opposed the Klan. The apposition, perhaps unintentional, suggested that "Honest Anti-Klan Farmers" could feel insulted if grouped with other targets of Klan malice. But the editor concluded his discussion with a hoot at Klan attempts to deny that it fostered "intollerance" and "narrow ignorance."[70] On another occasion he used a clearly anti-Semitic story emphasizing the greediness of Jews in order to attack the allegedly exorbitant power rates paid by the residents of Madill.[71] These, however, were isolated items amid the constant stream of derision he directed toward the pretensions of the local Klan.

In searching for the reasons why the countryside and its spokesmen displayed something like political and social tolerance, we are driven back to its general social ideology. Like the editor of the anti-Klan *Ada Bulletin,* Marshall County's anti-Klan editor was an inveterate Democrat, sympathetic to the "common man" but opposed to the merest hint of radicalism. He had previously been the editor of the *Marshall County News-Democrat* when that paper was the antagonist of the Socialist party in the county.[72] His objections were immediate and vehement when conservative Democrats accused anti-Klan Democrats of being reds. The *Enterprise* argued that the anti-Klan Democrats in question had never bolted the party ticket and had always upheld the cause of the farmers. They adhered to the traditions of "Jeffersonian Democracy" and "Americanism," not the snobberies and tyrannies of "Ku Kluxism."[73] The *Enterprise* was "for organized labor, but not for radicalism."[74] In short Americanism was fair play and open competition. On both counts the Klan was disqualified.

The climax of the social struggle in Marshall County came in the spring and summer of 1924. The first victory went to the anti-Klan in the Madill city elections where, according to the *Enterprise,* "a candidate on the avowed 'daylight' and no cow pasture platform who believed that the government at Washington was amply able to get along without the hooded and shrouded government at Atlanta" defeated an opponent sympathetic to the Klan.[75] An anti-Klan victory in the town of Madill was an ominous sign for the Klan's prospects throughout the county. And it was the county elections toward which everyone now looked and worked.

The Klan gave idolatrous support to its hero of the hour, the county sheriff whose name (ironically enough) was Tom Christian. The *Madill Record* praised Sheriff Christian's forays into the south end of the county, where the farmers in the sandhills just north of the Red River seemed to have a penchant for making, selling, and drinking corn liquor.[76] In a depressed area the distilled forms of corn may have provided more hard cash and happy hours than could be obtained from the sale of crops. It is clear from the descriptions that the sheriff was intruding into hostile territory. The editor of the *Madill Record*, Hiram Impson, when not assailing ethnic groups in distant cities, was always ready to disparage "inferiors" close to home. Although he acknowledged that Sheriff Christian's incursions into the countryside served to confirm that "factions" were present in the county, he was prepared to argue that factional strife was better than having men avoid moral necessities, sit upon their hands, confound license with tolerance, and tolerate still owners and liquor peddlers who "preyed" upon the people.[77] He fumed at those whom he called the "hopeless ignorant," the "wilful intolerant," and, in a moment of complete exasperation, "the most low down white trash.'"[78] In light of his well-known and tirelessly reiterated hatred of radicalism and bootlegging, both of which seemed to crop up repeatedly in the same locale, there can be little doubt that he was attacking the impervious residents of the sandhills.

Confronted with strong rural resistance, the Klan did not give up. The "Klanites" were reported to be making "herculean" efforts to win the south end of the county for their cause. Enemies alleged that the Klan had temporarily dropped its initiation fees in an attempt to induce farmers to join.[79] *The Madill Record*, on the eve of the 1924 Democratic primary, claimed wholesale defections from the FLU to the Klan in Willis precinct. Erstwhile supporters of the Farmer-Labor candidate for sheriff were said to be aiding the booze-fighting Christian.[80] With the approach of the Democratic primary in August 1924, the *Madill Record* defined the basic issue as "Whiskey or No Whiskey," and the *Marshall County Enterprise* countered with "Open Government or Invisible," two slogans that denoted and yet obscured by their very simplicity a social struggle of considerable proportions. Town leaders were seeking to assert a social and psychological mastery over a refractory countryside.

Edd Long, the acknowledged leader of the Marshall County FLU and its candidate for sheriff, sounded the theme of community defense when he announced that he would, if elected, take his orders "from the people with whom I live, not from some 'invisible' government in Atlanta or in the local cow-pasture." After expressing respect for the flag and the symbol of Christ, which the Klan "defamed," Long proclaimed himself a "genuine, blown-in-the-bottle Dirt Farmer" who believed in "the principles of Unionism."[81] He had joined the FLU when it was first formed. Taking his orders from the people among whom he lived, he would not be likely to regard them as "white trash" whose lives and neighborhoods must be invaded to keep the community morally in accord with standards external to its existence. In rejecting the Klan's version of the "public interest," Long and the FLU put forward their own: they would serve the working farmer and protect his neighborhood.

FLU candidates emphasized their attachment to local neighborhoods in the rural areas. The twenty-three-year-old principal of Shay School, drafted by the FLU for county treasurer (because, he said, "the union men knew me to be one of them"), informed the voters that his parents had lived on Marshall County farms, first at Lone Elm and then at Shay, for eighteen years.[82] The FLU candidate for county assessor said that he had come to the Indian territory in 1898 and had lived continuously in one neighborhood since then. He seemed proud to announce that he belonged "to that large class peculiar to the great southwest, known as the 'tenant farmers.' " He promised to assess both town and farm land fairly.[83] The candidate for state representative claimed that he had arrived in Marshall County in 1890 and, as a farmer, had both made and lost money, "lots of it, right here in Marshall Co."[84] The FLU candidate for school superintendant called for more money to be allotted to rural schools and less to state colleges.[85] The FLU endorsee for county commissioner from the south end professed no intention to favor one area over another but did believe that the south end ought to have its proper share of good roads. He had been a resident at Enos for twenty-five years and was the owner of a farm and cotton gin.[86]

In the primary election the FLU candidates won all but three offices, bringing jubilation to the *Enterprise* and desolation to the *Record*. "Boys from the forks won big victory; hoed their corn; routed the cyclops," proclaimed the *Enterprise*.[87] "A Good Fight Has No Defeat; the Closed and Prejudiced Mind," mourned the *Record*. The editor of the *Record* wrote that he could not understand the "prejudice" shown against the Klan. He concluded with an admonition to himself and to his fellow believers: "In the lands where the Nordic rules, the wish of the majority is respected."[88]

TABLE 5

Percentage Voting for Edd Long, FLU Candidate for Sheriff's Nomination (Marshall County), August 1924

Precinct	Percentage	Precinct	Percentage
Lark	96.1	Madill, fourth	44.2
Shay	83.1	Madill, third	49.3
Isom Springs	81.0	Woodville	52.9
Linn	48.8	Madill, second	59.6
McMillan	54.3	Kingston	51.6
Willis	58.6	Aylesworth	27.6

SOURCE: *Madill Record,* August 7, 1924.

The voting pattern of a decade, interrupted only by the extraordinary events of World War I, reappeared in these latest results. The onetime weakest Socialist precincts, which were *all* town precincts, contained all of Edd Long's lowest percentages in the sheriff's race. Only the rural precinct of Kinlock (35.4), which was also a relatively weak Socialist precinct, gave the FLU candidate a lower percentage. Lone Elm (89.8), Powell (82.1), Lebanon (76.1), Simpson (72.5), and Tyler (68.6) are further examples of previously strong Socialist precincts that voted decisively against the Klan candidate in 1924.[89] Some support from people in the towns—a support never available to the Socialists—was obviously necessary if a rural-based movement like the FLU was to defeat the Klan. In turn, Klan candidates picked up considerable support at the country boxes of McMillan and Willis, and even majority support in Linn. But the general tendency was for country voters, organized by the FLU, to protect their neighborhoods and to reject the version of the "public good" fostered by town elites in 1924, just as country voters in the same areas had rejected the "parasitism" disguised (in their view) as "patriotism" at the height of the Socialist insurgency in 1914. That political and cultural feelings were paramount in this resistance may be inferred from the fact that the price of cotton had almost recovered its wartime level in 1923 and 1924, exactly coinciding with the time of the bitterest battles between the agrarian radicals and the Klan.[90] Prosperity must have emboldened the country people to defy those who presumed to be their moral tutors and political bosses.

In the aftermath of the primary fight, a political situation developed that was significant because it forced the different elements in the Democratic party to place their partisan loyalty in the scale against the Klan issue. The *Marshall County Enterprise* accused the *Kingston Messenger* and the *Madill Record* of fomenting a "bolt" from Edd Long because he did not evince a satisfactory opposition to the local "whiskey" traffic. The *Enterprise* implied that the FLU could abandon three non-FLU incumbents who had been renominated and who had never denied being Klansmen. Always the good Democrat, the *Enterprise* editor was plainly trying to keep the warring elements in line behind all Democrats. He calculated without sufficient regard for the FLU's ideological opposition to the Klan. A "prominent farmer" from the south end, speaking officially for the FLU, informed the *Enterprise* man, who had endorsed the entire Democratic ticket, that the issue was whether a candidate supported or opposed the Klan, not whether he was a Democrat or Republican. The farmer recommended a vote for a Republican should he be an "anti" and his opponent a "kluxer." The FLU publicly challenged the non-FLU nominees to declare themselves on the Klan issue.[91]

In the absence of local results for the November general election, some insight into the potency of the Klan issue may be gained by studying the United States' senatorial contest between former Governor Walton, renominated by a minority vote in a furious Democratic primary, and William B. Pine, a Republican oil man from Okmulgee who was generally considered a Klan sympathizer, if not a member.[92] The Senate vote can demonstrate which Democratic registrants were more willing to switch to a Klan Republican in a county that had previously given an average of 24 percent of its vote to Republican candidates.

TABLE 6

Percentage Voting for Republican Pine (Klan) for United States Senate (Marshall County) November 1924

Precinct	Percentage		Precinct	Percentage	
Lark	(27.6)*	1.7	Madill, fourth	(24.8)	56.9
Shay	(7.1)	22.5	Madill, third	(23.8)	55.1
Isom Springs	(10.1)	15.1	Woodville	(12.5)	36.3
Linn	(16.8)	30.1	Madill, second	(17.2)	41.0
McMillan	(40.0)	41.7	Kingston	(32.2)	54.3
Willis	(36.5)	40.2	Aylesworth	(41.1)	74.4

*Republican presidential vote in parentheses.
SOURCE: State Election Board Archives, Oklahoma City.

Pine was elected with 61.5 percent of the statewide vote, but he received only 40.9 percent in Marshall County. Most of that support came from town Democrats, who showed the strongest tendency to vote for a Klan Republican. At this time even FLU voters would have had good cause to feel doubtful in voting for someone as mercurial as Walton. Although they believed that Klan legislators had railroaded "Our Jack" out of office primarily to stop his war on the Klan, FLU spokesmen acknowledged that some of the charges of gross corruption leveled at Walton during the legislature's impeachment sessions had been substantially proven. The strong vote in the country precincts for Walton, who had asked for election on virtually no basis other than his opposition to the Klan, provides impressive confirmation of strong opposition in this agrarian radical constituency to the style, the substance, and the social origins of Oklahoma Klan politics.

Marshall County was one of only three counties in the state where Walton polled a majority vote. In both the general election and in the primary that preceded it he ran well ahead of his statewide percentage in the counties that lay in the southern third of the state, especially on the east side. Even at that, his percentages in the southern counties were generally between 40 and 50 percent, far below the normal Democratic preponderance in the area. By contrast, Walton received no more than 28 percent in Oklahoma County and 29 percent in Tulsa County, both of which were urban areas in which the Klan had had great success and much influence.[93]

The FLU was successful in Marshall County where the Socialist party had not been because it restated the fundamental beliefs of "producers" in a manner uncomplicated by the enlarging and disturbing implications of Socialist analysis. Without questioning the small farmer's place in a capitalist society, the FLU could use the language of agrarian protest to mobilize the resentment of the countryside against the town merchants and landlords. By professing their desire to protect the homes and livelihoods of common men from the "open shoppers" and the Klansmen, the FLU could split the town vote in Marshall County to a greater degree than the Klan could split the country vote. Ten years before the Socialist party, lacking the protective drapery of Americanism, had only been able to split the country vote while losing almost the entire town vote.

In 1924 one of the Marshall County FLU candidates protested that the FLU was not "radical." He argued that the FLU program would benefit everyone, "for when the farmers prosper, all callings and professions prosper."[94] What may have been true for Marshall County and southern Oklahoma was increasingly untrue for a nation already industrialized and daily more urbanized. The FLU was correct: for all of its undeniable animus against local monopolists and distant big business, it was not "radical". When FLU candidates said that they were "for the masses as against the classes" and "for equal rights for all and special privileges for none," they were only reaffirming the "genuine, blown-in-the-bottle Dirt Farmer's" understanding of the traditional verities of agrarian America. Far from being a Socialist commited to a transformation of Oklahoma and American society, Edd Long was a defender—and a politically successful one—of his neighborhood community and of its neighborly way of life. The residents of the south end of Marshall County wished to be left to themselves, but in order to remain where they were, they had to take political action to win some relief and peace of mind. Devoutly wishing to be free from the exactions of "parasites" and the minatory intrusions of busybodies, symbolized by the booze-fighting Sheriff Christian, they resisted and defeated a Klan that seemed to embody both evils. For a few more years they would move about the countryside before unprecedented social changes would force them to migrate.

NOTES

1. The price of wheat (twelve month average) was $1.98 per bushel in 1918; $2.12 in 1919; $2.11 in 1920; $1.11 in 1921; and $.95 in 1922 and 1923. The price of corn was $1.70 per bushel in 1918; $1.58 in 1919; $1.26 in 1920; $.47 in 1921; $.56 in 1922; and $.88 in 1923. The price of cotton was 27.9¢ per pound in 1918; 29.0¢ in 1919; 28.1¢ in 1920; 10.9¢ in 1921; 18.1¢ in 1922, and 25.5¢ in 1923. T. R. Hedges and K. D. Blood, "Oklahoma Farm Price Statistics, 1910-38," *Oklahoma Agricultural Experiment Station Bulletin No. 239* (December 1939): 18, 19, 24.

2. *Oklahoma Leader* (Oklahoma City), June 7, 1922.

3. S. P. Freeling, *Does Socialism Menace Oklahoma?,* pamphlet reprint of a speech delivered at Chickasha, Oklahoma, October 20, 1922, Vertical File, Library, Oklahoma Historical Society. Freeling was attorney-general of Oklahoma during the Williams administration, 1914-1918.

4. *Oklahoma Leader*, February 4, 1922.

5. Ibid.

6. For the history of the league at the state level, see Gilbert C. Fite, "Oklahoma's Reconstruction League: An Experiment in Farmer-Labor Politics," *Journal of Southern History*, 13 (November 1947): 535-555.

7. See Oscar Ameringer's editorial denunciation of Walton's "apotasy" in *Oklahoma Leader*, July 27, 1923.

8. On the "Walton war," see Sheldon Neuringer, "Governor Walton's War on the Ku Klux Klan: An Episode in Oklahoma History 1923 to 1924," *Chronicles of Oklahoma*, 45 (Summer 1967): 153-179, for a judicious interpretation.

9. General discussions of the Oklahoma Klan may be found in Charles C. Alexander, *The Ku Klux Klan in the Southwest* (Lexington, 1965), and John Hunter Montgomery, "Oklahoma's Invisible Empire" (Senior thesis, Princeton University, 1962).

10. *Madill Record*, February 15, 1923.

11. *Johnston County Capital-Democrat* (Tishomingo), June 8, 1922.

12. *Madill Record*, June 14, 1923.

13. *Stonewall Weekly News*, April 26, 1923.

14. *Madill Record*, September 4, 1924.

15. *Stonewall Weekly News*, October 27, 1921.

16. Ibid., December 28, 1922.

17. *Madill Record*, February 1, 1923.

18. Ibid., February 28, 1924.

19. Ibid., May 1, 1924.

20. *Stonewall Weekly News*, October 5, 1922.

21. The best description of the Oklahoma Klan's techniques of organization and propaganda may be found in Montgomery, "Oklahoma's Invisible Empire".

22. *Fairview Republican*, November 24, 1924.

23. *Oklahoma Leader*, February 9, 1922.

24. For reports of Klan warnings and whippings, see the *Oklahoma News* (Oklahoma City), October 27, 1921, January 31, July 22, 1922, August 2, 11, 1923; *Stonewall Weekly News*, September 22, 1921; *Fairview Republican,* December 9, 1921. For reports of Klan charity, see *Fairview Republican*, December 22, 1922; *Johnston County Capital-Democrat*, June 15, 1922; *Madill Record*, July 27, August 31, 1922, August 30, 1923; *Oklahoma News*, December 22, 1921; *Allen Democrat*, January 27, 1922.

25. *Allen Democrat*, July 7, 1922.

26. *Elk City News-Democrat*, June 15, 1922, June 21, 1923; *Fairview Republican*, December 22, 1922; *Johnston County Capital-Democrat*, June 15, 1922; *Lamont Valley News*, November 2, 1922; *Madill Record*, July 27, August 31, 1922, August 30, 1923; *Ringwood Recorder*, January 26, 1923; *Stonewall Weekly News*, April 27, October 19, 1922.

27. *Ada Bulletin*, September 15, 1923.

28. *Madill Record*, February 23, 1922.

29. *Wapanucka Press*, June 22, 1923.

30. *Madill Record*, April 6, 1922.

31. Ibid., December 21, 1922.

32. *Marshall County Enterprise*, June 27, 1924.

33. *Oklahoma Leader*, December 19, 1921.

34. *Johnston County Capital-Democrat*, December 13, 1923.

35. *Stonewall Weekly News*, August 3, 1922. The *Allen Democrat* agreed that it was the rural folk who had brought about these dreadful results.

36. *Ada Bulletin*, May 26, 1922.

37. Ibid., June 30, 1922.

38. Ibid., January 19, 1924.

39. Ibid.

40. Ibid., June 9, 1922.

41. Ibid., January 3, 1923.

42. Ibid.

43. Ibid., May 23, 1922.

44. Ibid., May 30, 1922.

45. Ibid., August 25, 1923.

46. Ibid., May 23, 1922; see also *Harlow's Weekly*, December 12, 1917, for Judge Bolen's denunciation of Socialist "traitors" who did not deserve, in his view, the privileges of citizenship.

47. *Ada Bulletin,* May 23, 26, 1922.

48. Ibid., June 24, 1922. The pro-Klan *Allen Democrat* attempted to discredit the judge by publishing an affidavit of Nora E. Montgomery, who testified that the judge had fallen into an inebriated stupor outside her house one winter night in 1920. *Allen Democrat*, July 21, 1922.

49. For the history of the Farm-Labor Union and a critique of the economic theories and proposals of its leaders, see Robert Lee Hunt, *A History of Farmer Movements in the Southwest: 1873-1925* (College Station, Texas, n.d.), 145-192.

50. *Marshall County Enterprise*, September 6, 1923, July 4, 1924. FLU members in the country neighborhoods of Willis, Shay, Lark, Isom Springs, Powell, Lebanon, Enos, Cumberland, and Simpson were reported to be meeting regularly.

51. Ibid., February 7, 1924.

52. Ibid., October 26, 1923.

53. *Oklahoma Leader*, July 25, 1921.

54. Ibid., November 27, 1922.

55. Ibid., December 4, 1922.

56. *Marshall County Enterprise*, December 14, 1923.

57. *Madill Record*, October 25, 1923.

58. Ibid.

59. *Marshall County Enterprise*, November 2, 1923.

60. Ibid., November 9, 1923.

61. Ibid., November 16, 1923.

62. Ibid., November 23, 1923.

63. Ibid., August 30, 1923.

64. *Madill Record*, September 13, 1923.

65. *Marshall County Enterprise*, June 27, 1924. For more verses, see also June 13 and July 11, 1924.

66. Ibid., February 7, 1924.

67. Ibid., November 9, 1923.

68. Ibid., October 26, 1923.

69. Ibid., August 1, 1924.

70. Ibid., October 26, 1923.

71. Ibid., November 9, 1923.

72. Ibid., June 21, 1923.

73. Ibid., December 28, 1923.

74. Ibid., November 9, 1923.

75. Ibid., April 4, 1924.

76. *Madill Record*, February 14, June 26, 1924; *Marshall County Enterprise*, July 5, 1924.

77. *Madill Record*, July 19, 1923.

78. Ibid.; and ibid., May 1, 1924.

79. *Marshall County Enterprise*, May 16, 1924.

80. *Madill Record*, July 31, 1924.

81. *Marshall County Enterprise*, March 21, May 30, 1924.

82. Ibid., April 4, 1924.

83. Ibid., April 11, 1924.

84. Ibid., May 2, 1924.

85. Ibid., April 11, 1924.

86. Ibid., April 18, 1924.

87. Ibid., August 8, 1924.

88. *Madill Record*, August 14, 1924.

89. The precinct election results are available in the *Madill Record*, August 7, 1924. The computations of percentages are mine.

90. See note 1 above for cotton prices through 1923. The price advanced to 26.2¢ per pound in 1924. If a farmer brought in a good crop of cotton during 1924, he must have done well even if he lived in a period of general price inflation.

91. *Marshall County Enterprise*, August 22, September 5, 19, October 17, 1924.

92. Walton had won the Democratic senatorial nomination with a minority vote (30.7 percent) in a race with four other candidates. Oliver Benson, et al., *Oklahoma Votes, 1907-1962* (Norman, 1964), 115.

93. Ibid., 117. If the practitioners of political psephology wish more precision in stating these conclusions, they should compare Walton's 1924 Senate vote in the general election with the prewar Socialist party vote. In those southern Oklahoma counties where the Socialists had had strong rural support, Walton generally ran ahead of his statewide vote. But in northwestern Oklahoma counties where farmers had defected from the Republican party to the Socialists in the prewar years, Walton ran behind his statewide pace. Traditional Republican loyalty did not keep Republican farmers who had once voted Socialist from voting for a Klan Republican in 1924. Traditional Democratic loyalty may have kept some quondam Socialist voters in southern Oklahoma from switching to a Klansman because he was a Republican. The best way out of these explanatory thickets is to remember that the Democratic party vote in southern Oklahoma

showed a strong tendency to go for or against Walton on the basis of country versus town, conservative enterprisers versus agrarian radicals. It was only in southern Oklahoma that there was a strongly organized and politically conscious movement like the FLU. It is impossible to guess how the onetime Socialist voters in northwestern Oklahoma who had returned to the Republican party in 1924 would have behaved had they been organized by a strong agrarian political movement like the FLU. But, knowing the pattern of division in the Democratic vote, we may say, at the very least, that agrarian radical traditions and experiences must not be neglected in explaining the anti-Klan vote within the Oklahoma Democratic party in 1924. Party loyalty did not prevent large numbers of pro-Klan town Democrats from switching to a Klan Republican.

94. *Marshall County Enterprise*, December 28, 1923, April 11, 1924 (''Jeffersonian Democracy'' versus ''Ku Kluxism'').

Oklahoma's socialists in ————9
a capitalist world

The Socialist party rose and fell with a meteoric incandescence in the dawn of Oklahoma's history. Its light had already been extinguished when Oscar Ameringer undertook to explain, in a series of editorial articles in the *Oklahoma Leader*, why he would support the farmer-labor insurgency within the Democratic party during the 1922 elections. Ameringer's explanation was founded upon a careful analysis of the history of the Socialist party in Oklahoma.

Ameringer believed that the underdeveloped economy of a new frontier was politically decisive: "poor markets, low prices, lack of capital and high interest prevailed for many years in Oklahoma after prosperity had struck its northern neighbors."[1] Low prices and high interest rates insured the persistence of agrarian discontent and rebellion. "The socialist party," Ameringer argued,

> which grew so powerful in the first decade of this century was in fact a renaissance of populism. It adopted the phrases and slogans of the younger movement, but at bottom it rested not on a wage earning proletariat, but on the same rebellious frontier farmers who had given vitality to the populist movement.

As Oklahoma society developed, as crop prices improved, as oil fever spread over the state, there was "no room left for the discussion of economic problems, except from the purely individualistic and capitalistic viewpoint. Everybody expects to get rich by the short route, and social problems are forgotten."[2] And when the war brought "two dollar wheat, forty cent cotton, and five dollar oil," many of the wayfaring political rebels of former years subsided into a contented and prosperous domesticity. The moral debacle of European socialists during the Great War and the battering persecution of war opponents in America "finished the organized movement in Oklahoma."[3] Little could be accomplished in 1922 by indulging in "foolhardy and shallow bravado." Ameringer and his associates believed that they had saved both the *Oklahoma Leader* and their own political integrity: if this was treason to socialism, "then so much the worse for it."[4] Except for diehards like O. E. Enfield and Hector Sinclair, and 4,000 hardy perennials who shunned the farmer-labor option to vote Socialist in 1922 (only 0.7 percent of the total state vote), most of the old-time Socialist voters apparently followed Ameringer into the motley crowd supporting the promising populist, Jack Walton, now fully embarked on his ill-starred course.

The burden of Ameringer's argument was that the small farmers of Oklahoma were far more likely to be swayed in a politically decisive manner by the events of the market than by the proposal of conscious designs for a new society. The incomplete evidence of popular mentality reveals somewhat more of the short-term grievance and the temporarily disadvantaged interest than of the permanent alienation of the property-less worker. Bad men and their unconscionable manipulations had to be replaced by good men, who would remove corrupt influences from the market, thereby permitting it to deliver to the working farmer his natural and proper reward. One could carry Ameringer's argument to its logical conclusion: the country people's collective cultural perception of the variable events in an invariable marketplace helped to reinforce a social structure that ensured their objective and seemingly permanent dispossession. Predictably enough they were loath to concede the permanence of their lack of property and their disadvantages in the marketplace.

Local Socialist spokesmen might declare the struggling farmer to be one with the propertyless industrial laborer, but many of the farmers, whether owners or tenants, felt otherwise when the markets started to rise. They did not easily yield up the hope of making a killing, to the limit of their individual abilities, in a good market. Consequently, even in the Socialist press, there was an abundance of local talk about the reasons for rising and declining prices, and there was relatively little local discussion of a transformation of the principles and practices of farm ownership. A farming population that might be characterized as a movable peasantry confirmed Marx's dictum on peasants: they tend to lose interest in politics and retire into an isolating rural seclusion when they make good profits from their crops and acquire land of their own.

Some of the indigenous Socialist leaders in Oklahoma did see the need for socialism, and, having acted upon their perception, they came to know the great difficulty of achieving it. As provincial and incomplete as their articulation of socialist principles may have been, they did understand that the processes of the marketplace would have the ineluctable result of cumulative inequality. The possessors of property would continue to acquire advantages that would increasingly appear to be inherent and natural. Those few local Socialists who perceived that the market is a social construction over time could conceive of the conscious abolition of a capitalist social order that allotted brutally unequal life chances to those who possessed and those who lacked capital.

But many of the followers in the movement, as local leaders regretfully observed when the party's vote fell in 1916, had taken the "belly route" instead of the "head route" to the Socialist party. Crying out in anguish during hard times, the "belly route" Socialist abandoned the march to the Socialist republic for the quicker results of an improving market. Ingrained belief inclined the "belly route" men to hang onto the residual culture of individualism associated with the free market. These were not people whose lives had already been collectivized by the urban neighborhood and the factory experience. The experiential individualism of their small-holding ways persisted until far greater social forces uprooted these people from their country neighborhoods. Rural community they had, but prominent in their particular sense of community was the tradition of private activity and individual responsibility.

None of these observations should be taken to mean that the Socialists of Oklahoma did not severely disrupt their local society. The very fact that so many Oklahomans acted to support the Socialist party was a shocking departure from respectable political practice and from regional tradition. The Democrats never let the Socialists forget that their support for a radical party was an intolerable affront to American "patriotism." Socialism, its local opponents vehemently pronounced, was far worse then populism. Outright intimidation and persecution were soon to be the fate of those who persisted in this departure from the "Americanism" that served as both the measure and the scourge applied by the town middle classes seeking to cleanse their communities and to restore proper standards of citizenship. That the country people held out as long as they did against both the pressure mounted by aroused "Americanists" and their own American feelings may be attributed in large measure to the transcendental and millennarian strain of their thought—a strain that derived from the undoubted authority of a still fierce religion. In the Protestant tenets that conferred dignity upon the souls of the poor and the disinherited, the country people found the courage to launch political assaults upon the locally notable and powerful. In the experience of political rebellion organized by a radical party, the country people found a bridge that enabled them to cross over from their own customary beliefs in order to make a significant, if not a lasting, connection with a modern and radical political association. Freed momentarily from the unthinking acceptance of their community's enduring customs, they groped in difficult circumstances for an understanding of the novel idea of cooperation and social ownership. It is hardly surprising that their understanding of socialism was often incomplete, for they were to "learn" their lessons in the midst of the biases mobilized against such new departures—biases that, as any American can tell us, enshrine private rights and praise self-assertion, if not self-aggrandizement.

The experience of the Socialist party of Oklahoma was a small episode in the history of socialism, but its dismal fate may illuminate, if we take the long view, the ideological disarray and the political perplexity of socialist parties throughout the Western world in the last fifty years. It is important to remember that those socialist parties that have won electoral majorities and political power have had to dispense with much socialist principle and practice in order to draw support away from the parties of private enterprise. As Ameringer pointed out in the context of Oklahoma politics, such a strategy of ideological compromise bade fair to improve performance in elections even if the doctrinaire considered it treason to the principles of socialism. Liberal capitalism, with its capacity to create enormous amounts of private wealth (however unequally distributed), has proven to be tough and resilient almost beyond the comprehension of many socialists. It has been capitalism's ability, modified by public regulation and fiscal policy, to make plausible its promise of improving business and richer material life that has confounded socialists throughout North America and Europe as well as in the hinterlands of Oklahoma. Despite great differences in cultural tradition and work experience, Oklahoma farmers were probably not so much more resistant to a revolutionary collectivism than the industrial workers currently sitting in their living rooms, watching football on their color television sets, paying only occasional attention to the pronouncements issued from the offices of labor or socialist parties.

When taking the long view, one becomes aware that the most signifi-cant fact in the history of Western socialism has not been the peculiar weakness of the American variety and the remarkable strength of the European; instead, it has been the inability of doctrinaire socialists to win elections wherever they have advocated a strenuous and thoroughgoing implementation of socialist principles. Moderate and compromising socialists, everywhere more concerned with electoral success than with doctrinal purity, have frequently attempted to make capitalism work "better" or more "fairly," which is approximately what many of the local Socialists proposed for their countryside, even though they believed that they were revolutionaries. When business has declined in capitalist economies, hard-pressed social groups have often looked to labor or socialist parties for measures of relief but seldom for elaborate designs of new societies. When business improves, the cry quickly goes up not to tamper too much with a rising market and popular hopes for renewed prosperity. Against the resilience of capitalism, the imported and some of the local Socialists in Oklahoma could explain that capitalism is a contradictory system that produces abundance while (perhaps because) it periodically impoverishes many. They could explain that competitive individualism often made people who practiced self-help old before their time. But the explanations, however logical and well founded, were to become pale and unappealing when placed beside the entrancing prospect of "more" in the marketplace. Then as now, the periods of material prosperity seemed, for many working people, to be worth the wait.

Even during their days of despair, the country audiences were looking for something more exciting than logical social analysis. The heavy air of bewilderment and disappointment that pervaded their meetings would be dispelled less by persistent attempts at explanation than by urgent millen-narian vision. For a transitory moment or two, a people weary to the bone must have believed their dreams to be within reach. They had known more privation and pain than anyone should have to learn. A life without misery, distrust, and selfishness they devoutly wished and fervently sought, but, with the exception of the fleeting ecstasy of the camp meetings, their search turned away from novel proposals for a perfected society.

The small holders reverted fairly quickly to their habitual hope: a rising market that would carry them upward to a decent existence. Capitalism in America heaved and lurched its way ahead to its greatest boom and its worst depression. Keeping their faith in the recognizable village community and the small holder's independent way of life, the Oklahoma farmers stumbled forward to their doom, losing the struggle that so many had already lost before them. They would be Democrats, Christians, and Americans while they remained in Oklahoma. They continued to move, but they did not migrate until the tractors destroyed the basis of the old neighborhoods. Faced with the uncompromising plans of a consolidating capitalism, many of the country people were finally forced to take the roads leading west to California.

Like people everywhere who have known and enjoyed life in familiar communities where they wished to stay, the Okies were notoriously reluctant to leave their country life in Oklahoma. They took with them some important elements of their communal life. Observers in California noted their yearning for good preaching and their prickly belief in individual rights and community self-regulation. Wherever they could find a patch of ground free for use, they started little gardens to remind themselves of home.

The absence of any strongly manifested collective memory of socialism among people who had lived in rural areas where the movement had flourished for a brief time suggests that that particular form of "socialism" had indeed only been a transitory moment in the harried lives of southwestern tenant farmers.[5] Whatever they were destined to find in California, they had left far behind them that peculiar syncretic radicalism of their father's day—a radicalism with vivid dreams of a golden age when the lost souls of earth would roll away the stone that had too long hidden the Christ of humanity from those who worked and sweated for a meager living. Those were local dreams, born of the despair of existence, the warmth of neighborhood life, and the evangelism of the Socialist encampments down in the valleys of the Canadian and Red rivers.

Appendix I
Maps

Average Value of Land Per Acre (1910)

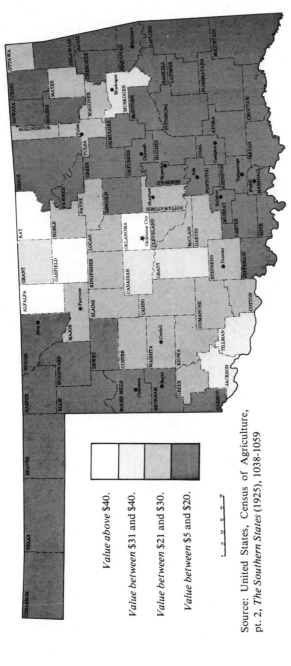

Value above $40.

Value between $31 and $40.

Value between $21 and $30.

Value between $5 and $20.

Source: United States, Census of Agriculture, pt. 2, *The Southern States* (1925), 1038-1059

Average Value of Land per Acre, 1910. Adapted from *Historical Atlas of Oklahoma*, by John W. Morris and Edwin C. McReynolds. Copyright © 1965 by the University of Oklahoma Press.

Percent of Farm Tenancy (1910)

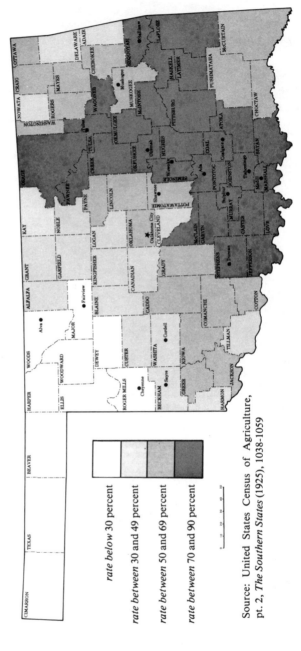

Source: United States Census of Agriculture, pt. 2, *The Southern States* (1925), 1038-1059

rate below 30 percent

rate between 30 and 49 percent

rate between 50 and 69 percent

rate between 70 and 90 percent

Percentage of Farm Tenancy, 1910. Adapted from *Historical Atlas of Oklahoma*, by John W. Morris and Edwin C. McReynolds. Copyright © 1965 by the University of Oklahoma Press.

1914 Socialist Voting Strength (*Gubernatorial Contest*)

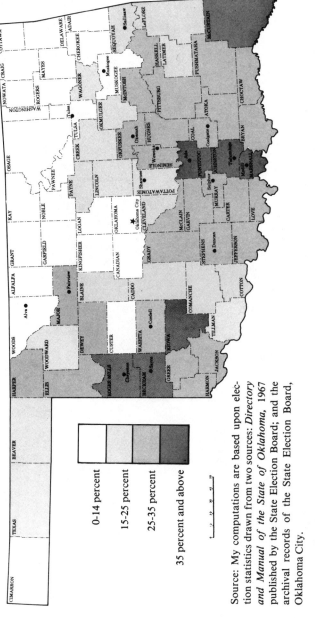

0-14 percent

15-25 percent

25-35 percent

35 percent and above

Source: My computations are based upon election statistics drawn from two sources: *Directory and Manual of the State of Oklahoma, 1967* published by the State Election Board; and the archival records of the State Election Board, Oklahoma City.

1914 Socialist Voting Strength. Adapted from *Historical Atlas of Oklahoma*, by John W. Morris and Edwin C. McReynolds. Copyright © 1965 by the University of Oklahoma Press.

1914 Election—Socialist Party First, Second, or Third

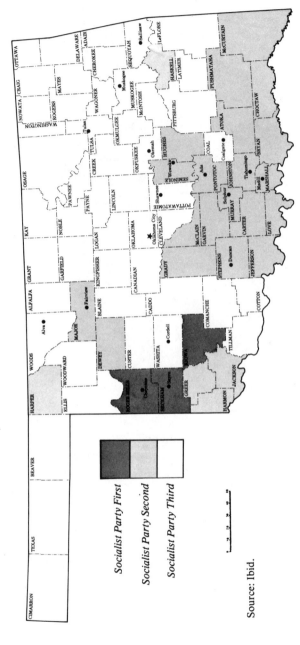

Socialist Party First

Socialist Party Second

Socialist Party Third

Source: Ibid.

1914 Election—Socialist Party First, Second, or Third. Adapted from *Historical Atlas of Oklahoma*, by John W. Morris and Edwin C. McReynolds. Copyright © 1965 by the University of Oklahoma Press.

1916 Socialist Voting Strength (*Presidential Contest*)

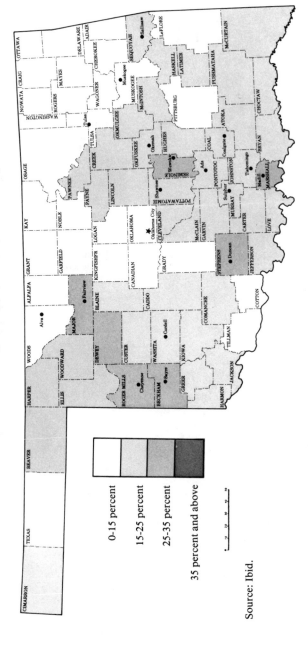

0-15 percent

15-25 percent

25-35 percent

35 percent and above

Source: Ibid.

1916 Socialist Voting Strength. Adapted from *Historical Atlas of Oklahoma*, by John W. Morris and Edwin C. McReynolds. Copyright © 1965 by the University of Oklahoma Press.

1916 Election—Socialist Party First, Second, or Third

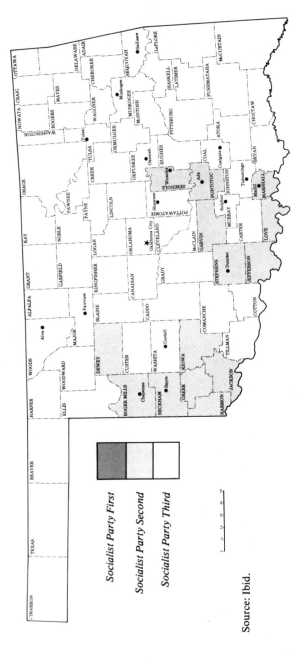

Source: Ibid.

1916 Election—Socialist Party First, Second, or Third. Adapted from *Historical Atlas of Oklahoma*, by John W. Morris and Edwin C. McReynolds. Copyright © 1965 by the University of Oklahoma Press.

Marshall County, Oklahoma, Circa 1910
(with towns, railroads, and roads outlined)

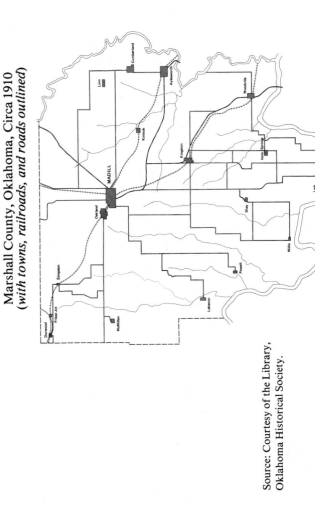

Source: Courtesy of the Library,
Oklahoma Historical Society.

Marshall County, Oklahoma, circa 1910. Adapted from *Historical Atlas of Oklahoma*, by John W. Morris and Edwin C. McReynolds. Copyright © 1965 by the University of Oklahoma Press.

Appendix II
Tables

TABLE 1

Fifteen Strongest Socialist Counties
(Rank based upon simple average of six elections, 1908-1918)

COUNTY	*Socialist Percentage of Total County Vote*					
	1908	*1910*	*1912*	*1914*	*1916*	*1918*
Marshall (se)	23	29	35	41	26	7
Beckham (sw)	16	23	28	40	27	7
Dewey (nw)	13	21	26	31	33	17
Stephens (sw)	19	21	28	35	28	5
Roger Mills (sw)	16	19	25	36	25	13
Major (nw)	17	18	22	29	27	21
Love (se)	17	15	30	35	21	3
Johnston (se)	21	19	29	36	21	4
Seminole (se)	15	16	28	35	28	4
Pontotoc (se)	18	17	27	35	22	2
Choctaw (se)	17	21	25	34	17	7
Coal (se)	24	14	26	28	20	6
Murray (se)	15	25	30	29	17	2
Okfuskee (ne)	15	17	31	29	20	3
Jefferson (sw)	12	17	31	31	22	2

(ne)—northeast quadrant   (sw)—southwest quadrant
(se)—southeast quadrant   (nw)—northwest quadrant

TABLE 2

Fifteen Weakest Socialist Counties
(Rank based upon simple average of six elections, 1908-1918)

COUNTY	*Socialist Percentage of Total County Vote*					
	1908	*1910*	*1912*	*1914*	*1916*	*1918*
Craig (ne)	2	2	3	3	5	1
Kay (ne)	2	3	6	7	7	3
Muskogee (ne) (lt)	2	3	8	9	5	1
Ottawa (ne)	4	4	6	6	6	2
Nowata (ne)	3	4	6	8	6	2
Adair (ne)	2	2	8	7	9	2
Mayes (ne)	2	2	8	8	8	2
Grant (nw)	2	4	7	8	8	2
Cherokee (ne)	2	3	6	13	8	1
Oklahoma (c) (lt)	5	6	6	9	8	2
Delaware (ne)	3	4	9	9	10	2
Garfield (nw) (lt)	4	5	7	9	11	3
Noble (ne)	4	7	10	8	8	4
Tulsa (ne) (lt)	5	6	10	11	9	2
Logan (c) (lt)	3	4	10	10	12	4

(c)–center of state　　　　　(sw)–southwest quadrant
(ne)–northeast quadrant　　　(nw)–northwest quadrant
(se)–southeast quadrant　　　(lt)–large town (over 10,000 population)

TABLE 3

Voter Turnout Percentages, 1907-1918

	1907	1908	1910	1912	1914	1916	1918
Oklahoma	67.8	66.9	55.1	54.2	51.9	57.4	36.7
Marshall County	62.2	53.2	65.3	69.3	81.3	76.8	39.2
Beckham County	68.3	72.2	58.0	63.3	58.0	67.9	41.6

TABLE 4

Percentage Socialist Vote, 1907-1918

	1907	1908	1910	1912	1914	1916	1918
Oklahoma	4	8	10	16	21	15	4
Marshall County	11	23	29	35	41	26	7
Beckham County	7	16	23	28	40	27	7

TABLE 5

Ballots Cast in Strong Socialist Precincts, 1916-1918

Socialist ballots, Marshall County

PRECINCT	1916	1918	NUMBER INCREASE/ DECREASE	PERCENTAGE INCREASE/DECREASE
Lark	54	4	−50	−92.5
Shay	47	4	−43	−91.4
Isom Springs	49	5	−44	−89.7
Willis	44	5	−39	−88.6
McMillan	33	4	−29	−87.8
Linn	23	2	−21	−91.3

Democratic ballots, Marshall County

PRECINCT	1916	1918	NUMBER INCREASE/ DECREASE	PERCENTAGE INCREASE/DECREASE
Lark	13	14	+ 1	+ 7.6
Shay	22	14	− 8	−36.3
Isom Springs	18	11	− 7	−38.8
Willis	87	42	−45	−51.7
McMillan	31	17	−14	−45.1
Linn	18	6	−12	−66.6

Republican ballots, Marshall County

PRECINCT	1916	1918	NUMBER INCREASE/ DECREASE	PERCENTAGE INCREASE/DECREASE
Lark	11	4	− 7	− 63.6
Shay	4	4	0	0
Isom Springs	20	7	−13	− 65.0
Willis	7	16	+ 9	+128.5
McMillan	15	16	+ 1	+ 6.6
Linn	8	14	+ 6	+ 75.0

TABLE 5 (CONT'D.)

Socialist ballots, Beckham County

PRECINCT	1916	1918	NUMBER INCREASE/ DECREASE	PERCENTAGE INCREASE/DECREASE
Emma	23	4	−19	− 82.6
Carter	25	0	−25	−100.0
N. Carter	103	7	−96	− 93.2
Hext	39	18	−21	− 56.7
Coyote	13	2	−11	− 84.6
Friendship (Bettina Twp.)	33	3	−30	− 90.9

Democratic ballots, Beckham County

PRECINCT	1916	1918	NUMBER INCREASE/ DECREASE	PERCENTAGE INCREASE/DECREASE
Emma	8	7	− 1	−12.5
Carter	20	11	− 9	−45.0
N. Carter	85	45	−40	−47.0
Hext	30	17	−13	−43.3
Coyote	12	15	+ 3	+ 25.0
Friendship (Bettina Twp.)	55	42	−13	−23.6

Republican ballots, Beckham County

PRECINCT	1916	1918	NUMBER INCREASE/ DECREASE	PERCENTAGE INCREASE/DECREASE
Emma	5	14	+ 9	+180.0
Carter	2	5	+ 3	+150.0
N. Carter	20	31	+11	+ 55.0
Hext	10	13	+ 3	+ 30.0
Coyote	4	2	− 2	− 50.0
Friendship (Bettina Twp.)	7	21	+ 14	+200.0

TABLE 6

**Percentage of Illiteracy among Native White Males of Voting Age
in Selected Oklahoma Counties (State = 4.0)**

Fifteen Counties with Highest Socialist Vote (1910-1916)		Fifteen Counties with Lowest Socialist Vote (1910-1916)	
Marshall	7.4	Craig	4.0
Beckham	2.8	Kay	0.7
Dewey	2.2	Muskogee	3.3
Stephens	6.5	Ottawa	4.4
Roger Mills	2.3	Nowata	2.8
Major	1.6	Adair	12.6
Love	9.7	Mayes	7.2
Johnston	9.3	Grant	0.6
Seminole	8.6	Cherokee	13.0
Pontotoc	6.6	Oklahoma	0.5
Choctaw	6.5	Delaware	8.9
Coal	7.3	Garfield	0.5
Murray	5.6	Noble	0.9
Okfuskee	4.3	Tulsa	2.0
Jefferson	4.4	Logan	1.0

Three Green Corn Counties		WCU Counties	
Seminole	8.6	LeFlore	13.9
Pontotoc	6.6	Sequoyah	14.5
Hughes	7.4		

SOURCE: U.S., Bureau of the Census, *Thirteenth Census of the United States,* vol. 3, *Population* (Washington, D.C., 1913), 467-479.

during World War I. As this study indicates, some of his biggest problems were caused by the obduracy of local Socialists. In the Western History Collection there were a few other small collections from state Democrats but nothing very useful for purposes of this study.

NEWSPAPERS AND PERIODICALS

In attempting to depict and analyze the attitudes of the people who gave varying measures of support to the Socialist party of Oklahoma, I was driven to the newspapers, where I spent months studying the impact that socialism made upon Oklahoma farmers and, conversely, the imprint *they* made upon the socialism that was carried to them.

The *Industrial Democrat* (Oklahoma City) reveals socialism with a local accent. The *Oklahoma Pioneer* (Oklahoma City) bears the strong imprint of Oscar Ameringer and the Milwaukee comrades. Between 1910 and 1912, when it folded, it gives the best overall view of the growth of socialism, including the growth of internal tension and conflict. In its editorials and major articles it provided probably the most sophisticated version of a secular and proletarian socialism to be found in Oklahoma. The *Sulphur New Century* (Murray County) was founded by southern Oklahoma Socialists to counter the influence of the Milwaukee group. It is an excellent window on the attitudes of local Socialists. The *Otter Valley Socialist* (Kiowa County) serves the historian equally well. The *Strong City Herald* (Roger Mills County) was purchased by a Socialist in 1914 and thus serves as a useful source on socialism in western Oklahoma until 1918, when it apparently went under. The *Ellis County Socialist* (Shattuck) illustrates the close connection between evangelical Protestantism and rural Socialism. Unfortunately, the *Madill Socialist-Herald* (Marshall County) is available only for three numbers in July and August 1912, even though I have found references to it as early as 1911 and as late as 1916. The *Okemah Sledge Hammer* (Okfuskee County) is useful for Socialist opinion in a county with a large minority of Negroes. Other local Socialist papers of some use were the *Boswell Submarine* (Choctaw County), the *Johnston County Socialist* (Tishomingo), and the *Taloga Times* (Dewey County). A few issues of the *Sentinel Sword of Truth* (Washita County) were available. And the *Sayre Social Democrat* (Beckham County) had a stormy career until its editor was arrested for libel. It was the forerunner of the *Social Democrat* (Oklahoma City), which gives us important information on the expansion of local organization and the changes of direction that took place in 1913 after the departure of Ameringer and his group for Milwaukee. Neither James R. Green nor I were ever able to discover any extant copies of the so-called Oklahoma edition of the *Appeal to Reason* (Girard, Kansas), which was probably a page inserted into the papers sent to Oklahoma addresses. The *Woods County Constructive Socialist* (Alva) illustrates an evolutionary socialist view in a northwestern wheat county where struggling small owners gave the Socialist local a "populist" flavor. The *Grant County Socialist* (Medford), reveals the tribulations of a Socialist editor in a prosperous county where socialism was hopelessly weak. For socialism in the last months of the Great War and the first months of peace, one can study the *Oklahoma Leader* (Oklahoma City) and the *Cleo Chieftan* [sic] (Major County).

Democratic response to the rise of socialism can be followed in a legion of dailies and weeklies. For views from the capital, one can look at the *Daily Oklahoman* (Oklahoma City) and *Harlow's Weekly* (Oklahoma City), both of which were extensions of the personalities of their respective founders and owners, E. K. Gaylord and Victor Harlow. Both spoke for a progressive agriculture as the best basis for business expansion in the capital city. Both were alarmed at the tensions generated by the high rate of farm tenancy in Oklahoma. The *Oklahoma News* (Oklahoma City) was for many years the only effective competitor against the Gaylord publications. It provides a useful check upon the tendentious reporting of the *Daily Oklahoman*.

The local Democratic weeklies were closer to the sources of tensions and were generally less analytical and more vituperative. Among the most interesting of these papers were the following: the *Marshall County News-Democrat* (Madill); the *Kingston* (Marshall County) *Messenger*; the *Beckham County Democrat* (Erick); the *Wewoka Democrat* (Seminole County); the *Wapanucka* (Johnston County) *Press*; the *Johnston County Capital-Democrat* (Tishomingo); the *Cordell Weekly Beacon* (Washita County); the *Fairview Leader* (Major County); the *Roger Mills Sentinel* (Cheyenne); the *Cheyenne Star* (Roger Mills County); the *Ada Weekly News* (Pontotoc County); the *Ada Star-Democrat* (Pontotoc County); the *Allen Democrat* (Pontotoc County); the *Stonewall Weekly News* (Pontotoc County); and the *Ada Morning Bulletin* (Pontotoc County). The latter four newspapers were especially useful in following the struggles between farmer-labor groups and the Ku Klux Klan in the early 1920s. In this regard the *Madill Record* (Marshall County) and the *Marshall County Enterprise* (Madill) were also very useful, indeed virtually indispensable, as the reader will know from careful study of chapter 8.

Republican newspapers were hard-pressed to exist in most parts of Oklahoma. Three of the best were the *Fairview Republican* (Major County), which had its readership in a solidly Republican northwestern county; the *Cordell Herald-Sentinel* (Washita County), whose pugnacious German editor persistently pointed out the iniquities and follies of one-party rule in Oklahoma; and the *Sayre Headlight* (Beckham County), which had to fight to make headway. The *Oklahoma City Times* was a Republican mouthpiece in the capital until 1916, when its recurrent financial difficulties finally delivered it into the hands of E. K. Gaylord, who harnessed it closely to the *Daily Oklahoman*.

Two farm journals, professedly nonpolitical and nonpartisan, provide essential information on the difficulties, social and natural, encountered by farmers in various parts of the state. The *Oklahoma Farm Journal* (Oklahoma City) was intelligently edited by John Fields, an agronomist who was also the Republican nominee for governor in 1914 and 1922. He sold his journal to the Capper publications of Kansas when he could no longer bear the financial losses. Fields had been driven out of business by the *Oklahoma Farmer-Stockman* (Oklahoma City), still another of E. K. Gaylord's successful publishing ventures. The *Farmer-Stockman* was especially useful because it contained much criticism of the practices of country bankers and landlords, reflecting the concern of Gaylord and the capital city businessmen who feared that rural social conflict would make the state unattractive to investors.

All of these newspapers are on microfilm and easily available in the vast collection at the Oklahoma Historical Society. Newspapers from all of the counties of Oklahoma have been filmed and are continuing to be filmed by that worthy society.

PUBLIC DOCUMENTS

The most important documents to mention are those that the historian unfortunately still cannot examine. Upon inquiry I discovered that the manuscript census returns for 1910 will not be available for scholarly study until 1980. This was a heavy blow to my hopes for doing an extensive collective biography of ordinary Socialist followers and of the people who opposed them. The local papers yield enough names of delegates and local secretaries but do not contain enough biographical information to support systematic analysis. Thus the possibility of uncovering underlying patterns of Socialist support and opposition within precincts went by the boards.

The United States Census volumes on population, agriculture, religion, and manufactures, as cited in the text, provide necessary information for counties as a whole, revealing general variations in different areas of the state. But the county aggregates simply do not permit the kind of precise analysis within counties that is necessary to correlate variations in conditions with variable political behavior and attitudes.

The *Reports* of the State Labor Commissioner were useful in establishing the composition of the Oklahoma City work force at the time of strong Socialist insurgency. The *Reports* of the State Board of Agriculture were marginally useful.

The official precinct returns for Oklahoma elections were critical to the development of the interpretation presented here. They are available at the State Election Board Archives in the Capitol Building, Oklahoma City. It would have been impossible to provide persuasive evidence of the political significance of the conflict between the county-seat businessmen and the small farmers in the countryside of southern Oklahoma if those returns had not been preserved. Unhappily full precinct returns were not available on some crucial state questions, the most important of which for this study was the grandfather clause amendment in 1910. The scholar should also be on the alert for the infrequent misprint in the precinct returns. Even with the precinct voting data, it is difficult to make precise statements about political behavior within counties. In some counties the precinct boundaries were changed frequently; in other counties not so often. In the few instances where I visited county election boards, I found that records of boundaries and elections "way back in 1910" were of no concern to the current county election officials. It was all dead politics to them.

VARIOUS SECONDARY WORKS

To begin with, there are two works that contain exhaustive and sophisticated research on my topic: James R. Green's monumental "Socialism and the South-western Class Struggle, 1898-1918: A Study of Radical Movements in Oklahoma, Texas, Louisiana, and Arkansas" (Ph.D. dissertation, Yale University, 1972), and Donald R. Graham's "Red, White, and Black: An Interpretation of Ethnic and Racial Attitudes of Agrarian Radicals in Texas and Oklahoma, 1880-1920" (Master's thesis, University of Regina, 1973). On many issues the research of these scholars has been essential to the development of my own interpretation. It is accurate to say that my argument emerged from a kind of dialectical discourse with their interpretations. In the text I have made clear my disagreements with their emphases; here, once again, I wish to emphasize my great indebtedness to their work. Another dissertation, which was being completed just as this book went to press, served to clarify my thinking about the origins and nature of the labor system created by tenant farming in Oklahoma. Ellen Rosen's sociological interpretation of Oklahoma's socialism will be available shortly from the Department of Sociology, The Graduate Faculty, City University of New York.

It would be easy if tedious to list every book on populism, progressivism, and American socialism that I read in graduate school and in the course of my research and teaching. The well-known works on populism, however, must be mentioned simply because they lured me into a fascinating subject. Foremost among these is Richard Hofstadter's *The Age of Reform: From Bryan to F.D.R.* (New York

1955). Frankly, Hofstadter's interpretation of populism and midwestern rural society offended my native midwestern pride. That I have changed my attitude toward his work without losing my pride should be readily apparent in the book itself. Norman Pollack's *The Populist Response to Industrial America* (Cambridge, Mass., 1962), strains to create a modern, radical Populist mind. Walter T. K. Nugent's *The Tolerant Populists* (Chicago, 1963) is informed by a more patiently empirical and judicious temper. Although both Pollack and Nugent criticized Hofstadter, neither did so with as much effect as Michael Paul Rogin in *The Intellectuals and McCarthy: The Radical Specter* (Cambridge, Mass., 1967). Rogin's work called my attention to the divisions within rural midwestern society that were obscured by Hofstadter's grand generalizations. Rogin also taught me to see even great historians like Hofstadter as human beings, with hopes and fears like the rest of us. His suggestion that Hofstadter's interpretation of populism perhaps revealed a conservative's discomfort at the specter of radical insurgency emboldened me to depart on my own critical venture. Two classic works educated me in the complexity of social and political conflict in the rural South. Roscoe Martin's *The Peoples Party in Texas: A Study in Third Party Politics* (originally printed as *University of Texas Bulletin No. 3308*, February 1933) has been given a well-deserved paperback reprint. He was years ahead of most historians in correlating social ecology and political behavior. C. Vann Woodward's *Tom Watson: Agrarian Rebel* (New York, 1938) evokes the pathos of a man trapped between past and future, trying to look forward when he really wanted to go back.

The American works on populism set me to thinking about the interpretation of nostalgic and/or forward-looking response on the part of social groups caught in the process of industrialization. Not until I began to place American capitalist development within the larger context of western capitalist development did I comprehend my subject in a truer historical sense. The English Marxian historians who have done so much to open up the study of ordinary people during periods of historical convulsion taught me a great deal. No historian interested in the lives of laboring people should deny himself an encounter with E. P. Thompson's *The Making of the English Working Class* (New York, 1963). While less exciting than Thompson's work, the writings of E. J. Hobsbawm (especially *Primitive Rebels: Studies in Archaic Forms of Social Movement in the 19th and 20th Centuries*) help the student of agrarian movements to sort out the often contradictory responses of people whose lives are disrupted by a consolidating capitalism. What Hobsbawm did for ''primitive rebels,'' George Rudé did for the urban artisans and laborers in *Paris and London in the Eighteenth Century: Studies in Popular Protest* (New York; 1971). Rudé and Hobsbawm combined their large talents to produce a provocative study of agricultural laborers struggling to starve off their doom as a class (*Captain Swing*). Their book significantly changed my perspective on my own topic. Finally, one of the seminal works in this great tradition must be mentioned: Karl Marx's *The Eighteenth Brumaire of Louis Napolean*. (New York; 1963, 1968, based on Hamburg 1869 edition). Taken together, these works make the student think that there is a process of historical development from the less complex to the more complex; that history, in all of its full contradictoriness, is moving forward.

Although some of its implications must be regarded with care, Robert Wiebe's *The Search for Order* (New York; 1967) prodded me into some new thought about the changing nature of American communities between 1880 and 1920. Relatively few books in American history seem to embody a persistent and searching concern with underlying social process. Wiebe's book is interesting precisely because it does present a theory about the submergence of communities in a larger society.

Recent articles have also helped to sustain my interest in my subject. Lawrence C. Goodwyn, "Populist Dreams and Negro Rights: East Texas as a Case Study," *American Historical Review* 76 (December 1971): 1435-1456, shows us that the history of the ordinary country people must somehow be captured out of the fastness of time and the obscure localities in which they dwelled. Goodwyn discovered an episode of political cooperation between white populist officials and black voters that would have remained unknown if he had not talked to an old black man with a good memory. James R. Green, "The Brotherhood of Timber-Workers: A Radical Response to Industrial Capitalism in the Southern U.S.A., 1910-1913," *Past and Present*, no. 60 (October 1973: 160-200, explains how the inhabitants of the pine woods in western Louisiana became militant and radical unionists when drawn into the disciplined industrial process of the lumber industry. Charles Tilly, "The Analysis of a Counter-Revolution," originally published in *History and Theory* 3 and conveniently reprinted in Don Karl Rowney and James Q. Graham, Jr., eds., *Quantitive History* (Homewood, Ill., 1969), 181-208, was a revelation. Tilly discusses his research into the history of the Vendée rebellion, which was, of course, a revolt in a backward region (relative to the surrounding area) against the centralized authority of the French Revolutionary government. His suggestions led me to rethink my own view of the Green Corn Rebellion. Equally important for my purposes was Tilly's advocacy of a sociological approach to historical events in which social structure is studied with as much care as historians have been wont to lavish upon conscious and intentional behavior. Finally, George Rudé's "The Changing Face of the Crowd," published in L. Perry Curtis, Jr., ed., *The Historians's Workshop* (New York; 1970), recalls the difficulties and affirms the importance of doing the history of the inarticulate. The lives of the common people are indeed "the stuff of history." Sooner or later leaders and historians must deal with the facts of their diverse lives

A number of works originating in Oklahoma yielded information useful in my own studies. Keith L. Bryant, Jr., *Alfalfa Bill Murray* (Norman; 1968), portrays the life and career of that obstreperous character. Edward Everett Dale and James D. Morrison, *Pioneer Judge: The Life of Robert Lee Williams* (Cedar Rapids; 1958), tends toward excessive admiration, but does effectively describe the life of a less well-known but important state politician during the period of Socialist challenge. Rex F. Harlow and Victor E. Harlow, eds., *Makers of Government In Oklahoma* (Oklahoma City; 1930), enables the scholar to attempt some collective biography. The Harlows apparently used the reputational method to identify leaders in each county and then provided brief descriptions of their origins, careers, and public offices. Even a few of the old Socialists appear in their volume. L. C. Snider, *The Geography of Oklahoma* (Norman; 1917), provides some useful description of topography and soil patterns. Oklahoma Council of Defense, *Sooners in the War*, (n.p., n.d.) is a summary of patriotic activities during World War I. Those activities ranged from making bandages to suppressing Socialists.

Howard Meredith, "Agrarian Socialism in Oklahoma" (Ph.D. diss., University of Oklahoma, 1969), is a useful political and organizational history of the Socialist party of Oklahoma. Meredith advised me to look at the local Socialist newspapers if I wished to see numerous instances of racially bigoted and segregationist socialism. Charles Bush, "The Green Corn Rebellion" (Master's thesis, University of Oklahoma, 1932), seems to be as much a primary document as a scholarly study. It adopts the point of view of the town middle classes who suppressed the rebellion.

Five statistical works were essential in establishing the basic social ecology of southern Oklahoma: J. T. Sanders, "The Economic and Social Aspects of Mobility of Oklahoma Farmers," *Oklahoma Agricultural Experiment Station, Bulletin No. 195* (August 1929); John H. Southern, "Farm Tenancy in Oklahoma," *Oklahoma Agricultural Experiment Station, Bulletin No. 239* (December 1939); T. R. Hedges and K. D. Blood, "Oklahoma Farm Price Statistics, 1910-1938," *Oklahoma Agricultural Experiment Station, Bulletin No. 238* (December 1939); H. A. Turner, "The Ownership of Tenant Farms in the United States," *United States Department of Agriculture, Bulletin No. 1432* (September 1926); and Oliver Benson et al., *Oklahoma Votes, 1907-1962* (Norman, 1964). Some comment on the preceding works may be useful to scholars. The Hedges and Blood study of farm price movements performs its task well but did not open the road to the bounty of insight that I had first imagined. One can make general correlations between the sharp decline of prices in 1914 and 1921 and the rise of agrarian discontent in politics, but these correlations cannot be established with great precision. Perhaps my disappointed expectations only reveal that I am much less the economic determinist than I was when I began the study! The Turner study of the ownership of tenant farms was almost a providential discovery, principally because Turner selected among his sample counties four southern Oklahoma counties in which I was especially interested. That a study of the ownership of tenant farms was undertaken is a great credit to the Bureau of the Census because the subject itself does have serious political as well as demographic implications. Benson's compilation of the Oklahoma election results is convenient in every respect but one: he adopted the infuriating method of lumping all third-party votes together. In those years when there was an exceptionally strong third party, as was the case before World War I, the scholar must tediously compare Benson's "third party" column with his own computations in order to separate fragmentary percentages from the much higher and more significant percentages of the Socialist party.

Index

About the Author

Garin Burbank, assistant professor of history at the University of Winnipeg, received his Ph.D. from the University of California, Berkeley. A specialist in twentieth-century American history, he has published in such journals as the *Journal of American History*, the British *Journal of American Studies*, and the *Chronicles of Oklahoma*.